Understanding
W. G. SEBALD

Understanding Modern
European and Latin American
Literature

James Hardin, *Series Editor*

volumes on

Ingeborg Bachmann
Samuel Beckett
Thomas Bernhard
Johannes Bobrowski
Heinrich Böll
Italo Calvino
Albert Camus
Elias Canetti
Camilo José Cela
Céline
Julio Cortázar
Isak Dinesen
José Donoso
Friedrich Dürrenmatt
Rainer Werner Fassbinder
Max Frisch
Federico García Lorca
Gabriel García Márquez
Juan Goytisolo
Günter Grass
Gerhart Hauptmann

Christoph Hein
Hermann Hesse
Eugène Ionesco
Uwe Johnson
Milan Kundera
Primo Levi
Boris Pasternak
Octavio Paz
Luigi Pirandello
Graciliano Ramos
Erich Maria Remarque
Alain Robbe-Grillet
Joseph Roth
Jean-Paul Sartre
W. G. Sebald
Claude Simon
Mario Vargas Llosa
Peter Weiss
Franz Werfel
Christa Wolf

UNDERSTANDING

W. G.
SEBALD

MARK R. McCULLOH

UNIVERSITY OF SOUTH CAROLINA PRESS

Published in Columbia, South Carolina, by the
University of South Carolina Press

Manufactured in the United States of America

07   06   05   04   03   5   4   3   2   1

Library of Congress Cataloging-in-Publication Data

McCulloh, Mark Richard, 1955–
    Understanding W. G. Sebald / Mark R. McCulloh.
      p. cm.
    Includes bibliographical references and index.
    ISBN 1-57003-506-7 (alk. paper)
    1. Sebald, Winfried Georg, 1944– —Criticism and interpretation. I. Title.

PT2681.E18 Z73 2003
833'.914—dc21   2002015452

In memory of J. S. Winkler

Contents

Series Editor's Preface

Understanding Modern European and Latin American Literature has been planned as a series of guides for undergraduate and graduate students and nonacademic readers. Like the volumes in its companion series *Understanding Contemporary American Literature,* these books provide introductions to the lives and writings of prominent modern authors and explicate their most important works.

Modern literature makes special demands, and this is particularly true of foreign literature, in which the reader must contend not only with unfamiliar, often arcane artistic conventions and philosophical concepts, but also with the handicap of reading the literature in translation. It is a truism that the nuances of one language can be rendered in another only imperfectly (and this problem is especially acute in fiction), but the fact that the works of European and Latin American writers are situated in a historical and cultural setting quite different from our own can be as great a hindrance to the understanding of these works as the linguistic barrier. For this reason the UMELL series emphasizes the sociological and historical background of the writers treated. The philosophical and cultural traditions peculiar to a given culture may be particularly important for an understanding of certain authors, and these are taken up in the introductory chapter and also in the discussion of those works to which this information is relevant. Beyond this, the books treat the specifically literary aspects of the author under discussion and attempt to explain the complexities of contemporary literature lucidly. The books are conceived as introductions to the authors covered, not as comprehensive analyses. They do not provide detailed summaries of plot because they are meant to be used in conjunction with the books they treat, not as a substitute for study of the original works. The purpose of the books is to provide information and judicious literary assessment of the major works in the most compact, readable form. It is our hope that the UMELL series will help increase knowledge and understanding of European and Latin American cultures and will serve to make the literature of those cultures more accessible.

J. H.

Preface

W. G. Sebald's first novel to be translated into English was in fact his second to appear in German; his first German novel was the third to appear in English; and his second novel to be published in English was in reality the third to be written. How, then, should a critical study proceed? Given that Sebald's work has received considerable attention in translation—not only in Great Britain, where Sebald spent the last thirty-two years of his life, but increasingly in North America and in the Commonwealth countries—it seems appropriate to treat his novels as a contemporary phenomenon of the English-language literary scene. This perspective is especially apposite for a series like *Understanding Modern European and Latin American Literature*, which is intended for the American reader and designed explicitly for general accessibility. Thus, the present study follows the chronology of the appearance of the English translations, since that chronology is most meaningful to the general readership here. It is not my intention to ignore the German reception of Sebald's books, however. I have tried to provide the reader with an accurate impression of the critical response to Sebald in German-speaking Europe as well as the English-speaking world.

A major challenge of this study is to pinpoint the features that make Sebald's prose unique. Sebald's distinctive narrative tone often sounds more like that of a nineteenth-century author. There is an unhurried, patient quality to that voice, and a maturity born of patient, unhurried observation. It is not far-fetched to trace this quality to Sebald's childhood experiences in a remote Alpine village. Sebald's fiction also contains a richness and variety of allusions, and, more to the point, a distinct *manner* in which he combines and connects these allusions. I have noted in Sebald's fiction, as well as in his critical writings, an affinity for writers with strong connections to their grandfathers, as was true, for instance, of Stendhal and Adalbert Stifter. Sebald himself often acknowledged the importance of his grandfather in his life. In an essay on the Swiss writer Robert Walser, he writes of his mother's father, Josef Engelhofer, who bore a physical resemblance to Walser. The companionship of his grandfather was so formative in his development because his own father was away much of the time during his youth. What exactly constitutes the special nature of such "trans-generational" relationships? The memoirist Gregor von Rezzori sees in them the kind of human exchange that is "cleansed of the passions between people of the same age and entirely given to perceptive kindness and unconditional trust." These words, it seems to me, best express the source of the empathy and altruism characteristic of Sebald's pensive narrators.

I have consulted the translations of Michael Hulse and, in the case of *Austerlitz*, Anthea Bell, but have returned to the original German in deciding on the final version of my quotations from Sebald's works. Although the translations in this book deviate from Hulse's and Bell's, the page number in the published translation is provided in an endnote so that the reader may compare the two versions. Original quotations of any length will be given in endnotes throughout, whereas short passages will include only the page numbers for the English-language edition. Self-explanatory and/or single-word quotations will not include either page numbers or endnotes. My intention is to approach as closely as possible the spirit and substance of the original for explicitly philological rather than aesthetic purposes. Also, certain British expressions have been replaced by more familiar American phrases and terms. Finally, it should be noted that translators invariably leave things out, for reasons that are not always clear. I take note of such textual changes in the discussion of Sebald's works that follows. Translations of German scholarly texts are my own, unless otherwise indicated.

Acknowledgments

My acquaintance with W. G. Sebald's work came about by a chain of odd coincidences. It was my friend and colleague Gill Holland who first directed my attention to James Atlas's article "W. G. Sebald: A Profile" in an issue of the *Paris Review* back in 1999. The article was essentially an interview with Sebald, a long one, and it contained a sampling of the enigmatic photographs—Sebald has called them "spectral images"—that are a prominent feature of his books. But the name was not familiar to me, nor were the titles of novels mentioned in the course of the interview. Sebald did not belong to the contemporary German "literary establishment," as far as I knew, by which I mean that his name had not yet been included among those of contemporary writers such as Martin Walser, Peter Handke, Hans Magnus Enzensberger, Ilse Aichinger, Peter Rühmkopf, and Günter Grass (who, coincidentally, had won the Nobel Prize for literature in the same year the article appeared). *The Rings of Saturn,* the most intriguing title mentioned in the interview, was not among the library holdings at Davidson College where I teach, but I did find *The Emigrants,* the first of Sebald's novels to be published in English. When I finally found time to begin reading, I realized immediately that the book was like nothing else I had ever read, and that I had happened upon some of the most compelling and original writing I had ever encountered. But it was yet another coincidence—a question put to my colleague Scott Denham during a technology workshop—that led me to renew my contact with James Hardin. I wrote him an e-mail message about a completely unrelated project. Soon we found ourselves discussing instead the Sebald project for the series *Understanding Modern European and Latin American Literature.* The present volume is the result of those electronic conversations.

In the long view, Walter Höllerer should receive credit for helping pave the way for my work on Sebald. It was he who introduced me many years ago, in a seminar at the University of Illinois at Urbana-Champaign, to the study of travel writing as a literary genre. His critical observations on a wide variety of travel descriptions have been especially helpful in approaching Sebald's work, in which travel is a fundamental element. T. H. Pickett of the University of Alabama has been a helpful correspondent, and occasionally a collaborator, since my undergraduate days. Other teachers, including H. G. Haile and James W. Marchand, deserve thanks for their inspiring devotion to literary study.

I am indebted to Davidson College for research support and to the staff of the E. H. Little Library, especially Joe Gutekanst. I owe a debt I can never repay to my wife, Audrey Rugg McCulloh. Her support of the project, expressed in the form of encouragement as well as proofreading, proved invaluable. A special thanks goes to Gill Holland, who first brought W. G. Sebald to my attention.

Introduction

In the course of the last decade of the twentieth century, W. G. Sebald published three books, which in their English translations have awakened the English-speaking world to the presence of a literary artist of the first rank. Sebald (1944–2001), whose novels read like intricately digressive travelogues grounded in impressionistic memories and associations, was quite possibly the first great new talent to appear on the German literary scene in the latter half of the twentieth century since Günter Grass. Sebald began his literary career by publishing poetry, but he is best known for his "hypnotic" and "haunting" prose. His fourth novel, *Austerlitz*, appeared in 2001, the year of his death.

Winfried Georg Sebald was born on 18 May 1944, in a region of southern Germany called the Allgäu, which, like Franconia to the north, considers itself a separate geographical and cultural entity from the rest of Bavaria, to which it officially belongs. The small town in which he grew up is called Wertach, which figures as "W." in the final section of the novel *Vertigo*. His parents were Georg Sebald and Rosa Genovefa Sebald, née Engelhofer. It was a quiet childhood in a quiet Alpine village, in a milieu that was very rural and very Roman Catholic.[1] His father was serving in the military—a profession that was regarded by the family as a mark of social advancement—when Hitler took power in 1933. In Sebald's early years his father was absent because of the fighting and, after the war, because of a lengthy internment in France. Once back home, Georg Sebald had to seek work in less economically depressed towns than Wertach, and spent much time away from his family. When a new German army was established in 1954, he decided to enlist, which led yet again to long periods of separation from the family. Sebald attributed his upbringing largely to his grandfather Josef Engelhofer.

As a boy, Sebald was sent to schools in Immenstadt and Oberstdorf from 1954 to 1963. He then studied German literature at the University of Freiburg and in French-speaking Switzerland, earning a *Licence des Lettres* from the University of Fribourg in the summer of 1966. Having become increasingly dissatisfied with German university life, with its overcrowded lecture halls and its faculty holdovers from the era of the Third Reich, not to mention the conspiracy of silence about twentieth-century German history, he found study in franco-phone Switzerland to be an intellectually and culturally liberating experience—one which marked the beginning of a lifelong devotion to French literature. After Fribourg, Sebald accepted a teaching position in England at the University of Manchester, instead of taking an assignment in Germany at the University of Hamburg. His application for the job was not the result of any special interest in England or the English; in fact, he knew little about Manchester or the United Kingdom, and his knowledge of the English language was rudimentary. In 1968 Sebald completed a master's degree in German literature and thereafter returned to Switzerland to teach elementary school in St. Gallen. In 1969 he returned to Manchester to teach German literature, and in 1970 took up residence perma-nently in England. He taught German and European literature at the University of East Anglia in Norwich until his death, with the exception of one year he spent at the Goethe Institute in Munich during 1975–1976. Sebald was not happy liv-ing in Germany again, and returned to England for good. It is understandable, then, that the theme exile (in his case voluntary) figures highly in his work. Though Sebald preferred England to Germany, he always considered himself a guest in his adoptive homeland. He died in an automobile accident near his home on 14 December 2001, ending a remarkable career as a scholar, poet, and nov-elist. He was fifty-seven years old.

Although he spent his adult life in England, Sebald wrote for the most part in his native German. His literary reputation in Germany was launched with the 1989 prose poem *Nach der Natur: Ein Elementargedicht* (*After Nature*), which won the Fedor-Malchow Prize for lyric poetry in 1991.[2] It is a collection of three groups of poems. The first depicts scenes from the life of the sixteenth-century German artist Matthias Grünewald, the second does the same for Georg Wilhelm Steller who accompanied Vitus Bering to Alaska in 1741, and the third is largely autobiographical, telling of his grandparents, his childhood, and wartime in Ger-many. All three refer throughout to man's relationship with nature and to the rela-tionship between nature and art. Although this work has undoubted merits, it did not serve to attract a significant following for its author—the historical portions seemed too distant from contemporary concerns and the autobiographical part was too obviously "poeticized memory."[3] Some recognized Sebald's originality, and he soon found himself enjoying the patronage of two prominent German writers, Christoph Ransmayr and Hans Magnus Enzensberger, who made certain his writing received the attention it deserved.[4]

Each of Sebald's subsequent prose works met with high acclaim, beginning with *Schwindel. Gefühle* in 1990. The book consists of four parts, the first retelling the artistic awakening of the author Henri Beyle, better known as Stendhal, the second, the narrator's journey to Italy, the third, Kafka's journey to

Italy, and the fourth, the narrator's return to his hometown in southern Germany. However it was not this work, which was not published in English until nine years later as *Vertigo*, but Sebald's second novel *Die Ausgewanderten* (*The Emigrants*) that launched his English-language career. *The Emigrants* was originally published in German in 1992. It was greeted as "among the greatest and most moving achievements of contemporary German writing" by the critic Ulrich Baron in the newspaper *Rheinischer Merkur*.[5] The book appeared in Great Britain in 1996 as Sebald's premier prose fiction work in English translation, and the following year it was published in the United States. The *Review of Contemporary Fiction* proclaimed *The Emigrants* "one of the best novels to appear since World War II."[6] The novelist and critic Susan Sontag praised the work as a remarkable new form of literature, and was joined by the novelists Cynthia Ozick in pronouncing Sebald's work "sublime."[7] It is the book that most clearly warrants the appellative often associated with Sebald, "documentary fiction." Its four parts explore the biographies of several people Sebald knew, most of them Jewish or part-Jewish, who suffered exile because of their ethnicity.

Sebald's third novel, *Die Ringe des Saturn: eine englische Wallfahrt* appeared in 1995, and was published in translation (*The Rings of Saturn*) in 1998 as the second novel to appear in English. It, too, garnered lavish praise from major critics. Sontag, for instance, called Sebald's writing "exotic and irrefutable" and ranked it as a rare example of literary greatness, countervailing with its "autumnal" maturity what she calls "the ascendancy of the tepid, the glib and the senselessly cruel as creative fictional subjects" of much modern literature.[8] *The Rings of Saturn* is a book even more "exotic" and difficult to describe than the other two, since it contains, in its ten chapters, so many multifarious narrative threads, historical links, and imaginative associations. Early reception of the book in Germany was not entirely enthusiastic, however, as indicated by a negative review in *Die Zeit* on 13 August 1996. The next two books Sebald published in German were not fiction. A collection of essays on the writers Johann Peter Hebel, Gottfried Keller, Robert Walser, Eduard Mörike, and others, appeared in 1998 under the title *Logis in einem Landhaus* (Lodgings in a country house). It was followed by another literary study *Luftkrieg und Literatur* (*On the Natural History of Destruction*) in 1999, a book actually composed of two essays, one concerning the rarity of depictions of urban destruction in postwar German literature, and one on the German writer Alfred Andersch. The next work of fiction, *Austerlitz*, which followed two years later, is the tale of an adult who must reconstruct his forgotten origins in order to unearth his true identity. It is an extremely personal book about the delayed and deferred sufferings of an orphan, but it is also a lengthy critique of European architectural and social history.

Sebald's poetry and fiction have been singled out for a number of literary prizes. He has been awarded the Berlin Prize for Literature, the Literatur Nord Prize, the Johannes Bobrowski Medal (all in 1994), the Mörike Prize, the Heinrich Böll Prize of the City of Cologne (both in 1997), and—signaling the attainment of truly international recognition as a notable contemporary artist—the 1998 *Los Angeles Times* Prize for Best Fiction Book for *The Rings of Saturn*. In 2000 he received the Heinrich Heine Prize of the City of Düsseldorf. More than once, in publications from the London *Times Literary Supplement* to the *New Republic*, Sebald's works have been called "masterpieces" and described as having attained that rarest of qualities in modern literature, the "sublime." In critic James Wood's words, "Anxious, daring, extreme, muted—only an annulling wash of contradictory adjectives can approach the agitated density of W. G. Sebald's writing. . . . This German who has lived in England for over thirty years is one of the most mysteriously sublime of contemporary writers."[9] Still, Sebald never seemed to become as much a part of the German literary scene as he did the American and British. Perhaps this lack of wholehearted acceptance in his own country is attributable to his acknowledged position as an outsider—by the time he was becoming known as a writer of German fiction, he had lived longer in England than he had in Bavaria.

Sebald spent his last years in a redbrick Victorian house on the outskirts of Norwich with his wife Ute, whom he met while at the University of Freiburg.[10] He was not the melancholy or depressed persona some of his readers have imagined, but a congenial, even "funny" person known to friends and colleagues by the improbable nickname "Max" (actually, Maximilian was the third of his three given names). Just as his childhood was ordinary, according to him, so was his lifestyle, despite the attainment of not inconsiderable fame in literary circles. Some of his personal modesty can be sensed in the voices of the unnamed narrators of his books, who are mild-mannered, compliant, and vulnerable to bouts of disorientation and depressive immobilization. As Anthony Lane suggests in an article in the *New Yorker*, modesty, not debutante virtuosity, exemplifies the tone of Sebald's narrative voice; he was a writer who "raised modesty to the brink of metaphysics."[11]

Sebald exhibited by all accounts a quiet cosmopolitanism and self-possession, but at the same time harbored a fascination with the strange, fantastic, and irrational. What he wrote about Hebel could just as well be said of Sebald himself, that the appeal of his writing arises less out of what he tells us about the nature of things than what he can show us about things beyond comprehension.[12] Sebald was fascinated with all forms of eccentricity and the allegedly thin line between genius and insanity. He even went as far as to spend portions of his summer vacations in a Viennese mental clinic observing the behavior of the inmates, one of whom is portrayed in *The Rings of Saturn*. His study of the many known and little-known forms of madness, oddity, quirkiness, and whimsicality informs his work to the same degree as does his more ordinary avocation—that of art history.

His reliance on visual representation in his texts and his many references to painting point to the importance of the visual arts in general for providing a domain from which Sebald draws much material for his work. One of the most striking characteristics of his prose texts is their unusual inclusion of captionless photographs and other images. Many are the sort of old photographs and post-cards one might find in junk shops, and indeed, Sebald discovered many of them on his meanderings through the towns and shops of East Anglia, and collected such things over a period of years. Indeed, Sebald combined the habits of a studious antiquarian with the imagination of a collector of stories about strange mythical beasts. He was drawn to make-believe per se, and he used to enjoy talking at length about such things. One interviewer has reported that being in his presence was like being in C. S. Lewis's *The Lion, the Witch and the Wardrobe*, "in which a gang of children climb through a closet door and find themselves transported to some other world."[13]

The kind of writing Sebald pursued since turning to poetry and fiction in the late 1980s is in many ways unique, though it demonstrates stylistic and thematic affinities with several innovative writers, including Franz Kafka, Vladimir Nabokov, Thomas Bernhard, and Jorge Luis Borges, among others. After the publication of *The Emigrants* in Britain in 1996 and in America in 1997, numerous critics variously proclaimed that a "new genre" had been created. Many commented that Sebald's work was like nothing they had ever read. Sebald's new type of fiction—part dream sequence, part travelogue, part photo album, part history, part memoir, part cultural-historical fantasy—confounded some and dazzled many, especially those already familiar with postmodernist genre-blending of Umberto Eco and Italo Calvino. But most who encountered the late-blooming writer in Germany and subsequently in the English-speaking world were in agreement regarding the uniqueness of Sebald's prose. The question remains, however, whether Sebald's accomplishments truly ascend to the level of an utterly new kind of literature.

Sebald blurs all demarcations—between past and present, reality and dream, art and life, fact and fiction. Yet others have done such things before. What sets Sebald so clearly apart for so many critics and readers? Joyce Hackett, a professor of creative writing at New York University, offers a succinct explanation in a review of *The Rings of Saturn*:

In narratives that blend reportage, memoir, art criticism, social chronicle, natural history, fiction, literary essay, personal anecdote and images, W. G. Sebald is literally reinventing the diary as his own genre. Not since Montaigne has an author bound such a breadth of passion, knowledge, experience and observation into such a singular vision.[14]

It is the accumulation of the various threads of his episodic narrative into one final "literary monism," as I call it, that seems to distinguish Sebald's work. His books weave and intertwine disparate or unlikely threads and images into a final oneness without giving away anything of the author's intention—the reader hardly notices what is happening, much less perceives how the result is accomplished. Most sections of his novels (all but *Austerlitz* have four or more component parts) end not so much with a flourish but a unifying crescendo. Or is it merely the illusion of a unifying crescendo?

Three salient features of Sebald's work have repeatedly caught the attention of critics: the scope of his cultural and historical knowledge, his exacting power of description, and, as mentioned, his ability to unite a multitude of narrative threads in a compelling way. With the exception of *Austerlitz*, which is, in its narrative structure at least, more traditional, Sebald's books initiate a new genre—something more than the journal-as-novel or the extended essay, the nuanced autobiography or the fictionalized memoir.[15] Sebald was among the first to write what some have called the "documentary novel."[16] He enlarged upon that new form, making it far more than the sum of its various eclectic elements. And it should come as no surprise that Sebald's content and style have much in common with documentary writing. The year Sebald enrolled in the University of Freiburg (1963) was the year of the publication and performance of Rolf Hochhuth's controversial play about papal acquiescence to Hitler. The drama was called *Der Stellvertreter* (*The Deputy*) and purported to document the passivity of the Roman Catholic Church and its complicity in Nazi crimes. This was followed by a spate of similar historical and documentary dramas by Peter Weiss, Hans Magnus Enzensberger, and others who effectively energized West German drama, which was until then, as Sebald argues in his 1987 study of German theater in the 1970s and 1980s, uninspired, uninspiring, and wholly without significance.[17] Sebald's remarks on documentary drama came the year before his first work of creative writing was published, a volume of poetry containing historical and documentary elements. Indeed, Sebald's early poetry in *Nach der Natur* embraces not only documentary technique, but many of the themes that would appear later in his prose: the relationship of subjective experience and objective representation, man's constant struggle with nature, the burden of personal depression, the relationship of solitary talent and society, the unreliable and autonomous nature of memory, the constancy and ubiquity of the phenomenon of combustion (e.g., starlight, renegade brush fires in the south of France or California, the intentional burning of rainforests in Brazil, the intentional smelting of ores, and the firing of pottery).

Still, any consideration of Sebald's stylistic originality must be balanced by recognition of those belletristic influences that are clearly reflected in his work. In the coming chapters, traces of the influence of writers as diverse as Sir Thomas Brown, Edward FitzGerald, Hugo von Hofmannsthal, Joseph Conrad, Thomas Bernhard, Adalbert Stifter, Stendhal, Kafka, and Chateaubriand, among others, will be identified and discussed, paying special attention to Sebald's explicit reconstructions of several of these artistic personas, their milieus, and their inner lives. The primary subject of Sebald's writing is, in the end, writing itself. The question that occupies his narrators is always lurking in the background, and occasionally comes explicitly to the fore: What, in the final analysis, is the nature and purpose of writing? To take a step further, what is a writer's undoing? Can one ever know that one is on the right track with one's writing? To judge from the acclaim Sebald has received in highly respected publications in Germany, the *Times Literary Supplement* in Britain, and in the *New York Times* and the *New York Review of Books* in the United States, he himself seemed to be very much on the right track with his writing when his life ended in 2001. In a time when literary critics and theorists make much of "crossing boundaries," Sebald traversed virtually all borders demarcating conventional categories of the written word, even adding visual representation to the mix. His writing is a unique combination of the documentary and the fictional, the dream diary and the historical record, the travelogue and the elegy, the case history and the revisionist critique, the postmodernist send-up and the respectful encomium, interspersed—sometimes wistfully, sometimes insistently, sometimes whimsically—with photographs of times gone by, drawings, old postcards, copies of paintings, and other images or portions of images.

If the comparison of Sebald's achievement with Montaigne's development of "a new genre" seems overstated, James Wood offers a more temperate assessment of Sebald's literary accomplishment:

> When *The Emigrants* appeared, one immediately recalled Walter Benjamin's remark, in his essay on Proust, that all great works establish a new genre or dissolve an old one. Here was the first contemporary writer since Beckett to have found a way to protest the good government of the conventional novel form and to harass realism into a state of self examination.[18]

In Sebald, literature turns an eye inward, examining itself, probing itself, exploring itself and its relation to the mind, leaving nothing untouched or unconnected. This universalizing and unifying process of examination accounts for the contradictory features in Sebald's writing—his work is both disquieting and quiescent, unsettling and reassuring, surreal and studiedly realistic, precise yet shifting. There is sublimity but also violence and grotesqueness. Sebald finds beauty all around, but also infirmity and decline, though decline takes on an almost consoling quality of constancy. It remains to be seen if the aforementioned comparisons—whether to Montaigne or Beckett or Proust—will continue to be invoked when discussing Sebald's work, but it is indisputable that his first three novels were recognized as a major development in European literature. For most critics, Sebald's first novel of the twenty-first century, *Austerlitz*, bore renewed testimony to the originality of his talent and the enduring power of his prose. His death, within a few weeks of the book's publication in Britain and America, was a tragedy for the literary world.

Chronology

1944	Born in Wertach im Allgäu, Germany on 18 May
1950–1954	Attends elementary school in Wertach and Sonthofen
1954–1963	Attends secondary school in Immenstadt and Oberstdorf
1963–1966	Enrolls in the University of Freiburg, studying later in French-speaking Switzerland, where he earns a *Licence des Lettres*
1966–1968	Travels to England, where he teaches German literature at the University of Manchester and earns an M.A.
1968–1969	Teaches German at a grammar school in St. Gallen in Switzerland
1969	Publishes book on the German-Jewish writer Carl Sternheim
1970	Returns to teach at the University of Manchester
1970–1975	Serves on the faculty of the University of East Anglia in Norwich and earns a Ph.D. in German literature
1973	Completes his dissertation on the German writer Alfred Döblin
1975–1976	Returns to Germany under the auspices of the Goethe Institute in Munich
1976	Returns to teaching German literature at the University of East Anglia
1985	Publishes *Die Beschreibung des Unglücks: Zur österreichischen Literatur von Stifter bis Handke* (The description of melancholy: Austrian literature from Stifter to Handke)
1986	Defends successfully his *Habilitationsschrift* (postdoctoral thesis) at the University of Hamburg
1988	Promoted to Professor of Modern German Literature at University of East Anglia. Sebald publishes *A Radical Stage. Theatre in Germany in the 1970s and 1980s*
1989	Publishes his first non-scholarly work, *Nach der Natur: Ein Elementargedicht* (*After Nature*). Establishment of the British Centre for Literary Translation with Sebald as its director
1990	Publishes his first novel, *Schwindel. Gefühle*, which would appear in English as *Vertigo* in 1999. Publishes *Unheimliche*

	Heimat: Essays zur Österreichischen Literatur (Foreign home-land: essays on Austrian literature). Receives the Feder-Malchow Prize for Lyric Poetry in recognition of *Nach der Natur*
1992	Publishes his second novel, *Die Ausgewanderten* (*The Emigrants*)
1994	Receives the Berlin Literature Prize and the Johannes Bobrowski Medal for *Die Ausgewanderten*
1995	Publishes his third novel, *Die Ringe des Saturn: eine englische Wallfahrt* (*The Rings of Saturn*)
1996	*The Emigrants* is published by Harvill in Great Britain
1997	*The Emigrants* is published by New Directions in the U.S. Receives the Heinrich Böll Prize and the Mörike Prize
1998	*The Rings of Saturn* appears in English. A volume of biographical essays, *Logis in einem Landhaus*, (Lodgings in a country house) is published in Germany. *The Rings of Saturn* is awarded Best Fiction Book Prize by the *Los Angeles Times*
1999	Sebald publishes a book of critical essays, *Luftkrieg und Literatur* (*On the Natural History of Destruction*), with the thesis that post-war German literature has failed to address the massive bombardment of the country during the Second World War
2000	Receives the Heinrich Heine Prize and (with Markus Werner and Ilse Aichinger) the Josef Breitbach Prize
2001	Publishes his fourth novel, *Austerlitz*, in Germany in February. English translation by Anthea Bell follows in October. On Friday, 14 December, dies in automobile accident near his home in Norwich. *For Years Now*, a volume of poetry in English, is published posthumously, followed by *After Nature*, a translation of *Nach der Natur: Ein Elementargedicht*
2002	Receives The Literary Prize of the City of Bremen and, in the U.S., the National Book Critics Circle Award for fiction, posthumously, for the novel *Austerlitz*. *On the Natural History of Destruction*, a translation of *Luftkrieg und Literatur*, is published after the appearance of *After Nature*

Understanding
W. G. SEBALD

CHAPTER 1

Blending Fact, Fiction, Allusion, and Recall

Sebald's "Literary Monism"

Toward the end of the novel *The Emigrants,* the narrator returns to his German homeland to visit locations described in an old diary given to him by a friend. On arrival, the narrator is struck by both the "mental impoverishment and lack of memory" that marks the Germans, and "the efficient skill with which they had cleaned everything up."[1] The narrator's impression, although clearly subjective, has some basis in fact. The contemporary visitor to Germany cannot help but notice the extent to which history seems somehow routinely ignored, especially compared to Britain and France, where the historical past seems ambient and is actively, if selectively, celebrated. This is not to say that there are no efforts to recall and perpetuate German customs and traditions in German-speaking lands. Indeed, there are many folk festivals celebrating indigenous music, crafts, and costume, but these are almost exclusively regional in nature. And while there are also public observations of certain tragic dates from the period of the Third Reich such as *Kristallnacht* or the anniversary of the bombing raid that destroyed Würzburg, these do not seem to be part of any communal, national acknowledgment of the calamities, not to mention the crimes, of the past. Despite the many commemorative plaques and the meticulously preserved concentration camp sites such as Bergen-Belsen in Lower Saxony or Dachau near Munich, life goes on very much as if the Third Reich never happened. From the perspective of someone like Sebald's narrator—a German who has lived a long time abroad—the population as a whole does not seem to perceive itself as part of a historical continuum, as do other Northern Europeans. The apparently passionless symbolism of official memorializing in Germany conceals an amnesiac void that became even more obvious to Sebald after he began living in England. In his adopted homeland the Second World War is still the topic of many conversations and the stuff of many references, whereas in Germany the first half of the twentieth century—during which virtually every major city was smashed by bombs and the Jewish population of Europe virtually eliminated—seems to be treated as irrelevant in view of the overwhelming economic success of the Federal Republic since the *Wirtschaftswunder* of the 1950s. Sebald's approach to the Holocaust in particular—but also to the aerial campaign that rained destruction on Germany—is aimed at resisting "the German desire to silence and end witness."[2] More generally, he resists the processes by which time itself seems to seek to end witness. It is not just in *The Emigrants,* but everywhere in Sebald's work, beginning with his poetry, that the author recalls the past, recovers the past, and seeks to depict how the present fades imperceptibly into the past. His narrators and many of his characters are convinced that the dead are with us still, a part of who we are, and he is intent on telling their often obscured or suppressed tales. Sebald's fictionalized pilgrimage is a painstakingly empathetic journey amongst the living in search of the ghosts of the past. He confesses to being driven by the occasional odd feeling of being "signaled from the other side."[3] His own narrative voice, as German readers have pointed out again and again, is archaic, that of a specter.

Often the question arises among critics and commentators as to how much of Sebald's writing is autobiographical. Indeed, much of the time the first-person narrator seems to be a thinly veiled Sebald. This is a reflection of a certain legerdemain in Sebald's treatment of the nature of identity. What is the "true" identity behind our socially and historically determined selves? The essence of identity, like virtually everything in Sebald's world (whether in the objective *or* subjective realm), remains uncertain. But one thing is certain, namely that Sebald finds the autobiographical form appealing, In fact, he once said that he often preferred autobiographical writings to novels.[4]

The tone of much of Sebald's work—often called "autumnal"—is undoubtedly related to the author's experience of having begun to write not as a young man, but in his forties, after having experienced more of life's full range. In the course of developing his own stylistic voice and thematic concerns, he had been exposed to more literary influences than a younger man. Authors who launch their careers in mid-life, almost as an afterthought, do not usually write with a youthful sense of invincibility; they are seldom as bold and unambiguous in their assertions about purpose and meaning. Death is often a more proximate possibility and looms larger as an eventuality. In the case of Sebald's writing, catastrophes, deaths, and illnesses exist alongside the affections, attachments, and passions of life. Sebald's objectification of the not altogether obvious omnipresence of suffering and disease echoes a passage from one of the novels of the Austrian writer Thomas Bernhard, in which a doctor tells his adult son it is wrong to refuse to confront the reality that sickness and sadness "are in reality everywhere."[5] But this kind of pessimism, while it has captured the attention of many, is, as James Wood points out, another primarily aesthetic aspect of Sebald's work, not a theological or metaphysical one:

> In the same way that Sebald's facts appear to exist only in the fictional form that Sebald gives them, so Sebald's pessimism is a mood that can

only express itself in the form of his own books. That is to say, in patterned fragments, haltingly, uncertainly. This mood is a kind of nineteenth-century melancholia, a tendency rather than a system.[6]

Sebald writes about people and things that have gone before. When he writes about the present, he is always conscious that it is a present in the process of ✓ passing away. But Sebald shirks any form of existential fatalism; rather, his writings explore the aesthetic experience of the dwindling present, evoked by his search for keys to the past and its meaning.

The Uncanniness of Everything

Sebald is also a writer fascinated by the strangeness of life, even ordinary life, and his narrators often tell their stories as if they were strangers in a strange land, extraterrestrials, as it were. Judging from the reactions of critics and readers, who often express the sentiment that Sebald's books are unlike anything they have ever read, it is this restoration of a sense of the uncanny (as well as the sublime) to everyday experience that accounts for much of Sebald's appeal. The narrative progresses from one mental association to another, following threads, skeins of thought, in much the same way that one experiences consciousness itself, but with a remarkable richness borne of elaborate intertextuality (and *intra*textuality). Sebald's literary, artistic, and everyday-life associations are considered by many to be quite extraordinary. Crystallized in his prose, they are the product of a remarkably rich and daring imagination that draws on a fertile cultural and historical background, as well as a heightened aesthetic consciousness of the mundane.

Free association, or the appearance of free association, is clearly fundamental to Sebald's psychological and aesthetic approach to narrative. Thus, one does not have to look far to find the influence of Freud, whose writings were well ✓ known to Sebald (his critical writings contain numerous references to Freud's ideas). It is Sebald's affinity for Freud (as much or more than for Kafka) that informs his emphasis on the uncanny, especially when the uncanny coincides with the everyday. Freud devoted an entire essay to the subject in an essay titled "Das Unheimliche" ("The uncanny"), which, by his own account, was one of his few writings on aesthetics. Freud's definition of the uncanny (the German word connotes the strange or eerie, not the purely gruesome) is based on a characteristic also present to some degree in all of Sebald's fiction: the latent or obscured familiarity of the strange. The uncanny, according to Freud, is often that which was once familiar (now long concealed or repressed) being suddenly revealed, as when the spirits of the dead return to walk among us.[7] Closer examination of

Freud's article goes a long way toward elucidating what creates the mood or atmosphere in much of Sebald's work. The uncanny is "that class of the frightening which leads back to what is known of old and long familiar."[8] It is this paradox of the strangeness of the familiar, or the "rediscovered" familiarity of the strange, that motivates Sebald's evocation of what Freud calls "a special core of feeling" present in the experience of the uncanny.[9] More significantly, Freud makes much of repetition and coincidence, which provide, along with the uniting enterprise of traveling, the narrative structure of Sebald's prose. As Freud puts it, "involuntary repetition . . . forces upon us the idea of something fateful and inescapable when otherwise we should have spoken only of 'chance.'" And in a passage that could have come from Sebald himself, Freud elaborates on the strange phenomenon we all know so well, the indisputable psychological significance of coincidence:

> We naturally attach no importance to the event when we hand over an overcoat and get a cloakroom ticket with the number, let us say, 62; or when we find that our cabin on a ship bears that number. But the impression is altered if two such events, each in itself different, happen close together—if we come across the number 62 several times in a single day, or if we begin to notice that everything which has a number—addresses, hotel rooms, compartments in railway trains—invariably has the same one, or at all events one which contains the same figures. We do feel this to be uncanny. And unless a man is utterly hardened and proof against the lure of superstition, he will be tempted to ascribe a secret meaning to this obstinate recurrence of a number; he will take it, perhaps, as an indication of the span of life allotted to him. Or suppose one is engaged in reading the works of the famous physiologist, Hering, and within the space of a few days receives two letters from two different countries, each from a person called Hering, though one has never before had any dealings with anyone of the same name.[10]

The resemblance of this passage to Sebald's style is itself uncanny, both in the original German and in translation. Freud speaks analytically about the most intimate (and non-analytical) thoughts, and cites convincingly mundane specifics, such as the unexpected, coincidental, and even repeated encounter with a name—an encounter that one surmises might well have happened to Freud in reality.

Sebald's merging of the everyday and the uncanny is characteristic of his work, and perhaps all the more appealing in an age when remarkable adventures are no longer even conceivable for most of us; the thrills of the late twentieth century and early twenty-first seem to be relegated to activist eco-tourism, organized white-water rafting, and jumping with a vine round one's ankle from great heights in exchange for a fee. In one of his critical books Sebald explicitly credits the literary critic Walter Benjamin for an observation that is an essential part of Sebald's approach to the uncanny in fiction: a true sense of mysteriousness is most effectively created not through pathos or fanaticism, but by locating it squarely in the mundane.[11] Thus, tourists walking through an Italian resort town at night can resemble a writhing procession of lemurs, the poet Dante can appear on a park bench, a water bug in the moonlight can cause one to shudder in horror, a word in a newspaper can momentarily take possession of one's very soul.

The Narrator as Peregrinator

Sebald's style, which is alternately elegiac, whimsical, unsettling, seems to reinvest everyday life with a sense that there remains much that is unexplained and inexplicable, a sense especially appealing to those who resist the banalities of contemporary commercial culture, the reductionism of professional science, and the fashionable cynicism prevalent in modern secular society. Although he condemns the crimes and shortcomings of former times, just as he does those of the present, Sebald finds the present wanting, and turns to the past with respect and empathy in his search for meaning and relevance. Thus we find in Sebald a predilection for reminders of bygone days, such as sprawling nineteenth-century hotels and great manor houses, which his narrator invariably visits on his journeys. Such places once possessed an inimitable and unrivaled glory in what seems like a brief moment now long past—they stand like grand hulking ghosts in his English and Irish landscapes. Some endure in their own quirky and dilapidated way, as if awaiting an estate sale, and some are merely ruins. Various "paradisiacal gardens" and palaces seem to be repetitions of the same horticultural and architectural patterns in Sebald, and he locates them both in Europe and China, displaying them before us in their dazzling, strange beauty. All were once centers of life and cultivation, yet they stood somehow above life in a way that seemed almost magical at the time and, in retrospect, seems magical again. But it is not just gardens and mansions that recur. One prominent version of repetition Sebald uses is the phenomenon of the doppelgänger, the identical double. In the novel *Vertigo* the narrator sees on the streets of present-day Italy not only Dante and Wagner's benefactor, King Ludwig II of Bavaria, but twin embodiments of a young Franz Kafka. This habit of glimpsing various doppelgänger is not only uncanny, but, as one critic has suggested, also recalls Marcel Proust's character Swann, "who is forever discovering servant girls to have faces identical to those canvasses by Old Masters."[12] Sebald, whose work has occasionally been compared to Proust's (and more often to Jorge Luis Borges's), uses these doubles not necessarily to the same effect as the prolific Frenchman. Proust sets out to retrieve the past, and does so in such a way that we feel we possess that past again, virtually in its entirety. Sebald, on the other hand, superimposes faces and moments from the past onto the present to highlight the vividness as well as the incompleteness and the variability of memory. In Sebald, even some of the most vivid memories show up with flaws of composition—anachronistic clothing such as the wrong hat, or the uniform of a period later than that of the battle being recalled. In Sebald's prose, "memory does not so much restore the past as take the true measure of bottomless loss. . . . [It] occasions vertigo—a sense of all that has vanished from under our feet—because it reminds us of the missing as well as the found."[13]

In addition to his preoccupation with the mystery of memory and the recurring sensation of the uncanny, the act of traveling—physically, as well as mentally, through time—is at the center of much of Sebald's fiction. To read Sebald is to make a journey, or in the case of *The Rings of Saturn,* a "pilgrimage," as the original German subtitle (*eine englische Wallfahrt*) suggests. His compositions have as their narrative premise peregrination in some form or another—extended walks, aimless boat rides under the stars, journeys by train and by airplane. Susan Sontag properly identifies the function of forward motion in Sebald's fiction: "Travel frees the mind for the play of associations, for the afflictions (and erosions) of memory; for the savoring of solitude."[14] In *The Emigrants, Vertigo,* and *The Rings of Saturn,* travel is the explicit means by which encounters with new scenes and stories are sequenced and digressions introduced. In this, too, there are traces of Bernhard's influence, especially when one considers a book like the 1967 novel *Verstörung* (translated as *Gargoyles,* 1970) in which Bernhard's narrator follows his father, a small-town physician, on his rounds to treat his patients, listening to their sometimes bizarre tales and learning about the strange circumstances of their lives. Many are utterly eccentric, others seem within the realm of normalcy but on second glance appear obsessed by a bizarre stridency or capable of some disturbingly lurid or cruel act.

In Sebald's works, however, there is much more than a mere retelling of stories encountered by a peregrinating narrator, as in the example of Bernhard's *Gargoyles.* Accompanying the peripatetic narrator on his journey, the reader participates in an act of studied observation at every juncture, even at those times when the narrator is immobilized by nervous exhaustion. The photographs interspersed throughout the text—split-seconds framed and captured—reflect and reinforce the notion that Sebald is attempting to regain the immediacy of a moment, on the verge of receding into the void of the past. The photographs often suggest a totality—the totality of a life's experiences—that would otherwise have been lost. This is especially true of portraits and domestic scenes, which contain imbedded in them the unspoken destinies of the persons pictured. The narrative potential of photographs was hinted at in *Vertigo,* but was made abundantly clear in *The Emigrants,* itself a kind of album dedicated to the lives and sufferings of people who surely would have otherwise been forgotten. In one specific episode the near loss is explicit: a German Jewish artist in exile in England gives the narrator his mother's diaries and notes, from which he composes a restrained but lyrical memoir of daily bourgeois Jewish life in the spa town of Bad Kissingen. Always in the background is the chilling knowledge that the artist's mother, the author of the diaries, vanished in the Holocaust, and that she wrote down her memories because she knew something dreadful was looming on the horizon.

The Heightened "Reality" of Fictional Reconstruction

Sebald's use of photographs evokes the feeling one has when coming across old pictures of unfamiliar, long deceased relatives. One is brought to the realization that not only stories and voices and blood relationships have been lost, but the names and identities themselves. These things are gone forever; that is, unless someone like Sebald endeavors to retrieve their memory, creating at the same time a work of art (i.e. a work of fiction) in its own right. A major theme in Sebald's work is the heightened or intensified reality created by fiction, in comparison to our actual experience of reality, an experience that is mostly devoid of the sense of destiny and significance literary art can offer. His is an aesthetic mind at work; he believes that fiction, although drawn from the experience of reality, can be eminently more "true." Writing by its very nature gives order (although not necessarily in Sebald an explicit or immediately comprehensible order) to reality by creating a separate, aesthetically formed reality. The "reality" of fiction requires nothing less than persuasive elements that reinforce the appearance of verisimilitude or are otherwise compelling to the reader. In Sebald's novels, photographs and other images are interspersed throughout the text to confirm a detail of appearance or to "document" an event, but more often to assist the reader in visualizing a dream or dream-like encounter of the real, to capture again for a moment what has passed, or is passing, away. Mazes appear, and brilliant pleasure domes, or vast imaginary (and real) cities in the distance. These are snapshots, greeting cards, charts, paintings, advertisements, engravings—eclectic, often mysterious, and nearly always fixating. The reader is shown everything from scenes of seventeenth-century naval battles to the life

cycle of the silk worm to piles of naked corpses at Bergen-Belsen. The largest
percentage of the photographs, Sebald believes, are directly related, and in that
sense documentary, although about one-tenth, he estimates, are drawn from
unrelated sources.[15]

Sebald's visually augmented texts demonstrate how photographs, even of
unfamiliar persons in unfamiliar settings and times, have a particular power over
people, provoking involuntarily questions about the significance and meaning of
the past. Who are, or were, these people looking into the camera? What became
of them? What else happened the day the picture was taken, moments afterward?
Influential in confirming Sebald's intention to use photographs in his texts was
Roland Barthes's use of a photograph titled simply "Ernest, Paris, 1931" in his
book *La Chambre claire* (1980; translated as *Camera Lucida,* 1981). An anonymous schoolboy dressed in knickers stands beside a desk and smiles. Barthes
asks the question: "Is it possible that Ernest is still alive today: but where? How?
What a novel!"[16] Sometimes one wonders if Sebald's photographs are simply
illustrating the narrative or in fact guiding it and propelling it onward by their
own evocative power while the author is composing his stories. In any case, photographs can have a life of their own in Sebald's world, as most clearly expressed
by the character Vera in his fourth novel, *Austerlitz:*

> One has the impression that something is stirring inside them—it is as if
> one can hear little sighs of despair, gémissements de désespoir . . . as if the
> photographs themselves had a memory and were remembering us and how
> we, the surviving, and those who preceded us, once were.[17]

Pictures of ourselves are especially affecting in the way they call for reaffirma-
tion of the intimate past and its many connections with those living and dead.
The persons in the images are beckoning to us to be remembered, according to
Vera, and they themselves possess memories that extend even farther into the
past. But the use of photographic documentation is not without ambiguity; pictures can be falsified, and false claims can be made about the identities of the
persons or events depicted. The evocative power of Sebald's use of pictures is
also associated with a sense of mystery—one wonders whether they really represent what Sebald seems to suggest. Writing about *The Emigrants,* the critic
John Tagg explains the effect of the uncertainty that is part of the relationship
between text and image:

> It is not clear that Sebald writes about the photographs that appear in the
> pages of his book. And it is not clear that the photographs that appear are
> about what his writing describes. Yet, is it not because these things are
> unclear that Sebald's "unclassifiable" book has filled its readers with the

sense of being moved by something that cannot be documented, something that has remained hitherto unsayable, something that has resisted coming to light? Could it otherwise have given witness to the unforgettable forgotten that declines to enter the tribunal of history, but has not vanished into the grave?[18]

In Sebald, documentation is used, paradoxically, to evoke that which cannot be documented.

Not all is poignant, melancholy, plangent, or grave when it comes to Sebald's pictures. Occasionally the author engages in visual jokes, slyly framed in plays on words, although these have mostly escaped translation into English, so that the German and English text formats differ somewhat. In the German original of *Vertigo,* for instance, the top of a painting is at the bottom of one page, and the bottom is at the top of the next. Readers thus scan downward twice, and there at the end encounter the phrase "wie ein Untergehender," a play on the present participle of the verb "to go under," a verb that also means "to end" or "to be lost."[19] Neither the verbal nor the visual witticism can be translated; the English version neither divides the picture nor attempts the pun. In the same book, a page from a pocket calendar is meant to prove an astonishing coincidence, yet it is obvious that it could easily have been forged. Other visual details are amusing for their darkly funny, if tenuous links. Confining our discussion once again to *Vertigo,* we notice that in the two instances where Sebald displays multiple duplicates of the same picture, one is (allegedly) a drawing of Stendhal probing the syphilitic ulcers in his mouth with a tongue depressor, while the other is a photograph of a statue of St. George plunging his lance into the dragon's mouth.

The images, like Sebald's prose, are indisputably concrete and vivid. In both his choice of artwork as well as his literary allusions, Sebald brings his vast erudition to bear. But the intertextuality of his creations is anything but effete. The use of these references contributes to a densely evocative fictional texture. Sebald's allusions to images, authors, and their work usually relate to larger issues such as colonialism, commerce, geology, predation, individual suffering, and the passing of time. Even obscure foreign phrases seem to be there for reasons that have more to do with authoritativeness than with showing that Sebald's aestheticism is fully grounded in reality.

Work in Progress

Books are central to everything Sebald does, whether in his professional or his literary life, which is why the subject matter of his prose is tightly bound up with the act of writing. His work creates the illusion at times of being just ahead of his readers, as if readers are part of the process themselves. Sebald's emphasis on the immediacy of perception and its interplay with memory—and with the distortion or the absence of memory—is brought to the fore in his specific descriptions of the act of recording, of writing. At the end of *The Rings of Saturn,* and at several points in *Vertigo,* for instance, Sebald refers to his literary production as writing notes. The translator, Michael Hulse, chose to use the word "notes," although the word Sebald employs (*Aufzeichnungen*) is actually more suggestive of something like "depictions," since the verb *aufzeichnen* means to write down or record, but also to draw, and thus, to make manifest a visualization. Rainer Maria Rilke's prose, similar to Sebald's in its solitary mood and evocative diction, called his fiction "notes" in the case of *Die Aufzeichnungen des Malte Laurids Brigge* (1910), which is known in English as *The Notebooks of Malte Laurids Brigge.* As with Rilke, the impression that Sebald's literary creation arises out of his notes does not leave us with a feeling of sketchiness or incompleteness, but with the sense that we are present in the making of the work. As the literary scholar Ernestine Schlant has observed about *The Emigrants*:

> The narrator describes the circumstances of his own life at the time he becomes interested in the lives of these "others"; he describes the note-taking and the travels necessary for his research, so that the narratives are always works-in-progress constructed in front of the reader.[20]

Sebald weaves the fabric of his narrative out of intertwining digressions on the present and the past, out of the strange threads of perception, memory, and dream, and, finally, out of the experiences of travel in a here and now that is alternately mundane, lyrical, and uncanny. All the while one is drawn in by the illusion that one is at the same time part of the experience the author is relating. The narrator even portrays himself in the act of writing. In the portion of *Vertigo* titled "All'estero," for instance, he is asked by an innkeeper what he is working on, to which he replies that he does not know for certain, but harbors "a growing suspicion it might turn into a crime story."[21]

To be sure, Sebald's novels fit the genre of the travel book, but they also fit that of the crime story; they refer obliquely or directly to the Holocaust (as in *The Emigrants*), to Belgian colonial atrocities (as in *The Rings of Saturn*), to local murders reported in newspapers, or (as in *Austerlitz*) to the "architectural crime" of the Mitterrand Library in Paris. All these crimes are woven into the fabric of the narrator's personal story. For this reason, and because his prose poses as the account of actual travels and actual encounters with authentic personalities, terms like "documentary fiction" or "the documentary novel," or even the amalgam "faction" have been used to describe Sebald's medium.[22] His use of documentation—and the illusion of documentation—is only part of an eclectic and syncretic whole that is far greater than the sum of its parts. In addition to his technique of weaving together threads of fact and fiction, of coincidence and disparity, some see in Sebald's work a thematic originality as well. Ernestine Schlant locates Sebald's significance for German literary history in the originality of his approach to the Holocaust in *The Emigrants*—although we should remind ourselves that the book is not devoted in its entirety to that specific theme. Regardless, Schlant credits Sebald with being the first (some forty-five years after the fact) to "mourn the destruction of the Jews in Germany" calling Sebald's accomplishment "a unique achievement in German literature."[23] He is the first, according to Joyce Hackett, to "give voice to the culture and the lives that were destroyed."[24] The melancholy, elegiac tone that many perceive in that book is a response to irreversible loss and to the fact that those who survived were damaged beyond repair. If Sebald has indeed succeeded in opening the way for true grief about what was done by the Germans (and others) to European Jewry, then his achievement is no small one. He achieves his effect most powerfully in his indirect portrayal of the damage done to individuals by racist totalitarianism. In one of the most poignant passages in *The Emigrants,* Sebald shows us a devoted teacher, Paul Bereyter, an utterly humane and sincere man tormented by what the Nazis did to him and others, in wrenching moments of inconsolable suffering. A former student named Brandeis, now attending a music conservatory, visits Bereyter's class and plays the flute. The young teacher stands by the window and cannot hide his emotion at the sound of the music. He is forced to remove his glasses because his eyes have filled with tears, and he turns away from the class to conceal the sobs that are rising in him. The narrator does not descend into sentimentality by focusing on the scene, but turns our attention to other similarly quiet, sad incidents he witnessed:

> It was not only music, though, that brought on such changes of mood in Paul; indeed, at any time—in the middle of a lesson, during recess, or on one of our school outings—he might stop or sit down somewhere, alone and apart from us all, as if he, who was always in good spirits and seemed so cheerful, was in fact neither of those things, but the personification of inconsolable anguish.[25]

We witness this solitary suffering *with* the narrator, as it were, and share his sense of helplessness that life, as we confront its saddest victims, seems intent on forcing upon us. We are helpless to do anything about the helplessness we witness. For Sebald, this acceptance must extend to nature and its calamities, even the smallest—*sunt lacrimae rerum.*[26] In *The Rings of Saturn* there is a scene

11

in which the narrator is departing after having viewed a large English country house; he encounters a solitary Chinese quail on the grounds. The bird seems to be in a state of dementia, "running back and forth along the edge of the cage and shaking its head every time it was about to turn, as if it could not comprehend how it had gotten into this hopeless fix."[27] This diminutive, tormented creature seems to embody haplessness itself—there is surely nothing sadder than an innocent creature suffering, until death can eventually overtake it, without the prospect of relief. Here, as elsewhere in Sebald's work, such unavoidable and anguishing scenes are mirrored, and the reader cannot turn away. Inevitably one wonders what caused the bird's dementia. But unlike cases where the human cost of fascism or natural catastrophe can be chronicled and, at least to a certain extent, explained, the bird's story can never be told. But, as in both examples—that of the tormented teacher Paul Bereyter and that of the demented Chinese quail— there is simply nothing to be done. This unalterable condition, the fact that it is too late for us to do anything but to take note, is both the source of Sebald's "mournfulness" and what he has called the melancholic's "resistance" in the face of tragedy, misfortune, or existential despair. What we find in Sebald is not a purely passive sadness. For him, the creative act of writing constitutes a form of active coming-to-terms with experiences such as these, of confronting the dark side of reality, but also moving forward. The literary depiction of melancholy is for Sebald *Trauerarbeit,* a German term that can be translated literally as the "work of grieving."[28] Sebald's books grieve for the victims of the Holocaust, but also for all victims of oppression, exploitation, and disease. Although far less openly accusatory, he nonetheless carries on in prose the work that was begun in documentary drama by radical German writers such as Rolf Hochhuth and Peter Weiss in the 1960s, work which set out to expose the people and motives behind the brutal crimes of twentieth-century Europe.

Remembering is of course essential to grieving. It is hard to imagine sadness and melancholy without a painfully felt connection to the past and the things and people now forever part of it. But Sebald as a writer also focuses on memory as such. He is interested in its associative character. The ramifications of such associations hold an obvious fascination for him. He explores again and again the mysterious workings of memory and the question of how we can know anything at all for certain. This preoccupation with mnemonic ambiguity reflects to some extent the postmodernist obsession with ambiguity in general, and Sebald can be both philosophical and playfully sardonic in his use of narrative uncertainty. In this his prose sometimes exhibits the dark playfulness of Bernhard. The title of Bernhard's 1983 play *Der Schein trügt* (Appearances can be deceiving) might as well stand as Sebald's motto, since we often find in his prose not only ambiguity and the absence of verifiability, but outright deception. Appearances can and do lie, deceive, distort. As noted earlier, this is true even of the "documentary" media. Photographs can be retouched or misrepresented. Video footage and films, as selective and limiting technologies, by their very nature alter the reality they purport to convey, and they too can be intentionally falsified, especially in our age of computer manipulation of images.

Grim Humor

The occasional dissonance between the sign and the signified is not without its lighter side in Sebald's writing. Misunderstandings are often a source of humor, although it can be a grim form of humor indeed. Growing up in a southern German village after the war, the narrator of *Vertigo* thinks the newsreel scenes of "mountains of rubble in places like Berlin and Hamburg" are merely "a natural condition of all larger cities."[29] In the railway station cafeteria in Venice he encounters the alien incomprehensibility of a Kafkaesque procedure for the simple act of selling drinks and snacks to travelers. The circular coffee bar and neighboring check-out lines form a "steadfast island," holding out against its customers, who are swaying "like a field of grain in the wind, passing in and out of doors, pushing against the food counter, and surging on to the cashiers who sat some way off at their elevated posts."[30] The ensuing passage describes with fastidious detail the inimitably Italian chaos of purchasing receipts, then returning to "plead" for an item in exchange.

> The impassive corps of all male attendants, like their sisters, mothers and daughters at the cash registers, resembled some peculiar assembly of higher beings sitting in judgment according to the laws of some dark order of things, deciding the fate of a whole species that has been hopelessly corrupted by endemic greed.[31]

Clearly the scene is exaggerated to take on a monstrous absurdity (his attainment of a cappuccino constitutes "the supreme victory" of his life), yet virtually anyone who has traveled has come upon situations of similarly mind-boggling irrationality and inconvenience. The humor arises not merely from grimly comic exaggeration but from the apparently self-sustaining quality of the absurd around us; things that should hardly exist do exist, and they seem to have a life of their own. In another train station in Austria, a scene generates itself in which "down-and-outs" appear, one after the other, until there are a dozen of them (the original German specifies a thirteenth, a female). A case of beer materializes within their midst, as if out of thin air, while the bums hold forth on current events as well as the meaning of existence. Here the homeless enact what can only be called a caricature of normal bourgeois social interaction—the train hall becomes a free-of-charge venue for a plenary session of outcasts. That such a gathering takes place in public seems both mad and overtly routine, as in the case of the Venetian railway cafeteria, and the question a visiting extraterrestrial might ask is: How did this wholly unlikely madness come about in the first place?

Is Sebald Plotless?

Sebald has been criticized for offering the reader little in the way of plot. What happens in Sebald's books? Narrative movement in Sebald, aside from the associative and digressive, is, as we have noted before, primarily generated by travel. Travel literature, of which Sebald's work is an original and peculiar sort, has a favored position in German literary history, owing its status in large measure to Goethe's famous account of his journey to Italy, *Italienische Reise* (1816–1817). Indeed, Germans have long been known for their penchant for travel; one of the best known travel guides in the world remains the *Baedeker,* which first appeared in 1835. More recently, German literary travel descriptions were penned by the likes of Alfred Andersch, Wolfgang Koeppen, and Heinrich Böll.[32] In German literary criticism one lately speaks of travel literature as an example of "literarische Fremderfahrung," a term that can be translated as "the literary experience of the strange." The word "fremd" is similar to the English word in that it connotes both the "strange" and the "alien." It does not matter that some of the strange and alien things encountered in Sebald are encountered not in distant lands, but right at home. The notion is implicit in Sebald's work that life itself is a form of travel—a journey through time. Wandering, moving forward, listing in a storm or in the doldrums—these are all aspects of travel, and, by metaphorical extension, of living. It is no accident, then, that Sebald's texts contain frequent similes in which buildings are compared with ships. A home for the aged and infirm is likened to a liner on a "heaving sea" (*Vertigo,* 45); madmen on the hospital island of La Grazia seem to be "aboard a great ship sailing away" (66); a sugar-beet processing plant in a distant field resembles a moored freighter (*The Rings of Saturn,* 29), train cars glide away into the night like silent ships (*Austerlitz,* 49), and so on. One is reminded of one of Sebald's favorite authors, Joseph Roth, whose novel *The Radetsky March* (1932) includes an elaborate description of a nineteenth-century Austrian army garrison resembling a great ship. In the dusk its white walls and petroleum lamps at regular intervals make it appear like a liner "rocking gently . . . in the steady rhythm of waves on an unknown ocean."[33]

In Sebald, as prefigured in Roth, it is as if seemingly solid, stable phenomena like buildings and landmarks are not firmly in place, as they appear, but in constant motion. From the extraterrestrial perspective, of course, they *are* in motion. The earth spins, and revolves around the sun. But there is another dimension to motion as such. The motif of movement also translates into colonization, which is central to the global perspective of *The Rings of Saturn*. But colonization is not just a human enterprise. All things—even the trees—are on the move, spreading outward over centuries. Sebald's constructs often have the effect of a double-edged sword, and the phenomenon of movement is no exception; it brings life but also annihilation. Populations move outward, mostly westward for new territory, but diseases do the same. In *The Rings of Saturn* Sebald describes, with quiet power, the perfect and complete destruction wrought by Dutch elm disease in Britain.

It is not so much that Sebald's books lack plot, for the action moves forward —and backward and outward and upward—in its idiosyncratic way. The critic Fin Keegan has remarked astutely on Sebald's avoidance of traditional novelistic artifice:

> Sebald's linking method . . . is purely related to the deep structure of [his novels], by which I mean that the surface relations are as arbitrary as possible, in keeping with the writer's disdain for fictional contrivance: rather than trouble the reader with artful hinges bereft of thematic purpose or meaning, Sebald furnishes the scantiest of excuses for moving from one subject to the next. Like comedians (and seducers, for that matter) he knows that these links are fundamentally unimportant and, like punctuation, a mere matter of convention.[34]

What the books lack, as several critics have pointed out, is the satisfaction of "resonance." The uncanniness of so many of the narrator's encounters and his sense of dislocation contribute to the impression that the ever shifting context leaves one with "nothing to hold on to, nothing to be sure about except perhaps those seraphic visual scraps that interrupt the text."[35] Uncertainty is both an element of the author's skeptical viewpoint and of the explicit experience of his narrators and other characters, who are all essentially exiles, as title *The Emigrants* expressly suggests. The other effect of having "nothing to hold on to" is the instability suggested by another title: *Vertigo*. The writer David Auerbach explains the function of Sebald's intentional avoidance of resonance:

> Rather than functioning as a factual mirror to current and past reality, [Sebald's books] refract the facts into something that resembles a mirror

of reality but which lacks any resonance whatsoever, so that [they] become a model for the process he is attempting to describe. The ultimate resolution of this process, and what we can learn from it, are the questions Sebald poses, and not ones he has yet answered.[36]

The author manages to construct a world, a world that is related by "refraction" to what is commonly called reality. At the same time he acts to destabilize reality by placing virtually everything—knowledge, experience, memory, reason, history—in question. But the absence of resonance or stable contextual orientation does not imply that Sebald's books are devoid of warmth and emotion. However, rather than demonstrated outright, human attachments and contacts are generally indicated or suggested in his narratives. Sometimes there is even sex. While the rare appearance of intercourse in Sebald's books occurs in such a way as to underscore the bizarreness of the sexual act, most intimacies are only indirect and, largely for that very reason, all the more poignantly evoked. Characters discuss their affection for others, acts of kindness are described, and the narrator exhibits nothing if not empathy for his subjects. The friendship and affection the narrator feels for fellow author Michael Hamburger in *The Rings of Saturn,* while clearly understated, is heartfelt. Likewise the sympathy of the narrator for the subjects of *The Emigrants* is present mostly in the background. The unsentimental detachment of his storytelling is especially pointed in Sebald's depiction of his return to his hometown in the last part of *Vertigo.*

Sebald's profound alienation from contemporary culture, manifested in his preference for the past, has nothing to do with resignation. There is a mood of transcendence in Sebald's melancholy tales, with their focus on the dwindling present and the experience of loss. This is particularly evident in his elegiac passages. Sebald's writing is predicated on the possibility, through attending to the plangency of the past, of finding meaning that transcends the banalities of the present. But contemporary life is not entirely severed from the sublime in Sebald. He has an eye for pure and uplifting scenes of beauty in the present, and a voice for their lyrical description. It is once again travel that permits Sebald's narrator to experience such moments of intense beauty, as when the narrator of *Vertigo* leaves a dreary station café in Innsbruck for a trip into the landscape of his childhood:

I marveled at the slopes, strewn with boulders, reaching from the heights down into the forests like pale fingers into dark hair, and I was astonished again at the mysterious, slow motion quality of the waterfalls, which, for as long as I could remember, had been cascading, unchanged, over the rock faces. At a hairpin bend I looked out of the turning bus down into the depths below and saw the dark turquoise surfaces of the Fernstein Samaringer Lakes, which, even when I was a child on our first excursion . . . into the Tyrol, had seemed to me the essence of all conceivable beauty.[37]

Besides the radiant beauty of the scene, there are two things to note about this passage. First, the perspective is from on high, almost aerial, and second, there is an association of sublimity with the fluid motion of water. Several critics have noted that Sebald's narrator often views the world from "higher ground" or, as one puts it, from a "giddy-making vantage point . . . but also an angel's perspective."[38] It is the perspective of memory. As for the association of fluidity with the sublime, water can be the very embodiment of beauty in Sebald, but it is sometimes a terrible beauty, to be sure. Consider Sebald's description of the European hurricane of 1987 in *The Rings of Saturn;* he looks out the window towards the end of the garden, "where the crowns of the large trees . . . [a]re bent and streaming like aquatic plants in a deep current."[39]

Staid Hyperbole

The elegiac nature of Sebald's style is a product not only of the manifest transience of his subject matter and mournful mood of much of his work, but of hyperbole. As discussed earlier, Sebald's brand of humor is rooted in exaggeration. And here too the influence of Bernhard, as well as (although less frequently cited) Bernhard's aesthetically "quiescent" fellow countryman, the aforementioned nineteenth-century novelist Adalbert Stifter, can be felt.[40] As the literary critic James Wood observes, "for all the apparent quietness of Sebald's prose, exaggeration is its principle, an exaggeration he has undoubtedly learned in part from Bernhard."[41] Likewise, the pessimism in Sebald's works Wood likens to Bernhard's, except that Bernhard's "principle of exaggeration" is applied more consistently to the grotesque, whereas Sebald's concentrates more commonly on the elegiac, although the grotesque is by no means lacking. Sebald acknowledges the significance of Bernhard for his literary life and refers to Bernhard's particular brand of literary "extremism" as "periscopic writing."[42]

Both Bernhard and Sebald share a sense that even the domesticated, everyday life most of us live is permeated with a bizarre or surreal quality that is seldom acknowledged. Indeed, in Bernhard's work the mundane can even merge with the surreal. Bernhard gives explicit form to this strange union in the belief of the physician father in *Gargoyles* that the whole world is completely and utterly surrealistic—nature, human affairs, everything. Bernhard and Sebald have in common, then, not merely the narrative device of traveling from place to

17

place listening to tales, but the tone of the bizarre that so easily spills over into the surreal. In contrast to Bernhard, however, Sebald does not dwell on the repellent and disgusting with as much "periscopic" detail and elaboration, but tends to treat them with succinctness and brevity before moving on. Another feature of Bernhard's writing that finds its way into Sebald's is the furtive use of *italics*. He sometimes uses italics to baffling effect, since the likeliest as well as the unlikeliest of words receive emphasis, a feature also of another influential book for Sebald, Stendhal's *Life of Henry Brulard*. Finally, Sebald, like Bernhard, eschews paragraphing. It is no wonder, then, that some critics consider Sebald to be Bernhard's legitimate successor in German-language literature.[43]

The exaggeration of elements of the real into the form or shape of the surreal does not, of course, originate with Bernhard. German literature is known for its share of overstated writers, so exaggeration in itself is nothing new or rare. Literary immersion into twisted minds, for instance, goes back at least to Georg Büchner's *Lenz* (1839). And what other literature has produced a work like Elias Canetti's *Die Blendung* (1936; *Auto da Fé*, 1946), a book that is as insistently prolix as it is relentlessly insane? But Sebald employs exaggeration in a different way from Bernhard's and that of others: "Where Bernhard uses a Nietzschean hammer," Wood continues, "Sebald's exaggeration is squeezed through a dreamlike reticence, yielding the novel effect that characterizes Sebald's prose."[44] Life is seen through the lens of a dreaming eye, and what the mind behind that eye perceives is a world passing away before it. This "plangent dwindling" is perhaps most variously and insistently portrayed in *The Rings of Saturn,* but it is true of all of Sebald's creations. Wood is at least partly right about the source of Sebald's stylistic originality, his "haunting" way of telling a story. One seems to get to the place one is going, often a most bizarre place, through virtually unnoticed transitions. Everything the author shows us comes to us "narrowly, . . . by way of the dreamiest indirections."[45] Tim Parks, writing in *The New York Review of Books,* echoes Wood's analysis of Sebald's abiding stylistic principle: "There is a back and forth in Sebald's writing between the wildest whimsy and the bleakest realism. One extreme calls to the other."[46] The extremes do indeed seem to call to one another from unexpected directions and from around otherwise unnoticed corners, creating an essential tension in Sebald's work. They frequently take readers by surprise, "startling" them, as one critic put it.[47] In the end, however, hyperbole is simply an intrinsic part of the telling of a tale, according to Sebald.[48] One narrates, after all, for effect. It is only natural that the superlatives stick in one's mind.

The paradoxical combination—"exaggerated reticence"—seems especially well suited for generating Sebald's characteristic mood and imagery. He creates an impressionistic, sometimes surreal verbal canvas of contrasts: the mundane and the bizarre, the placidly familiar and the vividly grotesque, the farcical and the tragic, the lyric and the insane, the criminal and the kind, the constant and the transient. For those with Sebald's aesthetic sensibilities, his prose holds up a mirror to experience and captures the fleeting essence of the moment, which paradoxically extends to and includes the past. If anything, Sebald's fastidious attention to mundane details creates a sense of authorial reliability that serves as a narrative balance to the bizarre, surreal, and grotesque.[49] But the overriding mood many perceive in Sebald's work is still the melancholy, the mournful, the autumnal. If one examines Sebald's corpus as a whole, however, it becomes apparent that similar appellatives such as "melancholy" and "somber," also often used in describing his work, are simply too sweeping. There are satirical elements that emerge in his prose, products of his humor and astute powers of observation. There are moments of the profoundest beauty. What Sebald does is display openly, from the perspective of a wandering outsider who happens to have certain literary leanings, the very oddness of people, of history and its calamities, of the very predicament of being alive. Sebald's subject is in large part the routine strangeness of the past and present, but it is in the last analysis the unsettling strangeness of the familiar.

The tone of Sebald's narrative voice accommodates his literary encounter with the world's overwhelming strangeness by being in the main sedately reassuring—another feature of his writing noted by a majority of critics. He accomplishes this effect in large measure through his diction, and the same sedate reassurance is relayed by his translator as well. Sebald's choice of words is often just old-fashioned enough to distinguish it from contemporary speech, giving his voice a detachment that is at once serious and inviting. Randolph Stow has called Sebald's style "staid," but at the same time "smooth."[50] Blake Morrison writes that Sebald's narrator speaks with the voice "of a wistful, highly cultured mid-European, a man of 54 who sounds 120 at least."[51] Indeed, in his works Sebald restores a kind of nineteenth-century pithiness to life, refusing to accede to twentieth-century superficiality. Little or no notice is taken of the commercial clutter, the disposable plastic, and the pointlessly harried pace of contemporary life. The reader is spared, for the most part, references to shopping malls, video stores, slang, bad grammar, and mobile telephones. Such acknowledgment of modern gadgets as does exist in Sebald is either whimsical (a combination alarm clock and teapot appears in *The Emigrants*) or blasé (more than once the narrator of *The Emigrants* awakens in his chair to see the television test pattern and realizes he has fallen asleep.) Although Sebald's work clearly belongs to postmodernism, both chronologically as well as in its rejection of traditional narrative conventions, it is free of the irreverence characteristic of many postmodernist writings. The dominant chord is reverential. Sebald's deference comes through in his attitude toward history especially, which for him is worth the painstaking effort of discovery and reconstruction, and is not to be manipulated for contemporary purposes external to it. And with the knowledge he has gleaned in his years of study comes the authoritative quality of his voice, the source of its reassuring timbre. It is also the voice of the traveler, recording his travels, on whom we rely for all we know of strange, faraway lands.

Ambient Oneness

The strange lands Sebald describes are part of a world to which we all conceivably have access—through literature, history, and fantasy. Many of the strange places to which he guides the reader are wholly imaginary, as was "Zembla" in Nabokov's novel *Pale Fire* (1962). They include the lands on the planet "Tlön" and the unchartable earthly region "Uqbar" from the Borges story "Tlön, Uqbar, Orbis Tertius," which Sebald mentions twice in *The Rings of Saturn.*[52] In Sebald's play of interconnections and possibilities, as with any memorable fiction, what goes on in the author's mind becomes part of the reader's mental cosmos. The interrelatedness of all things takes shape in the merging of many currents, threads, memories, even identities. In *The Rings of Saturn* there is a key scene in which the narrator visits his friend, the author Michael Hamburger. During the visit the narrator senses his own identity converging with the other man's. (145) It is as if the narrator himself had lived in the same house long ago, and the desk, writing implements, and spectacles had belonged not to Hamburger but to him. Everything—body and soul, mind and matter, present and past—belongs to one continuum. There is no real external and internal, subject and object, there is only oneness. In Borges's "Tlön, Uqbar, Orbis Tertius," we find, among the precursors for Sebald's motifs of fluid identity and coincidence by secret design, a lengthy description of the "monism"—the word is used explicitly—that characterizes the belief system of the fantastic, invented world called "Tlön." "To explain or to judge an event is to identify or unite it with another one," Borges writes, "the present is undefined, . . . the future has no other reality than as present hope, [and] the past is no more than present memory."[53] And in an observation that anticipates Sebald's concepts of memory, predestined order, as well as his use of "ghostly" sepia photographs, Borges's narrator reports that one school of thought on Tlön "declares that the *whole of time* has already happened and that our life is a vague memory or dim reflection, doubtless false and fragmented, of an irrevocable process."[54] (What better illustration of a "dim reflection" than a series of dark and often slightly out-of-focus photographs?) Borges even adds another note on the interchangeability of identity: "Another [school] believes that, while we are asleep here, we are awake somewhere else, and that thus every man is two men."[55] Both these ideas have a strange irrationality to them, but the most all-encompassing principle is the rejection of familiar assumptions about temporal reality—of time as a series of points in the present that recede and are "lost" in the past. Sebald writes about time most explicitly and at length in *Austerlitz*. At one point the novel's eponymous protagonist remarks that he believes, more and more, that time does not really exist. The character Austerlitz posits an incomprehensible, higher, quasi-spatial reality in which "various chambers are enclosed one inside the other," and through which "the living and the dead may and do pass back and forth."[56] Elsewhere he says:

> If Newton thought . . . that time was a river like the Thames, then where is its source and into what sea does it finally flow? Every river, as we know, must have banks on both sides, so where, seen in those terms, where are the banks of time?[57]

He asks if the weather doesn't govern human life more profoundly than the idea of time, which seems somehow not to be a single phenomenon at all, standing eternally still in some places, rushing headlong in others, and in yet others, swirling in eddies. It is his hope that "time will not pass away, has not passed away, that I can turn back and go behind it, and there I shall find everything as it once was, or more precisely I shall find that all moments of time co-exist simultaneously."[58] Time is not the fictional quantity measured by clocks, but something more like what the existentialist theologian Paul Tillich (1886–1965) called "the Eternal Now." Underlying Sebald's art is not just an aesthetics, then, but a metaphysical monism, an entire "intellectual world," as one scholar has put it.[59] As always when dichotomies are exploded, the rational must join with the irrational to form a new logic—the nature of light, to give one famous example, must be understood not as *either* a particle *or* a wave, but as having the properties of *both*. In addition, the traditional categories of subject and object are destabilized in Sebald. Just as the physicist must acknowledge, according to Heisenberg's principle, that the act of observation is an act that by its very nature alters the object observed, so too the observer—that is to say, Sebald's narrator—must stand on the brink, apart, examining and depicting scenes of uncertain reality. Sometimes subject and object even threaten to conflate, as with the strange thoughts of converging identities at the home of Michael Hamburger. It remains a typically Sebaldian paradox, however, that the narrator has no choice but to describe the oneness of all things from a detached and objectifying point of view.

In the case of his sensation of merging identities, to yield would be to abandon the role of observer and succumb. By merging with the Other, consciousness would enter a realm that otherwise recedes from us—the realm of final certainty. Such certainty would be complete and irresistible, however, and would surely mean a descent into madness, as the narrator acknowledges. Still, even madness is within the continuum, and, as Sebald's narrator matter-of-factly observes, "such thoughts are usually dispelled as quickly as they came."(185) Sebald's narrator then once more moves on, taking up yet another narrative thread. Authority is restored. And the narrative continues down another path, follows another allusion, or arrives at another fork, always pursuing what Nabokov calls "that blissful anastomosis provided jointly by art and fate."[60]

The Final Word is Never Final

There is much that is puzzling, astonishing, and even "startling" in Sebald's writing. However, his style is eminently accessible. "The shocking truth," to cite Anthony Lane's colloquialism, is that "the guy is an easy read."[61] This is true in translation, perhaps, but far less so in the original German, which is highly hypotactic in structure and employs more archaic vocabulary. What comes through in both languages, however, is Sebald's precision and sense of detail, both reminiscent of Kafka. And while Sebald cannot be accused of underestimating his audience—readers must bring to the text a taste for a narrative that depends on a flow of incidents, coincidences, and uncanny events seemingly governed by hidden, unknowable laws—nonetheless, the readers' "task of detection never sinks into hardship."[62] Sebald repeatedly intrigues his readers with the enigmatic and unexplained, presenting little in the way of certainty about the veracity of memory or the substance of meaning. The "authoritative unreliability" that characterizes many of the images and events in Sebald is perhaps the most important underlying principle of Sebald's literary monism; everything belongs together somehow, everything is interrelated by some secret orderliness, but even the author isn't certain precisely how. If he is, he isn't telling. In any case, there are too many coincidences, too many currents flowing in upon themselves, for life to be merely a random chain of events compatible with philosophical materialism.

It would be surprising if there weren't detractors of the monism of Sebald's books—books which are, as some have argued, indescribable except in their own terms.[63] Those who find little to praise in his work consider it prolix, plotless, and pointless. The *New York Times* critic Margo Jefferson, in assessing Sebald's first three novels, believes the author has exhausted the "landscape of rarefied solitude" and that his approach has become monotonous—while his achievement is impressive, she considers words like "greatness" and "masterpiece" too hyperbolic to describe his works.[64] The writer Andre Aciman, in a long essay in the *New York Review of Books* claims Sebald's work belongs to a particular brand of recent European fiction that is, in the end, sterile and inconsequential:

> They are works about how works impart meaning, about how relative all meaning is, and about how inadequate all literary constructs are destined to remain. But they are seldom about anything else—which is why, once you remove the patina, and the dream-making, and the intertextual cross-references to keep students and critics at bay for another forty years, these works are really about very little other than our wish that they might have been about more. . . . What they lack, above all other things, is the depth of vision and the unencumbered impulse to come up with what is probably the most necessary thing a good author needs: which is a form.[65]

Aciman acknowledges that in *The Emigrants* Sebald came close to creating such a new form, as many critics wrote at the time of its publication, but he denies that honor to the novel *The Rings of Saturn*. Perhaps the best response to the criticism of the indirectness of Sebald's overriding "message"—or lack thereof—is to acknowledge outright the role that the concept of indeterminacy has increasingly played in modern critical theory and fiction since the idea began to assume its contemporary form in the field of physics in the first quarter of the twentieth century.[66] Commonly acknowledged in intellectual circles is the indeterminacy of the text—that is, the multiplicity of possible readings evoked by a given text. An even more profound but related skepticism posits the nature of our "reality" as a purely social construct; there is no true objectivity, only intersubjectivity. But to fully appreciate the purposes and effects of texts such as Sebald's books, one must also take into account the widely accepted principle of the inadequacy of language—*die Unzulänglichkeit der Sprache*—as elaborated upon in fiction by Hugo von Hofmannsthal and systematically developed in the work of early twentieth-century philosophers such as Ludwig Wittgenstein.[67] European discourse of the most sophisticated stamp has long been mindful of the difficulty of employing the flawed medium of human speech to make explicit assertions such as those Aciman seems to think Sebald should be able to offer if he is to be credited with truly creating a new form. However, postmodern European discourse avoids confident certainties not only for theoretical or conceptual reasons, but for important historical reasons. European writers and thinkers are painfully aware of the appropriation and perverse manipulation of language and culture for ideological purposes in the course of the last century. The example of Martin Heidegger is certainly instructive on this score: his reputation as a philosopher, like that of the critic Paul de Man, has been undermined in the estimation of many by revelations of his overt sympathies for the cause of fascism.

There is no doubt that Sebald's novels are specifically concerned with what it is to be a European—and, moreover, to be a European writer—in a time when European culture, despite the ubiquity of its remaining architectural monuments, literature, and artworks, is vanishing. Since Aciman in his review does not name the European authors he believes resemble Sebald for postmodernist inconclusiveness, a concrete comparison is not possible. It is certainly true, however, that much experimental fiction in Europe, while "superbly crafted," studiously avoids conventional narrative certainties—Aciman himself acknowledges Sebald's "intricate skein of interwoven themes, of private symbols piled upon collective images, of patterns and would-be patterns of cryptotechnics," although he is dissatisfied with what many other readers perceive as Sebald's uniquely appealing unity of voice and subject, his captivating melding of literature and life.[68] In the final analysis, as we have recognized, Sebald attempts so many different feats with his blend of essay, explication, and fiction that he does not fit in any category or even combination of categories. What does one make of a writer who alternately digresses on biographies, criticizes architecture, laments tragic loss, hallucinates, reports speech, investigates animal species, solves crimes, exposes deceptions, and extolls the beauty of landscapes? Where some readers find in Sebald a distinctive expression of wonder at the sadness and sublimity of existence, a skeptical reader asks "where is the point?" The point is in the final result—the completed yet paradoxically open-ended experience Sebald relates in his enigmatic books, with their haunting pictorial homage to the past. The critic Pico Iyer observes that the theme of all of Sebald's books amounts to:

> the effects [they] pass on to us—of restlessness, of panic, of being pursued through an echoing dream. And the feeling of dislocation is intensified by the fact that Sebald robs us of a sense of before or after, of cause and effect. There is no explicit context to his inquiries, and there is nothing in them that seems susceptible to reason. The reader is left in precisely the state that Sebald has made his own—unmoored, at a loss, in the dark.[69]

The statements the books make—and this is perhaps the final paradox of Sebald's work—are inexpressible as anything less than the totalities of the books themselves. They are, emphatically, examples of their own syncretic genre. And they are meant to reflect the way consciousness acts, by visual and thematic association. Narration of past lives is crucial to the mind's attempt to make sense of our own lives. In Sebald, consciousness is a theater that blends memory, hallucination, counterfeit memory, dream, soliloquy, and the unending stream of immediate perceptions. The possessor of that inner theater is at once actor, audience, and playwright. Externally, life is a journey, and Sebald's narrators are always ostensibly underway. But Sebald's is a modern pilgrim's progress, and there is no end in sight. To borrow a phrase from the title of Leonard Woolf's autobiography, in Sebald's fiction it is the journey, not the destination, that matters.

In sum, Sebald may be described as a writer who draws on his knowledge of several literatures and literary periods to create a new kind of documentary fiction that owes much to the expansive unconventionality of Borges, the diction and mood of Kafka, the deliberate narrative density of Bernhard, and the autobiographical sweep of Nabokov and Stendhal. In imaginative power, Sebald comes close on the heels of postmodernists such as Umberto Eco and Italo Calvino, although in manipulating biography and history he does not share their motivations. As to the latter point, whereas a writer such as Eco fictionalizes fact, Sebald proceeds in the opposite direction, making "facts fictive by binding them so deeply into the forms of his narratives that these facts seem never to have belonged to the actual world."[70] Ironically, despite numerous literary prizes in his homeland, he seems to have struck a chord with English-speaking readers to a greater extent than with his fellow Germans. Part of the reason for this is precisely his "Europeanness" in the minds of English-speaking readers; his idiosyncratic prose has a distinctly exotic appeal. On the German literary scene, however, reception in some quarters has been unwilling to use superlatives to describe Sebald's work, despite the fact that those who have done so, such as the poet Hans Magnus Enzensberger, are figures of national prominence. But it is also true from the perspective of some that Sebald, having lived abroad for so many years and having explored so many different literatures, simply marched to a different drummer. His subject was seldom contemporary Germany, except insofar as contemporary Germany—a dim reflection of pre-1933 Germany— arose out of the ruins of a terrible war and the shambles of a vast plan to exterminate a race of fellow human beings. It is safe to say that Sebald will never find favor with Germans who insist on only looking forward, never looking back.

CHAPTER 2

The Emigrants

In Search of the Vividly Present Dead

There is a fundamental contradiction in Sebald's commemorative approach to fiction: in searching for the meaning of the past, his narrators are seeking to recapture what is only *apparently* absent. They are attuned to the world around them and know that history is barely concealed beneath the surface of things. They are seeking an encounter with lives that have only ostensibly vanished into the past. By the same token, these lost lives—once examined with Sebald's allusive literary lens—often seem more intensely real than anything we can know in the present. This recollected, reconstructed vividness is in part a reflection of the self-contained, completed quality of the subject matter itself. Those lives that are over and done with—or virtually over and done with—lend themselves by their completeness or near-completeness to coherent, organic description. But true vividness emerges only when a life is shown to be more than the sum of its narrative parts—when a fictional creation seems very nearly to bring someone to life all over again. To the extent that fiction such as Sebald's can recreate or suggest the conditions that affected past lives, as well as the features that characterized the personalities in question, the illusion of a resurrected past can be achieved. Sebald's artistry is directed at discovering the secrets that regenerate past lives in imaginative form. Those secrets are constantly being threatened by the advancing frontiers of loss. The reader must be willing to participate in the salvaging of personal histories on the basis of documented historical reconstruction. That reconstruction is subject to Sebald's empathetic but covert fictionalizing. The "membrane" separating the true, or biographical, from pure invention is a porous one. Sebald's art requires a reader who knows the distinction between fact and fiction is often spurious.

The Emigrants is the second of Sebald's novels, but the first to appear in English. In the U.S. it was widely reviewed as a book about victims of the Holocaust, though the categorization of the novel as Holocaust literature obscures the nature of the book's content. As the critic and translator Gabriele Annan says of the book, "It is more general than that: it is about time, distance, absence, isolation, loneliness, depression."[1] It remains true, however, that the painful predicament of being Jewish in twentieth-century Europe forms one of the dominant themes of

The Emigrants, next to the toll taken by loneliness and depression, and the implications of exile for individual lives. The title of the novel, like all of Sebald's titles, is not without an ironic—in this case, sadly ironic—quality. None of the emigrants described in the book, whether Jew or Gentile, actually emigrated voluntarily. They were all in some way forcibly exiled. One of the emigrants, Paul Bereyter, remained in Germany, having been exiled not in the physical but in the spiritual and emotional sense.

The First Coincidental Encounter

The first character to be introduced in *The Emigrants* is the Lithuanian Jew, Dr. Henry Selwyn. He settled in England in the autumn of 1899, when his family left their Baltic home for New York City. Not knowing they had yet to reach their final destination, they disembarked too early—in London. In a nod to one of Sebald's favorite themes, the deceptiveness of mental "reality," Selwyn remarks that the Lithuanians as a group wandered the English streets assuming they had arrived in New York, even though the Statue of Liberty, which they had fully expected to see, had never appeared while the ship was approaching the city.

The narrator first meets Dr. Selwyn in the process of searching for a place to live in an area of Norfolk near the village of Hingham. The Selwyn episode, the shortest of the four in the book, begins in medias res, "at the end of September 1970," as the narrator and Clara, presumably his wife, visit Selwyn's property. The otherwise hopeful mood is contradicted by the first visual image of the book, a black-and-white photograph of a dark tree in a somber graveyard, presumably (this too is never explained) the same "grassy graveyard" in the churchyard next to Selwyn's house, a house that seems deserted when they arrive. In a typical Sebaldian association, the dark, "blind" window panes of the silent house recall for the narrator a bizarre domicile he once saw in France. Two "crazy brothers" in the Charente had built a replica of the façade of the palace of Versailles, creating an "utterly pointless stage set" that made a sightless, if imposing, impression.[2] When the couple finally ventures into the garden they find an elderly man lying under a tree, apparently contemplating blades of grass. As he rises, another characteristic of Sebald's way of seeing becomes apparent— the author makes a point of undermining or reversing initial judgments about appearance. Thus, the somewhat embarrassed gentleman is not what he appears: "Though he was tall and broad-shouldered, he gave the appearance of being stocky. One could have said he appeared to be a quite small person."[3]

The general state of things in Selwyn's estate is one of disorder and disrepair. Yet nature seems to carry on; a group of adopted horses eat their fill in the field, neglected vegetable plots and asparagus beds nonetheless yield produce of the finest flavor. There is a gloomy beauty to all that Sebald describes here, including the idiosyncratic apartments that the couple arranges to rent and renovate. The high windows with their inspiring views add a more uplifting note to the ambience, however. The cast of characters increases in number: Selwyn's wife Elli ("Hedi" in the original), an industrialist's daughter from Biel in Switzerland, then the maid Elaine ("Aileen" in the original), who seems to be virtually the only person inhabiting the rambling, mysterious house on a regular basis. Strangely, the maid never seems to prepare a meal, though she is occupied with countless unspecified chores throughout the course of each day. The narrator sneaks a glimpse of her bedroom as he is passing in the hall, and sees that it is full of dolls. At night she can be heard speaking with them. The house and its inhabitants exude eccentricity.

Selwyn's story unfolds slowly, revealed by means of occasional visits or chance meetings in which he recollects his distant childhood, which now seems more vividly real to him than the present. A photograph depicts the stone guardhouse with ramparts where Selwyn spends most of his time. This anachronistic "hermitage" is in a remote corner of the estate and the old man calls it his "folly." The reader expects this narrative line to be developed, of course, but as so often with Sebald, there is a sudden unexpected twist. The narrator, always an observer on the edge of things, chances upon Selwyn not at his hermitage, but standing at a window in the west wing of the house, aiming a double-barreled rifle at the sky. Finally he fires the weapon, and the roar of the discharge shatters the silence of the estate. Later Selwyn tells the narrator the history of the gun and his reason for firing it after many years of disuse: he was checking to see if it was still in working order. The scene is unsettling, but remains ambiguous, as Selwyn's explanation seems eminently plausible and his tone is matter-of-fact. But his conclusion that the recoil alone could kill someone points ominously toward the possibility of suicide.

Sebald staves off any foregone conclusions, however, with a companionable interlude in which Selwyn's friend Edwin Elliot appears. Elliot, a man who in his posture and his personality seems the opposite of Selwyn, is a well-known botanist and entomologist. The narrator and his wife join the two for a dinner prepared from vegetables Selwyn has harvested from the fertile chaos of his garden. Elliot turns the conversation to Switzerland, and Selwyn relates how in 1913, after finishing his medical studies, he journeyed to Bern to do postdoctoral work. There he met his future wife, whom he married after the war, and also a mountain guide named Johannes Naegeli, who later disappeared somewhere on the Aare glacier. A picture of the glacier—one presumes they are one and the same, in any case—is provided in the text. Sebald introduces a theme here in *The Emigrants* that we will encounter again and again in his fiction: the unreliability of memory. Selwyn imagines Naegeli waving to him from the platform of the Meiringen train station the last time they saw each other, but he knows the image probably isn't authentic. With this common phenomenon of false or wishful memory Sebald connects an observation more specific to Selwyn's individual story. The old man remarks again on the vividness of the distant past compared to the years leading up to the present. More precisely he speaks (with a lowered voice and a note of sadness) of how his wife has come to seem a stranger to him, while Naegeli now seems closer to him than ever. The death of Naegeli was a crushing blow to him. In this and later passages, Selwyn's tendency toward depression is becoming increasingly marked.

One of Sebald's favorite memoirists, Vladimir Nabokov, makes the first of several appearances in *The Emigrants,* his butterfly net tucked under his arm. Sebald provides the picture because, he writes, it resembles, down to the last detail, one of the pictures of Selwyn that appears on the screen while the men are showing slides of their trip to Crete. With that we have entered into another Sebaldian chamber: the realm of coincidence. Even the timing is strangely coincidental; the narrator had clipped the picture of Nabokov from a Swiss newspaper "just a few days before." (16) Moreover, this image simultaneously touches on another of Sebald's principal concerns: the "floating" nature of identity. As the narrator examines the landscape, the knee-length shorts, the boots, the stature of the men and their faces, it becomes clear that, for all we know, the figure of Selwyn could well be that of Nabokov and Nabokov could well be Selwyn. Highlighting the fluidity of identity is a fact the reader learns only later, as Dr. Selwyn is finishing the narrative of his life, that his real name was not Herry Selwyn, but Hersch Seweryn, and that he concealed his Jewish identity from his wife for many years. This deception is counted among the probable reasons for the deterioration of their relationship. Elli is often away on business while Selwyn stays home, solitary and aimless in his retirement.

This scene contains another typically Sebaldian visual reference. There is a moment while Elliot and Selwyn are showing the slides of their trip to Crete when the narrator mentions as a point of comparison an image from a film that is of immense importance for understanding the "extraterrestrial" narrative perspective found in all of Sebald's novels. It is also typical of Sebald that the reference is understated, almost hidden away. But if examined more closely, it provides keys to understanding Sebald's perspective as narrator as well as the intentionally enigmatic impressionism of his style. In this scene, as the host and his guests view the image on the screen of the Lasithi Plateau, the narrator

29

relates how he forgot the image completely in the years afterward, until he saw the movie *The Enigma of Kaspar Hauser* in a London cinema. This film, directed by Werner Herzog, first appeared in 1974. It is based on the true story of a young man who appeared on a Nuremberg doorstep in 1828 with a cryptic letter of introduction in his hand.[4] He could not talk; he had to be taught to speak. Nothing about his origins or childhood was ever learned, except that he had been locked away in a dark place. Kaspar sees everything around him in a completely new light as he learns for the first time to communicate with and commune with other human beings (to the extent that it is possible for him to do so). He is truly like the man who fell to earth. Herzog strengthened the film's sense of Kaspar's struggle to overcome the incomprehensibility of the new world around him by using not an actor but an inmate from a mental hospital, who is referred to only as Bruno S. in the film's credits. Sebald's narrator retells the scene in which Kaspar has begun to realize the distinction between dream and reality. He explains to his teacher Herr Daumer that in his dream he was in the Caucasus. Sebald's narrator relates what happens next:

> The camera pans from right to left in a sweeping arc and shows us the panorama of a high plateau ringed by mountain peaks. It looks very much like an Indian landscape, with pagoda-like towers and temples rising up with strange, triangular façades from amidst green forests and other lush foliage: these structures were follies, in a pulsing dazzle of light on the screen, that kept reminding me of the sails of those windpumps of Lasithi, which in reality I have still not seen to this day.[5]

Dream landscapes like this film sequence recur in all of Sebald's works, beginning with *Vertigo*. Such "follies"—gardens, monuments, temples, palaces—are perhaps both the natural creation of a subconscious utopian drive as well as a manifestation of man's tendency to repress transience and mortality. Sebald is concerned both with the workings of the mind—in this case, the mysterious impressions that arise from its dreaming state—as well as the nature and fate of artifacts that sentient beings craft from the stuff of nature. But Sebald's allusion to Kaspar Hauser, like many of his allusions and references, actually refers to much more than what is explicitly stated. In the film *The Enigma of Kaspar Hauser,* there is a sequence of scenes that might well be one of the most important clues to deciphering the code of "Sebaldry," to use critic Anthony Lane's coinage.[6] A succinct summary of the striking film sequence appears in a retrospective published twenty five years after the film's release:

> In a key scene, the mysterious foundling Kaspar (Bruno S.) is sitting with Käthe (Brigitta Mira), housekeeper to his tutor Prof. Daumer (Walter

Ladengast). He proposes to tell her a story about the desert, but admits he doesn't know the ending. Käthe reminds him that Prof. Daumer believes that stories should be told from start to finish, so Kaspar gives up the attempt. It is only on his deathbed, following his stabbing by an unknown assailant, that he tells the tale, illustrated by what looks like rough, flickering found footage. A caravan loses its way crossing the Sahara. Its leader, an old blind Berber, tastes the sand and tells his people that the mountains they see are imaginary. The caravan goes on, reaches the city— and then, says Kaspar, the story begins. But what happens next he does not know.[7]

Kaspar Hauser, always naturally and utterly honest in his new-found use of language, feels no need to finish a story where no end exists. He is immune to the compulsion to please others or honor convention. He simply relates his dreamlike tale, and draws no conclusions. Similarly, the incompleteness of unfinished stories is for Sebald a characteristic that is desirable, not a sign of insufficiency or imperfection. Even where his narratives end with a crescendo, suggesting at least provisional or interim closure, there is nevertheless a sense that the story, like life, is still going on. We don't know the ending. Even where Sebald's prose recaptures a personality from a bygone period, with the benefit of hindsight as it were, the story still retains an unfinished quality, and in that sense mirrors life. So it is with Dr. Selwyn; Sebald constructs a comprehensive view of his life by the end of the story, but at the same time suggests that we were not being told all we need to know to understand the character and his actions—that perhaps no one is ever told all they need to know in order to understand a person's actions.

However, it is obvious from Selwyn's discussions with the narrator that a terrible burden resulted from his decision as a young immigrant to hide his Jewishness. It is perhaps the main reason for his estrangement from his wife. But even his suicide, in retrospect so obviously predictable, does not mean the end of his story for Sebald. A strange coincidence resurrects the narrator's memory of Dr. Selwyn years later. He is in Switzerland taking the train from Zurich to Lausanne, passing the Aare glacier where Johannes Naegeli disappeared. He opens his French-language paper to find an article in which the recovery of the remains of the alpine guide is noted, and the fact that he had been missing since summer 1914. A copy of the article is displayed in the text as proof of the unlikely scenario. Sebald concludes the first part of his unfinished story with the following memorable words:

And so in such ways the dead are always returning to us. Sometimes they come back after more than seven decades, emerging from the ice and lying

31

at the edge of the moraine, a pile of polished bones and a pair of hobnailed boots.[8]

The story ends like a contemporary rendering of Johann Peter Hebel's story "Unverhofftes Wiedersehen" (Unexpected reunion), in which the corpse—in Hebel's version, quite well preserved—of a long dead miner is rediscovered decades after his mine's collapse, when his fiancée has long since become an old spinster.[9] As the motto of this chapter suggests, nothing, it would seem, has the power to erase the evidence of the dead—the "remnants" we inherit—like the power of memory to restructure and revise the past. Thus, the very function we depend on for preservation of the past can deceive us in the profoundest way. Sebald is in the company of Stendhal and Nabokov and many other memoirists in highlighting the uncanny ability of memory to alter and even expunge the past. Though memory is essential for living, and certainly for writing, it is an unreliable, mercurial friend.

The Teacher

Bereyter, a surname that can be found several times in Stendhal's *Life of Henry Brulard,* is the name the narrator of *The Emigrants* gives to an influential teacher from Sebald's childhood, the highly cultivated "Paul," as he was known to adults and children alike. Paul Bereyter was the third-grade teacher in the town of "S.," which is in reality Sonthofen, approximately ten miles from Sebald's birthplace of Wertach. The family moved to "S." in December of 1952. But this is not meant as an autobiographical narrative so much as a fictionalized biographical study of Sebald's former teacher, whose suicide came soon after that of the writer Jean Améry in 1978 (the date of Paul's death is however given in the text as January of 1984). The narrator attributes his motivation for finding out more about Bereyter's life to two factors: the drastic nature of his death, as mentioned in the obituary, and the seemingly unrelated fact that, as the article stated, Bereyter had not been allowed to teach during the Third Reich. The latter was due to his quarter-Jewish ancestry, and the former refers to Bereyter's choice of means to his end: at the age of seventy-four he threw himself in front of a train. The second part of *The Emigrants* thus begins with this terrible fait accompli. In a similar reversal of narrative order, the section on Dr. Henry Selwyn began with an ending too, though the reader may not have realized it fully at the time. It is a visual, not a verbal ending, however, a photograph of a great tree rising above headstones in a cemetery, followed in the German version by the first word of the first sentence, "Ende," which can mean both "at the end of" and "The End."

Sebald's purpose in the section on Paul Bereyter is to show something of the idiosyncratic appeal as well as the barely hidden sorrow of the title character's personality and to retrace a life's journey that ends, for reasons that include the individualized effects of the Nazi persecution of the Jews, in self-destruction. The sympathy the author feels for his teacher is understated in the text, but ever present. Still, he insists his reasons for writing about Paul stemmed from a pre-occupation with memory—he recognized that the will to recall Bereyter's life, a life which he as a child had encountered only temporarily and on the periphery, seemed in the end presumptuous. These attempts to recall were part of an effort at *Vergegenwärtigung* or a "bringing into the present." It seemed best to find out what really happened and put it in words once and for all. Sebald the narrator tells us he wrote about the Paul Bereyter he knew, and about what he was able to learn about Paul since his death.

In spite of his misfortunes, Paul retained a childlike quality throughout much of his life. The narrator takes note of this childlike quality when he remarks that the use of Bereyter's first name by everyone was for contemporaries a sign that they considered him not quite grown up, while for the schoolchildren it meant that he was "like an exemplary older brother, and belonged to us and we to him."[10] The cheerful tenderness of Paul's relationship with his pupils masks a sadder, more depressive side to his character. He displays moments of solitary grief even amidst a crowd, and one is reminded of the motto at the beginning of the story: "There are some mists that no eye can dispel."[11] He will become very nearly blind in later years—the "mists" will expand to make his vision one great blur. But the sadness of his teaching years is of a different sort. It is associated with the aesthetic experience of music or natural beauty. He also experiences frustration and impatience. When the children's inability to comprehend gets the better of him, he pulls a handkerchief out of his pocket and bites on it. But his greatest contempt is reserved for the two Roman Catholic priests who take turns teaching religion class on a weekly basis. He disappears shortly before they arrive and reappears only after they have left. He erases whatever they have written on the blackboard with visible vehemence. He obviously regards their pedestrian, sanctimonious, anti-intellectual brand of religion as a prime example of the provincialism and willful stupidity he struggles to combat in his teaching. And to be sure, his approach to teaching is unconventional, designed to give the pupils in his care an enlightening and uplifting educational experience, as opposed to the stifling, rote drudgery typical of the more authoritarian schools of the time. The class spends many hours out-of-doors, hiking, examining flora and fauna, touring nearby castles, and visiting local tradesmen and businesses. He teaches the pupils French words for the things around them. Whenever they stop

33

to rest he plays his clarinet. Similarities with Ludwig Wittgenstein, who taught primary school at one point in his life, are not unintended. Paul instructs his pupils in arithmetic far beyond the official guidelines for the grade, but ignores the prescribed reading textbooks, assigning stories from a classic anthology, Hebel's *Rheinischer Hausfreund*.

The reasons for Paul's apparently inconsolable loneliness become comprehensible to the narrator only after he gets to know a woman named Lucy Landau, who, he learns, made the arrangements for Paul's funeral. Here the narrative shifts from the perspective of the child and observer to that of the adult companion; the voice we hear now is largely that of recorded speech. In paraphrasing the remarks of Mme. Landau, Sebald relates the testimony of another, better-informed witness, with an eye toward completing, and thereby making sense of, Paul's story. The narrator visits her at her villa by Lake Neuchatel at Yverdon. As is so often the case with Sebald, the old house holds a fascination, and the narrator tells the story of Mme. Landau's move there as a child and her memories of the capacious emptiness and the silence of the place by the water. Her father had spent most all he had on the purchase, relocating the family from Frankfurt, and there was little left over to buy furniture. As she looks back on her life, she notes that the two people she remembers in her life as possessing the highest degree of decency and discretion were Ernest, a devoted friend of her youth, and Paul Bereyter, whom she met, far too late, in 1971 at Salins-les-Bain in the French Jura.

Paul confided in Mme. Landau a number of things the narrator could not have otherwise known. For instance, Paul revealed to her the depth of his contempt, in the last years of his career, for the provincialism of the pupils, who despite his affection for them came to seem more and more repugnant and worthy of contempt as time went on. He felt claustrophobic in the classroom, and even experienced feelings of malice toward the children at times. He told her of his own suicide attempt, dismissing it in an ironic tone as a stupid and embarrassing act. Yet the reader suspects this nonchalance is either a ruse or, at best, wishful thinking, knowing in advance how Paul will end up. Adding to the impression that Paul is hiding some terrible defect is Sebald's classroom memory of his teacher's voice—it seemed to come from his chest rather than the larynx, evoking the feeling that some clockwork inside was powering him, rendering him vulnerable to a complete mechanical breakdown at any moment.

Mme. Landau remembers long walks during which they discussed architecture and the human need to dream of utopia. This theme will be encountered again in *The Rings of Saturn*. More precisely, it is the paradox that the quest for utopia has in modern times led to the progressive destruction of natural life.

Mme. Landau recalls a sublime view, shared with Paul, from the mountains above Lake Geneva. She remembers marveling at the tiny trains and houses far below, the broad glaciers and high mountains in the distance, with the contrast evoking in her for the first time, clearly, "the contradictory dimensions of human desire."[12] Such was her experience on excursions with her sensitive and eminently thoughtful companion. Mme. Landau is also the source of a collection of photographs from Paul's life, including a photograph of Sebald's own class —surely scarcely indistinguishable, the narrator suggests, from the class Paul would have taught in Sonthofen as part of his pedagogical training in 1934. There are pictures of an Austrian girlfriend; the contented couple seems poised on the brink of a bright and boundless future in 1935, both unaware that Paul will soon be dismissed from his new teaching position because of the recently proclaimed racial laws. A subsequent picture shows a remarkably thin Paul Bereyter, and one is reminded of an earlier passage in the story in which Sebald's classmate, who has become a chef, remarks to the narrator years later that he never once, in all their days together in school, saw Paul eat anything. Mme. Landau relates how Paul, frustrated that the Nazis had succeeded in blocking his employment in his hometown, took a job as a private tutor in France until 1939, when he returned to Germany—for reasons that are never entirely clear—and was soon drafted into the army.

From remarks about Paul's Jewish paternal grandfather and his family we gain a deeper insight into what is concealed, at least in this specific instance, under the immense blanket of silence that descended on German history after the end of the Second World War. What Sebald regards as a thoroughgoing conspiracy of silence will be revisited in the novel *The Rings of Saturn* and in the critical study *Luftkrieg und Literatur*. One is struck by the facility with which the story "Paul Bereyter" recreates an entire milieu, virtually untraceable, of assimilated Jewish life. The integration of the Jews into German society, also evident in the succeeding chapters of *The Emigrants,* makes the fate that awaits them seem all the more heinous.

Paul's contradictory feelings—pedagogical devotion on the one hand and contempt for willful stupidity on the other—plagued him increasingly in the years after he was allowed to return to service in the school at "S.," and he spent most of his free time in Switzerland at Villa Bonlieu with Mme. Landau. At the same time he was unable or unwilling to give up his home in "S." In his retirement he gardened at Yverdon and read vociferously until his eyesight began to fail, mostly books by writers such as Kurt Tucholsky, Georg Trakl, Walter Benjamin, Ludwig Wittgenstein, and Arnold Zweig—all of them suicidal and most of them successful at their attempts. Paul's notebooks are full of accounts of various suicides, lending weight to the notion that he had been considering ending his own life long before he went blind. Mme. Landau movingly narrates the final trip to "S." They journeyed there to pack and move Paul's things and finally give up the apartment. The weather contributes to a mood of sinister foreboding, she recalls, and when she awakes from an afternoon nap, she notices in the weak crepuscular light that Paul's windbreaker, which had been hanging on the same hook for the last forty years, is missing. She knows she will never see him alive again.

In the last pages of "Paul Bereyter" the meaning of his manner of death becomes clearer, and a connection with the narrator's life is revealed. Though it has only been hinted at before—in Sebald's narratives there is always the illusion that the reader and the narrator stumble upon their discoveries at virtually the same time—the railway had always been imbued with deep significance for Paul. In an unused room on the north side of the apartment he had kept a Märklin model railway for years, "the very image and symbol of his very German tragedy."[13] Though the narrator does not expand on the "Germanness" of the tragedy, suffice it to say that the always punctual Germans possess one of the most extensive railway systems in the world. The narrator recalls Paul's insistence that his pupils learn about train stations, signals, freight warehouses, and the like; an example of a child's drawing of a station layout is provided in the text.

Paul's personality, paradoxically, is characterized by both the profoundest depression and the most expansive optimism. The former eventually leads to his suicide, while the latter is epitomized in his devotion to teaching. In spite of the odds, he remained—or tried to remain—a believer in the limitless potential of a rational, child-centered approach to education. Sebald's brief mention of a book by the Swiss educational reformer Johann Heinrich Pestalozzi suggests much about the life of Paul Bereyter. Mme. Landau, who coincidentally had been reading Nabokov's autobiography when she and Paul first met at Salins-les-Bains, at one point offers to read to Paul from Pestalozzi's *The Evening Hour of a Hermit,* a book of observations on teaching and living published in 1781. Paul welcomes the offer with the assertion that he would gladly give up his eyesight for such a gift. If one delves more deeply, one discovers that Paul had much in common with Pestalozzi: a rationalist's disregard for religious doctrine, a pedagogical focus on objects as opposed to language, and a temperament ill-suited for administrative organization. With Sebald, important hints are often embedded in details to which little attention is called. Yverdon, for instance, where Mme. Landau lives at Villa Bonlieu, is also the place where Pestalozzi established his last school. It finally had to be closed, like all the others he founded, but it lasted a full twenty years, from 1805 to 1825. Idealistic and energetic, both teachers were doomed to failure in their lifetimes, but the written record preserves their legacy. In the case of Pestalozzi, many consider his writings the single most important influence on modern pedagogy.

The Great-Uncle

The section "Ambros Adelwarth" concerns a great-uncle whom the narrator saw only once or twice in his life. It begins with a motto, quoted in English in the German original as well as the translation, taken from Chidiock Tichborne (1558–1586), who wrote, "My corn is but a crop of tears" shortly before his execution at the Tower of London. From the beginning, then, the reader is apprised of the stoic fatalism ahead. This portion of *The Emigrants* is the story of a life stalked, then set upon, and finally conquered by psychiatric depression. Unlike the other characters encountered so far, Ambros recognizes his depression not as an existential despair but as a pathological condition, and seeks treatment, though in seeking treatment he ensures his demise. Not just thematically, but visually, this text differs to a degree from the previous two. The variety of photographs and other images displayed on the pages of "Ambros Adelwarth" is greater than in the previous two stories. This visual eclecticism is more marked, presumably to reflect the increased role of the narrator's own travels as he retraces many of his uncle's journeys. There are antique pictures of family members who grew up with Adelwarth—in contradistinction to Paul Bereyter, his last name rather than his first is almost always used—but there are also pictures of the most exotic and idiosyncratic character: a pagoda, the Chrysler Building, a seaside villa, the Brooklyn Bridge, a young man in an Arabian costume, numerous hotels, various interiors, an image of ancient Jerusalem by night, and several group pictures in which clothing serves as an indicator of the historical period.

Ambros Adelwarth stood out among the narrator's emigrant relatives for his elegance and commanding presence. His diction was unaffected by dialect or accent—or so it seemed to Sebald at the time (in the year 1951, when he was going on seven years old). Adelwarth left after a few weeks for Switzerland, and the narrator would never see him again. It was Aunt Fini who had the closest relationship with Adelwarth, and her return visits to her homeland in the following summers always brought news of his whereabouts. It is she whom the narrator sets out to visit in New Jersey when he decides to learn more about Adelwarth's life and death.

Central to Adelwarth's personality is the question of homosexuality, although that aspect of his life is approached obliquely in the narrative, until Fini's husband Kasimir says as much. He states that Adelwarth was "of the other persuasion," in spite of the refusal of his relatives to acknowledge the fact. Adelwarth spends most of his career with the Solomon family in New York, and develops an evidently deep and committed relationship with the somewhat younger son, Cosmo Solomon. He serves as Cosmo's valet and traveling companion. But Cosmo dies tragically, destroyed by mental illness, and Kasimir remembers Adelwarth in subsequent years as increasingly crippled by depression, an "empty man . . . held together only by his clothes," living aimlessly in the large house the Solomon family had bequeathed him.[14] In any case, Adelwarth's attachment to Cosmo seems more than platonic, and it is also true that he had spent a long period in the employ of a Japanese bachelor. But the issue is never entirely settled, given Adelwarth's discretion and the times he lived in, not to mention Sebald's insistence on uncertainty as a guiding principle of representation. Suffice it to say the issue will not go away. And as the narrator learns more and more about Adelwarth, their two lives begin to blend, the same way the past and present become intertwined in Sebald. For instance, he dreams of visiting Deauville, the French resort where Cosmo and Adelwarth had their best times together, in the summer of 1913. The place is full of visitors. It is so full that the men and boys sleep in the lobbies and on the billiard tables. He searches among the silent guests for Cosmo or Ambros but they disappear before he can approach them. Sebald's use of contemporaneous detail—he has, among other things, researched the newspapers of the day—paints a convincing and alluring picture of Deauville in Adelwarth's time, while at the same time retaining a dreamlike mood, with "swaying diners" who speculate in a rising collective murmur as to the nature of the relationship between Cosmo and Ambros, who sit in the middle of the ballroom eating lobster. Are they brothers, master and man, friends, or something else? (Later Cosmo will sign the register of their hotel in Constantinople with the word *frères*—brothers.)

The theme of dislocation and exile pervades this story, as it does all of *The Emigrants*. One need only think of Paul Bereyter's postcards to his parents from the front—regardless of where he was, he always wrote that he was 2,000 kilometers away, to which is added (by Paul? by the narrator?) the question: but from where? The same notion is expressed in the scene where Sebald and Uncle Kasimir are standing on the beach and conversing in English. The older man, having turned pensive, remarks that he often comes out here because it makes him feel that he is a long way away, though he never quite knows from where. The plight of the exile is depicted in even starker terms when he adds, "This is the edge of darkness."[15] The "edge of darkness" is a metaphor for the foreboding year of 1913, in which Adelwarth and Cosmo made their most extensive travels. It was a chronological calm before the storm. This year appears also in Sebald's chapter on Kafka's visit to Italy in the novel *Vertigo,* and serves as an implicit historical watershed. It represents the last period in which nineteenth-century European culture and society was still intact, the last year before the "civilized" nations unleashed an apocalypse of modern technological warfare that sent an entire generation of young men to their deaths. Sebald's reconstruction of the journey, which is enriched by references to the writings of Chateaubriand, follows the two companions across the Mediterranean to the Holy land, where a lyrical ending to the chapter highlights the peaceful contentment once possible for both Cosmo and Adelwarth.

However, much of the story is devoted to Adelwarth's worsening condition as an older man, which was preceded by Cosmo's decline. The origins of Cosmo's mental deterioration, which was much more dramatic than Adelwarth's, lie in his agonized response to the terrible news from Europe as the Great War dragged on. The world he loved was ending. Many of the depressive personalities in Sebald seem to suffer empathetically in this way; like Paul Bereyter, they cannot keep their feelings in check the way most people can. Another mark of the isolated and depressive personality that recurs in Sebald is the inability to distinguish between dream and reality, an inability which grows worse as time goes on. Cosmo's final descent is initiated in a cinema, where he is watching a German film about a gambler—Fritz Lang's *Dr. Mabuse* (1922)—in which the villain is able to hypnotize and manipulate an entire public to his evil ends. Cosmo is overcome by the sensation he is being drawn into the labyrinth of the film's nightmare world, as if the whole production had been devised as a trap to destroy him. The scene that most disturbs him is one in which there is a caravan reminiscent of the one in the Kaspar Hauser film mentioned earlier in "Dr. Henry Selwyn." It is actually a conjuror's illusion, and disappears as quickly as it came. Cosmo insists the caravan has taken his true soul with it.

According to a prevalent modern conception of depression as a symptom of defective brain chemistry, there is of course no "will" powerful enough to retrieve a soul sinking into the depths. Only medication and therapy can help. Sebald's depressive characters often serve to confirm the utter helplessness of those with this condition, as they decline in what seems a most deterministic and ineluctable way. No matter what is undertaken, the result is often the slow disappearance of individual personality. Samaria Sanatorium in Ithaca, New York, for many years tried electric shock therapy, which was presumably the ultimate cause of Adelwarth's death after he committed himself to that institution, where Cosmo too had ended up years before. Ithaca thus figures as one of the stations on the narrator's journey. Sebald's insertion of the figure of Nabokov into the narrative is no mere gratuitous apparition, however, since Nabokov was in fact teaching at Cornell University in Ithaca in the 1950s, the period when Adelwarth was being treated. The figure of the novelist and lepidopterologist is an intra- and intertextual allusion linking the story with Dr. Selwyn's, while at the same time suggesting the possibility of a hopeful triumph over the tragedy of exile. It also points to the intricate design and coloration of short-lived, elusive creatures such as butterflies—creatures that harm no one, while at the same time exhibiting a natural beauty for which evolutionary explanations seem utterly insufficient. On one level the appearance of Nabokov is plausible and even mundane, on another it is a complex allusion to a master of the complex allusion. The reader cannot help but surmise that this is not the last time "the butterfly man" will appear. He is one of the repetitive threads that link the quartet of stories.

Samaria Sanatorium is another of those places that seems to be a character in the story as much as a setting. The place resembles the immense "pinewood lodges . . . that Austrian archdukes and princes built all over their hunting grounds in Styria and the Tirol in the nineteenth century," but now, years after Adelwarth died there, it is an empty hulk, showing unmistakable signs of decay.[16] The former director, Dr. Abramsky, is in some ways Dr. Selwyn's double— an elderly contemplative, a loner, an inhabitant of a ramshackle, neglected compound. Convinced that his treatments were doing more harm than good, he closed the clinic in 1969. "Giving up Samaria," says Abramsky, "was the condition I had to fulfill in order to be released from involvement in life."[17]

The visit with Dr. Abramsky occasions a lengthy description of the early days of electric shock therapy. The details are chilling. Not only was the experience itself violent and physiologically traumatic, but the side effects could be brutal: dislocated shoulders and jaws, broken teeth, fractures of various kinds. Many patients had to be dragged to the treatment room as if to a place of execution. That the efficacy of such therapy should have been frequently evaluated seems obvious, though Abramsky says his predecessor and colleague Dr. Fahnstock kept only cursory records that were surely destroyed long ago by the mice that took over the abandoned sanatorium. "My hopes lie with the mice," he concludes, then tells of a recurring dream in which vermin have bored through and so weakened the structure that it finally falls in on itself, ever so slowly, leaving only "a pile of powdery, pollen-like wood dust."[18]

It would be hard for a narrative to remained fixed much longer on so much hopeless depression (shock therapy was for Adelwarth a decorous method of suicide), and Sebald seems to know it. The subject of considerable amusement is contemporary Deauville, which is now nothing like the noble resort once visited by Adelwarth and Cosmo. In his descriptions we sense that Sebald's complaint about what popular culture has done to Deauville is at base a lament for the absence of dignity in contemporary life. He is in no way nostalgic for the social inequalities of the past, but finds a contemptible, mindless banality in the democratized distractions of popular culture. Sebald's descriptions of the hundreds of Japanese tourists—bused in from the airport, and bused out three days later, only to be replaced by another homogeneous group—are hilarious at first glance, though upon closer examination full of pathos. Buildings of various disharmonious architectural styles blight the landscape, and automobiles fill the once placid streets.

Nature is never totally defeated by man's despoilations, however. Carefully worded nature descriptions dominate in the final, uplifting pages of the story. While the world may have changed since Adelwarth's travel diary was written, one can still experience the ultramarine blue waters on the way to Constantinople, which is described as a stunning maze of a city with an "inconceivable variety of greens—the crowns of pines high aloft, acacias, cypresses, sycamores, cork oaks, eucalyptus, laurels, and junipers."[19] And although Jerusalem, their destination, is already a tawdry tourist trap—a 1913 counterpart to Deauville in 1991— its environs possess a serene beauty. The city itself is only beautiful in the form of an idealized image of a mystical, moonlit Jerusalem. The unreliable relationship of appearance and reality is highlighted again by the pair's visit to the Dead Sea. None of the things they had heard about toxic fumes, motionless waves, or green phosphorescence turns out to be true. Yet stranger things do; a white line, for instance, is visible in the mornings running the length of the Sea and vanishing an hour or so after daybreak, and the terrain where they camp at Ain Jidy is almost paradisiacal. Cosmo and Adelwarth both are still in control of their lives, still observing, still capable of treasuring experience. This is where fiction accomplishes the transcendence of hopelessness and melancholy—the depression and catatonic dementia that we know are yet to come are still very far away at Ain Jidy in 1913. Even the harbinger of their future plight—a young quail that flies into the tent and alights on Cosmo's lap while he is sleeping "as if it had found its rightful place"—is a thing of beauty.[20] Shortly before sunrise it realizes its mistake and flies away. It had not found its rightful place after all.

The Artist in Exile

Though all the lives into which Sebald delves in *The Emigrants* appear in some way connected to his own, the fourth and final chapter of the book is doubtlessly the most personal. It is also the longest. It begins with Sebald's own expatriation to England, and includes a narrative of his return to his German homeland to visit the places where the title character and his family once lived. That character, Max Aurach, is modeled to a large extent on the English Jewish painter Frank Auerbach, renamed Max Ferber in the English edition.[21] The name "Ferber" in turn is one of Sebald's plays on words—*Färber* in German is a dyer or

41

literally "one who colors." The use of the word hints at Sebald's authorial role as one who "colors" actual reminiscences with fictional hues, altering and expanding on reality, rendering—as we have said before—facts fictive. An additional overlapping with the narrator in this story is that Ferber, like Sebald and his other narrators, is an exile from Germany. Both first arrived by plane: Ferber in 1939, and Sebald in 1966. Sebald's description of the flight over the moonlit Midland landscape combines the mundane detail of a routine flight with an increasing sense of the strangeness of the scenery below: a mountain resembles a "monstrous prone body that sometimes seemed to rise up or sink," while the city of Manchester, "spread over a thousand square kilometers . . . built of countless bricks and inhabited by millions of souls, living and dead," glows dimly under a shroud of fog.[22] If the comparison of Sebald's perspective to that of an extraterrestrial observer was ever apt, it is certainly so here. Once in Manchester, the overwhelming atmosphere of the hotel where he settles in, as well as the city itself, is one of silence and emptiness, which is so smothering, especially on Sundays, that the narrator finds himself trying to cope by venturing out on long walks through the seemingly abandoned city.

Ever focused on the secrets of the past hidden just beneath the present's surface, Sebald discovers what remnants there are of the former Jewish community of Manchester. The many Jews who lived in Manchester left the inner city during the years between the two World Wars. As a stranger, the narrator is more sensitive to his new, alien environment's features than one who is at home there. Therefore it is no surprise that certain signs that might not interest the native intrigue the narrator, leading him to a hidden art studio where he meets "the artist, who has been working there since the end of the forties, ten hours a day, day in, day out, the seventh not excepted."[23] It is the artist's method, as much as his personality, that seems to interest both the author and his narrator. Max Ferber uses large amounts of paint, which he constantly applies and scrapes off, leaving on the floor a central mound of steadily increasing height and expanding breadth. Nothing is removed, cleaned, or otherwise touched. Everything in the studio is collecting dust and has been doing so for almost twenty years. Ferber regards this steadily growing mass of colors, rather than his paintings, as the *true* product of his continuing efforts and the obvious proof of his failure. Ferber's paradoxical assertion recalls Nabokov's image of an aging swan's repeated and futile attempts to climb into a moored boat—its "agony was so much closer to artistic truth than a drooping dancer's pale arms."[24] Failure and repetition are the constant companions of the true artist. On one of Sebald's visits Ferber explains his peculiar thinking, telling the narrator that nothing changes in his place of work, that everything remains as it was, "that he never felt more at home than in places where things are left undisturbed and allowed to lie muted under the grey, velvety sediment that collects as matter dissolves, little by little, into nothingness."[25] Ferber is a man in the grip of a compulsion, who continues to work day after day in spite of his conviction that his work is one long exercise in failure. The German edition provides an example of one of his charcoal drawings, which, like his paintings, are always the result of scores of preliminary versions. The drawing is recognizably a portrait—or two portraits—with seemingly unrelated lines superimposed, suggesting in turn yet another, larger portrait. At second glance the various levels of dissonance seem to form a unity after all. In any case, its suggestive, representational qualities are only visible from afar—close up the painting's subject is unrecognizable. The picture, which seems to be an emblem of the protean elusiveness of identity, is not included in the British or American edition.[26]

As elsewhere in *The Emigrants,* the first person pronoun shifts from the narrator to the protagonist and back. No quotation marks are used—an omission not unusual in modern German fiction but somewhat less common in English-language literature. Ferber speaks of his attachment, even "bondage," to Manchester. Since going there he has traveled abroad only once, to see the Isenheim Altar in Colmar, France. These paintings, by Matthias Grünewald, which are *not* shown in the text, have always fascinated him. These are the paintings that Sebald wrote about earlier in his collection of poems *Nach der Natur,* and here Ferber, the visual artist, responds to them, and especially to "The Entombment of Christ," in words that echo Sebald's own fascination with Grünewald's art:

> The extreme vision of that strange man, penetrating every detail, twisting every limb, and infecting the colors like an illness, was one I had always felt apt and right, as I had always known, but now I found my feeling confirmed by the sight of the actual work.[27]

Ferber goes on to say that the depiction of pain and suffering and its pervasive influence extending into nature itself expressed for him a central truth about consciousness: after a certain point, pain blots out everything, even the experience of pain itself. His own experience with a damaged vertebra immobilized him, putting him in excruciating pain for hours, pain that he gradually realized was distinctly reflective of his own inner constitution. Standing with his head pressed against the wall at an angle, he remembered a photograph his father took of him in the second grade, a young boy leaning over his schoolwork. In the photo his head was at the same angle. The picture, a close-up, appears in the text. But is it really Ferber, or is it someone else as a child? In spite of the many pictures interspersed throughout the book, we have few recognizable images of the main characters in these stories, with the exception of Paul Bereyter.

Lake Geneva, a setting in all of Sebald's works, appears in "Max Ferber," though its sublime beauty does not have the usual benign effect. Ferber describes a kind of sensory overload he endures while there; a feeling of foreboding overcomes him. As in Sebald's other novels, a breakdown occurs in which the narrator, or one of the main characters, is immobilized in an almost catatonic state. In this case, Ferber shuts out all the light by closing the curtains and pulling the blinds in his hotel room in Montreux. He remains inside for several days. In the course of the worsening of his nervous condition he realizes that only "the reality outside" could save him. He decides to go out and climb the Grammont again, just as he and his father had done in 1936. The brilliant day reflects the day in his memory, and as he surveys the deep blue lake below he fears its powerful attraction will jolt him away forever. The tension is broken by the sudden appearance, or rather reappearance, of the butterfly man, who admonishes Ferber that it is late in the afternoon—time to descend and return to Montreux before night falls. But at this point memory again plays its tricks, and for some reason the Nabokovian intervention, as well as the memory of the day on the Grammont, dissolve into a "lagoon of oblivion"—Ferber later cannot recall the descent, the remaining days in Switzerland, or the journey back to England.[28] The fruitless attempt to recapture the period plagues him to the point of near madness. Tranquilizers only contribute to his bizarre hallucinations, culminating in an elaborate dream in which Ferber recalls accompanying Queen Victoria to the 1887 art exhibition in nearby Trafford Park. Subconscious associations from Ferber's childhood mingle with historical detail from 1887, and the dream is crowned by the vision of an intricate model of Solomon's temple, which is presented to Ferber by a mysterious Herr Frohmann of Drohobycsz. Though Sebald is silent as to the source of this reference, the character is in fact taken from a description in the Austrian novelist Joseph Roth's collection of essays, *Juden der Wanderschaft* (1927; *The Wandering Jews,* 1976). Peering into the miniature temple, Ferber realizes for the first time, he says, how a true work of art looks.

Memory is equally problematic for the narrator. During his years away from Manchester, Ferber still stands out in his mind, though he cannot seem to picture Ferber's face. Yet Ferber's persona virtually obsesses him. Similarly, the reader will recall, Ferber himself can't seem to pinpoint identifying features when attempting a portrait. This characteristic uncertainty is dispersed once the narrator encounters one of Ferber's pictures in the Tate Gallery, "G. I. on her Blue Candlewick Cover." At least two points should be made in connection with this painting. Sebald's view of art, as we have seen, assumes that the experience of a book or the perception of a painting can be potentially more vividly "real" than the experience of reality. For the narrator of *The Emigrants,* seeing the painting in the Tate Gallery has the power to restore to his memory Ferber's appearance, where nothing else could. Second, there is an element of intratextuality at work here, as is so often the case in Sebald.[29] For instance, the fabric known as candlewick, as in the title of the painting, is mentioned several times earlier in the story. Its conspicuousness for Sebald is attributable to its being found, he learns, only in working-class English bedrooms. In another instance a description of Ferber's right eye (accompanied by a photograph in the German version only) represents a counterpart to Adelwarth's helplessly wandering left eye after his treatments at the Samaria Sanatorium.

According to an article the narrator comes across many years after leaving Manchester, Friedrich Maximillian Ferber (Friedrich Maximillian Aurach in the German original) left his home in Germany in May 1939 and came to England. The narrator realizes that the common nationality of Ferber and the narrator had never—oddly, for they both surely recognized each other's accents—become a topic of conversation between the two. They had never talked about Ferber's parents, his siblings, if any, or his past in any respect. The narrator had been totally unaware that Ferber's father was an art dealer in Munich who sent his son to an uncle in London when the boy was fifteen, several months before the war broke out. When the narrator revisits Manchester he addresses the subject of Ferber's past. One of the main ideas that emerges from these conversations is the deceptive nature of time, a theme Sebald also addresses in his next two novels. Ferber insists there is really no past or future, at least not for him, and that our idea of time is merely a "rumbling disquiet of the soul."[30] Remembering his past inevitably gives rise to a meditation on Germany—it was his homeland, after all —and the period in German history that he experienced as a boy. He never once returned, so Germany for him is frozen in the 1930s, a period of countless parades and flags, as well as a stifling silence about what was happening and what lay ahead. As if to emphasize the borderless continuum of time—no past or future—a gray lady wearing a muted ball gown, fashionable during his childhood, appears to Ferber almost daily, approaching him while he sits resting in his chair. The beautiful apparition removes her hat and gloves and bends over him, he swoons, and she is gone. Though this vision from deep in his past is profoundly vivid, his memory of past events also contains profound inconsistencies and tremendous blind spots. The time before the age of eight or nine is a complete blank. The most vivid scenes, however, seem to be associated with the feeling of his family's isolation from the rest of society. He recalls how certain topics of conversation were suppressed in his household, such as the loss of his father's share of his store to his Aryan partner and the suicide of his grandmother, Lily Lanzberg. Uncle Leo, dismissed from his position as a teacher in Würzburg, is the only relative willing to speak openly. The dichotomy of appearance and reality is one of the lessons Leo teaches young Ferber, as when he asserts that a photograph from a newspaper—a copy appears in the text—is counterfeit. The image, allegedly of the Nazi book-burning on the square in front of the Bishop's *Residenz* in Würzburg, is demonstrably a picture from another occasion, to which smoke from yet another picture has been added, as well as a dark night sky. When the books were in fact burned, on the night of 10 May, the darkness would have made taking a photograph with such sharp detail impossible. The benign counterpoint to this deception is the masterful ceiling fresco by Giambattista Tiepolo (1696–1770) inside the same residential palace in Würzburg. Uncle Leo spends an entire evening studying a picture book of the Tiepolo frescoes with a magnifying glass, amazed at how the artist achieved the visual suggestion of the infinite. The ironic subtext, however, suggests that the ceiling fresco itself is a deceptive medium; in order to achieve the illusion of verticality and infinity as perceived at a distance from below, fresco artists must distort and distend their painted forms on the flat as well as the rounded surfaces.

In Ferber's narration of the last months he spent with his parents, the tremendous power of denial becomes clear. Even after *Kristallnacht,* the "night of broken glass," in November of 1938, when Ferber's father is taken to Dachau, the family will not openly acknowledge that fate is closing in. After his release, the family even takes a skiing trip; the text shows a picture of the father posed on a snowy mountaintop, looking as if he were just another vacationer. The sad culmination of Ferber's father's behind-the-scenes efforts to arrange his child's escape is reached when Ferber finds himself with his parents at the airport at Oberwiesenfeld. There, he remembers, they bid him farewell, but he cannot remember a single word, an embrace, or an expression. The physical details of the airport and the airplane are, however, as fresh in his mind as if the event had happened yesterday, a fact which points to the central significance of the power of vision for Ferber—not only because it is key to his art, but also because it is key to memory. Remembering can involve all the senses, of course, but for most it is overwhelmingly visual. Sebald's visual emphasis is multifaceted; it is expressed in his verbal descriptions, in the actual images interspersed throughout the text, and in his depictions of his characters' use of their sight. Many of Sebald's characters are depicted in the act of searching for something (although it is often unclear what they seek). Leo examines the frescoes intently and at length, trying to see deeper and deeper into them. Likewise, when Ferber changes planes in Frankfurt, a customs officer stares at his opened suitcase for an inordinate amount of time, as if the shape and order of the neatly folded clothes held some secret meaning.

One thing that is certain about identity in Sebald is that his characters remain forever exiles. The condition is immutable. Ferber's attempts to conform to English life and "fit in" did not meet with success in the long run. At the same time, he quit speaking German the day he arrived in England, and once the letters from his parents stopped coming, the bond with his native language was broken entirely. Yet the news that would finally come, confirming their death, was at first utterly incomprehensible. In time he felt the meaning of it more and more acutely, and he withdrew inwardly, to "immunize himself against the suffering they endured and against my own."[31] While his repression of the pain by means of self-seclusion gave him a temporary sense of balance, it formed such deep roots that the effects of the tragedy, he says, "rose up again and put forth evil flowers that formed a poisonous canopy arching over me. It has kept my world shadowed and dark in these last years."[32] With this image of pullulating evil, Sebald provides a negative example of interconnectedness, of anastomosis.

The notes made by Ferber's mother in the last months before she was taken away form the basis for the rest of the story. She evidently recognized the hopelessness of her and her husband's situation, and as the efforts to acquire visas and permission to leave continued to bear no fruit, her thoughts turned to her childhood in the Franconian towns of Steinach and Bad Kissingen. These notes are lovely, Ferber tells the narrator, but also like "one of those evil German fairy tales, in which, once caught in its spell, you are forced to carry on with whatever work one has begun—in this case, remembering, writing, and reading—until your heart breaks."[33] The ambiguity of Ferber's sentiment will not be lost on many readers, for the twentieth century brought forth the fullest expression of such "evil German fairy tales" in the form of the camps at Auschwitz and Treblinka. The "forced work" there, however, was of a deadlier kind.

The narrator in the remaining pages relates Luisa Lanzberg's intimate reminiscences of a bygone age, acting as a kind of ghost writer. The reader is unaware, of course, of the extent to which the author (Sebald) is responsible for endowing the memoir with its truly lyric quality, but one may assume that the original document is written with sensitivity as well as painstaking detail. Sebald interjects phrases like "Luisa writes" or "so the memoir before me reads" throughout, suggesting the authorship is primarily hers. What emerges is a literary will and testament, written in the face of looming disaster. Luisa places her Jewish family, which can be traced to the seventeenth century, in the landscape of Lower Franconia, the area around Bad Kissingen. One is reminded that the Jews in Germany were not exclusively city dwellers by any means, but had businesses and homes in many small communities like Steinach, where Luisa lived until her family moved to Bad Kissingen in 1905. One begins to understand that the tragedy of the Jews in Germany is tinged with a terrible irony—these people, whom the Nazis considered utterly foreign, were for the most part assimilated and integrated into German society. Luisa Lanzberg's youth is characterized by nothing if not a comfortable—and comforting—feeling of belonging, a feeling that would have made it difficult for anyone growing up in such circumstances to accept, years later, the drastic intentions that motivated the Nazis. This sense of assimilation is exemplified by the picture of Luisa's father's sister that hangs on the living room wall. She is "the most beautiful girl far and wide," the memoir reads, and everyone calls her a blonde beauty, "a true Germania."[34] In that same vein, Luisa's mother treasures the works of the nineteenth-century poet Heinrich Heine, who is also, she asserts with pride, the favorite bard of Empress Elisabeth. Such ironies are painful. Yet, as is so often the case with Sebald, there is much more that is left unsaid. It is not even mentioned, for instance, that Heine was a Jew, nor that he fled to France to escape Germany's political oppression, nor that his oeuvre would later be largely extracted from the German literary canon by the Nazis. Some of his works were too firmly ensconced for the Nazis to expunge, however. In cases such as that of Heine's famous poem "The Lorelei"—too popular as a folk song to be suppressed—the Nazis simply suppressed Heine's authorship, attributing the song to an "unknown poet."

With Luisa Lanzberg's retelling of her childhood memories, a lyrical crescendo of sorts is reached. The intact world of small-town Jewish life in Steinach is described with affection and sympathy; the overriding tone is of serenity and contentment. Seasons change, and time is marked by the celebration of religious holidays. Special gifts arrive from relatives. A masked ball is held at a local beer garden. And in an echo of the previous story, in which Sebald describes Paul Bereyter's classroom, Luisa spends many lines telling her son what her exclusively Jewish school was like. Life will never again be as it was. Looking back, she is wistful:

> Time. In what time did all that take place? And how slowly the days passed then! And who was that strange child, walking home, tired, with a tiny blue and white jay's feather in her hand?[35]

The question of the girl's identity, left unanswered, implies yet other questions, especially that of her fate and the fate of her loved ones. These are the same questions "posed" by any photographs of a stranger from the past, the kind of photograph preferred by Sebald. But as in the case of Dr. Abramsky's parting gesture (the wave of a feather), the ultimate significance of the scene is left for the reader to puzzle over. This too is often the case in the novels of the French writer Claude Simon, whom Sebald admired (Simon is mentioned explicitly in *Austerlitz*).

Sebald's literary monism can be clearly perceived in Luisa's elegiac picture of the Steinach years. For her, those simple, seemingly endless hours of her childhood seem to have expanded outward in all directions over the boundless expanses of time, present even as she was writing her recollections many years later. In memory everything that is gone still exists, suspended in time and somehow indelibly real. There is no temporality, only the oneness of everything. During a stroll with a young suitor named Fritz Hansen in the park at Bad Kissingen, she encounters a young Russian boy with a butterfly net, and we presume to have encountered—quite plausibly, for his family visited German spas in the summers—the incipient writer Nabokov once again (In fact, something like the incident occurs in Nabokov's autobiography *Speak, Memory*). When Fritz later proposes to Luisa, the image of the butterfly boy appears before her eyes, and we learn more of the possible meaning of the figure Sebald inserts into his stories:

> "Everything around me blurred [and I saw] the Russian boy, whom I had long forgotten, leaping about the meadows with his butterfly net—a messenger of joy, returning from that distant summer day to open his specimen box and release the most beautiful red admirals, peacock butterflies, brimstones, and tortoiseshells to announce my final liberation."[36]

This youthful version of the butterfly man embodies an enviable lightness of being, and a soul directed outward, fixed not on itself but on the search for intricately beautiful objects of nature. This passage is the key to understanding the significance in Sebald of Nabokov—he is the ebullient alter ego to every melancholy exile.

A Cracked Bell: Returning Again to the Present

Beauty and tranquility characterize Luisa Lanzberg's images from the past. The denouement that follows, as Sebald's narrator embarks on a 1991 trip to visit the stations of her life, demonstrates that no remnants of Luisa's world remain. The privations and inconveniences of the traveler set the initial tone of this final portion of Ferber's story, as the narrator repeatedly changes trains and waits long hours in numerous station halls. Such experiences are not without a certain stoic humor, as, for instance, when the narrator boards the last train, from Gemünden to Bad Kissingen, and takes a seat in an almost empty car. A large square-headed man with close-set eyes and a red, puffy face chooses to avail himself—despite the many unoccupied seats—of the one directly across from Sebald. He sits, legs apart, with his rotund belly stuffed into summer shorts, and runs his tongue around his mouth, all the while breathing noisily. The sight is a far cry from Luisa Lanzberg's image of skaters gliding in wonderful, sweeping curves, and serves to illustrate the lack of dignity in the bearing, dress, and appearance of contemporary people. Luckily for the aesthetic sensibilities of the narrator, the "monster" exits at the next stop. But the surrealism of contemporary culture does not end there. Utterly indifferent to the beauty of the descending dusk outside the train windows, another traveler slices an apple and eats it piece by piece, spitting the peel into a bag on her lap after every bite. Arriving in Bad Kissingen is like arriving in a ghost town. The narrator climbs into the only taxi waiting outside the station and is taken to a recently renovated hotel, where more strange—but perfectly credible—creatures await his arrival. And if the people of the town are not in some way utterly bizarre, then they are ancient. A quotation from Goethe in the local paper the following day seems to express the central point of Sebald's comparison of the Bad Kissingen of yesteryear with that of today: "Our world is a cracked bell that no longer sounds."[37]

But Sebald has a purpose in his contemporary description of the spa town that is more than coolly detached parody. His narrator has come there to inspect the Jewish cemetery. He reads the names on the gravestones, among them Blumenthal (a literal translation from the German would be "valley of flowers"), Seeligmann ("blessed man"), Goldstaub ("gold dust"), Hertz ("heart"), Grünwald ("green forest"), and Leuthold ("lovely people"). Though Sebald doesn't mention the history of these names, they were, in point of fact, family names *assigned* to the Jews as a result of the laws of emancipation that were enacted in the first quarter of the nineteenth century. Sebald muses that in the meantime the Jewish surnames came to be thought of as a kind of slap in the face throughout German-speaking Europe: "The Germans begrudged the Jews perhaps nothing so much as the beauty of their names, so intimately bound up with the land they inhabited and its language."[38] Neither of the well-marked keys to the cemetery fits, however, so the narrator is unable to enter except by subterfuge. This situation is especially ironic in a country where keys are often meticulously labeled, and the prevailing mentality insists nothing can go wrong if you take such measures to ensure good order. Finally the narrator simply climbs the wall.

His visit to the graveyard affords Sebald the perfect occasion to consider again questions of transience and identity. One of the names listed is Auerbach, the surname of the painter upon whom the story "Max Ferber" is ultimately based. Sebald is startled to see that one Maier Stern died, by coincidence, on his own birthday, the 18th of May.[39] A writer's quill marks the grave of Friederike

Halbleib, prompting him to imagine her bent over her writing as Sebald is himself bent over his work, penning the words we are reading. As he is about to climb the wall and leave, he discovers a marker for the Lanzberg family, which he surmises was put there by Uncle Leo. The date of Luisa and Fritz's deportation is inscribed, November 1941, as is the fact that Luisa's father Lazarus Lanzberg died in the concentration camp at Theresienstadt in 1942. One can only surmise what happened to Luisa and Fritz. We learn the name of Luisa's mother, to whom she referred throughout the narrative as, naturally, "mother" or "mama." It is Lily. The tragic dimensions of the story expand as we learn that she committed suicide, and hers are the only remains in the grave. We are left to surmise, once again, how, and under what conditions, she took her own life. It hardly matters, of course. These past lives, reconstructed through the narrator's researches, are irrelevant to the Bad Kissingen of today. The names of the Jews who once lived here are concealed in an overgrown graveyard nobody visits. Increasingly, Sebald remarks, his head and nerves are "attacked" by "the spiritual impoverishment and lack of memory of the Germans" and "the skill and efficiency with which they had cleaned everything up."[40]

All in all, the visit has the unsatisfactory feeling of a homecoming to a permanently altered place, a place that has been drained of its meaning. The dissonance of personal tragedy and contemporary indifference begins to weigh on the narrator, and he decides to accelerate his departure. Even under these circumstances, the comic element is unavoidable; the sublime, what little there is, gives way almost completely to the ridiculous. The final part of the visit, a trip by boat to the salt vapor frames described by Luisa in her memoir, takes place in a completely empty motor launch. The portly woman piloting the boat, pictured wearing her sea captain's cap, had been waiting all morning for passengers. She is a Turk, and thus a member of Germany's largest minority, and a figure that could ✓ not have existed in Luisa's time. With playfulness, but also genuine respect, Sebald describes the idiosyncratic helmswoman, who philosophizes that there is no end to stupidity, adding—in stark contrast to common attitudes and stereotypes among the Germans themselves—that the Germans are just as stupid as the Turks, maybe even stupider. Finally the boat reaches the salt vapor frames, and the reader, who has surely been wondering what in the world these structures represent, is invited to inspect two large photographs of them. There is also a photo of one of the blackthorn twigs that are bound together to form the high wall that serves as a fibrous network from which the salinated air emanates. There the narrative of the visit abruptly ends. The story becomes a story of the writer's effort to complete the story. Sebald's work, according to the narrative, left him little time for writing in the winter of 1990–91. He was dissatisfied with the "patched up" final version of Max Ferber's life and was hesitating to send it to him for approval, when he learned that Ferber was gravely ill.

Once more Sebald assumes the persona of the solitary traveler, visiting a relic of the past. In this case, it is a relic that only Max Ferber, or someone like him, could love: the Midland Hotel in Manchester. The windows are covered with a thick layer of marbled dust, the steam heat barely works, the plumbing is antiquated, and whole sections are closed off. One seldom encounters another guest or a member of the staff in the halls. But in its state of near ruin it still possesses a distinctive character—one could say it is yet another of Sebald's character/settings, functioning in the way so many of the places in Sebald function, as personalities. Like the people who tell him their stories, buildings too have a history that intrigues him. This is even more explicitly demonstrated in the novel *Austerlitz,* for instance, in which architectural history is one of the fundamental subjects of the narrative. But even here in *The Emigrants,* Sebald effectively portrays grand structures like hotels and pavilions and train terminals by tracing their origins, their heyday, and their decline into a kind of geriatric state, as with the case of the Midland Hotel. Its potential rebirth as a Holiday Inn is the only likelihood for its future, Sebald laments. Sitting in one of the worn plush chairs in a hotel room that reminds him more of Poland than of contemporary Britain, the narrator has an aural hallucination. He thinks he hears the orchestra tuning up in the Free Trade Hall next door. Suddenly Manchester's music hall world comes to life. He hears the voice of an opera singer he admired when living there in the sixties, and he recalls the amateur performances at the Wine Lodge. There are echoes of his German origins as well—his memory conjures up a small man in a herringbone jacket who would take the stage and sing in Sebald's native language, acting out scenes from operas with all the theatricality expected of a heroic tenor. The association with Poland turns out to bear more fruit than the reader may have expected, as Sebald creates a hallucinatory segue into an image (pictured) of the Litzmannstadt ghetto of Lodz. There is an inner logic to this impressionistic transition that becomes obvious when Sebald adds that Lodz was once known as *polski Manczester*—the Polish Manchester. The narrator goes on to describe an exhibition he saw years ago, with the clear intention of exploring contemporary ideas about the significance of photography. In this exhibition were various pictures of the Jewish ghetto in Lodz during wartime, which was—and this "innocence" of the future is always the salient feature of old photographs—a time of cooperation with the German war effort. Many are pictures of people engaged in factory work or handicrafts, looking up for a split second so that the photographer can capture their faces. They seem content. Their lives seem normal. Of course, the reader knows what they cannot know. In the moment their images are captured, they do not suspect the horrific nature of the future that awaits them. And so Sebald's story of Max Ferber ends, with a final picture, not provided in the text, of three young women seated at a loom. They look intently out toward the photographer and, by extension, the beholder, the narrator, who cannot meet their gaze for long. Since this has been a tale about names, he asks what theirs might have been—Roza, Luisa (!), and Lea, or the somber-sounding Nona, Decuma, and Morta? Clearly the latter appellations, along with the author's reference to their "spindle, scissors, and thread" suggest the Fates of classical mythology, but the names actually correspond to the Latin words for ninth, tenth, and death. In the last line Sebald calls them "daughters of the night."[41] The moment is strangely triumphant; the dead, these unwitting victims at their looms, have been brought back from the brink of oblivion. Although Sebald provides many photographs for his readers, this image is too powerful to be left to anything but the imagination.

Reception

When *Die Ausgewanderten* first appeared in Germany in 1992, Sebald had already established his reputation there with the publication of *Nach der Natur,* and *Schwindel. Gefühle,* both of which had received considerable critical attention. In Germany, the reception of *Die Ausgewanderten* more or less served to confirm that Sebald was indeed a major new talent on the German literary scene. Epithets such as *Meisterwerk* ("masterpiece") were being applied to *Die Ausgewanderten* early in its reception.[42] Reviews were predominantly laudatory, stressing the originality of Sebald's idiosyncratic brand of documentary fiction. In Britain and America the book marked Sebald's literary debut. When *The Emigrants* was first published in 1996, the English-language readership was unfamiliar with Sebald. A few professors of German and perhaps a handful of graduate students had read *A Radical Stage,* a collection of various articles on German theater in the 1980s. But with the appearance of his first translated work of fiction it became obvious that a genial and original talent had entered the literary arena. That entrance was all the more striking for reason of his prior obscurity and the unfamiliarity of his stylistic techniques. In England the critic Philip Brady praised Sebald's unique "blend of empathy, distance, and imagination."[43] *New York Times* critic Larry Wolff called *The Emigrants* "a profound and original work of fiction, . . . an end-of-the century meditation that explores the most delicate, most painful, most nervously repressed and carefully concealed lesions of the last hundred years."[44] Susan Sontag's enthusiastic praise, quoted on the book's dust jacket, was instrumental in advancing Sebald's reputation, but the novelist Cynthia Ozick also contributed significantly to the critical success of

The Emigrants with an article in *The New Republic* in December of 1996. Like many other reviewers, she did not hesitate to use the word "sublime," and yet she hastened to expose the problematic nature of literary melancholia and its appeal:

> The heard language of these four stories—memories personal, borrowed, invented is . . . sublime; and I wish it were not, or if that is not altogether true, I admit to being disconcerted by a grieving that has been made beautiful. Grief, absence, loss, longing, wandering, exile, homesickness: these have been made millennially, sadly beautiful since the Odyssey, since the Aeneid, since Dante ("You shall come to know how salt is the taste of another's bread") and, more venerably still, since the Psalmist's song by the waters of Babylon. Nostalgia is itself a lovely and piercing word, and even more so is the German *Heimweh,* "home-ache." It is art's sacred ancient trick to beautify pain, to romanticize the shadows of the irretrievable.[45]

Nowhere in the critical literature is the universality of Sebald's particular brand of prose more forcefully argued. But Ozick barely touches on the rich tradition of peculiarly German melancholy in literature; she might have mentioned any number of Central European writers, from Adalbert Stifter and Theodor Fontane in the nineteenth century to Robert Walser and Peter Handke in the twentieth. And despite Ozick's lavish praise, there is a moment of substantively negative criticism. The final scene of the book (the one discussed above, in which a photograph of three young Jewish women sitting at a loom is described by the narrator) is, Ozick says, "the only false image in this ruthlessly moving and profoundly honest work dedicated to the recapture of phantoms."[46] The identification of the Jews themselves—the victims—with the makers of destiny, seems wrong to Ozick, though she is well aware that the author comprehends the problem—that such a picture, as sad as it is, can never adequately represent the reality of the subjects' tragic absence, or the unthinkable reality of their suffering and extermination in the camps. The absent photograph represents only a tenuous and poetic association with the Fates, however. These women of the Lodz ghetto are weaving "literally (but as we know, in vain) to save their lives."[47] The moment captured on film is a moment of counterfeit security and well-being.

American reviewers have found parallels in Sebald's writing where there is little real sign of influence (Henry James, Herman Melville), but most have correctly noted the significance of memoirists such as Nabokov and Chateaubriand. Only a few have delved more deeply into the ideological and critical content of Sebald's fiction. The translator Martin Chalmers is one of them. In a review in *The New Statesman* in the summer of 1996, Chalmers made much of Walter

Benjamin's influence on Sebald, especially in regard to the paradox of the author's efforts to preserve something of the past while at the same time emphasizing the dominance of destructive forces in history. Chalmers quotes from Benjamin's "Ninth Thesis on the Philosophy of History," in which progress is seen not as a chain of events stretching into the future, but as "one single catastrophe which keeps piling wreckage upon wreckage."[48] If there was any doubt about the appropriateness of drawing a parallel between Benjamin's perspective on history and Sebald's in *The Emigrants,* it would be dispelled two years later with the appearance of *The Rings of Saturn.* No book could be more befitting of the image of Benjamin's angel of history, driven inexorably away from the past by a "storm out of paradise." The angel's wings are filled by the storm winds, and, tellingly, he faces the past with his back to the future.

In the years after the publication of *The Emigrants,* Sebald's work became the subject of academic study in Britain and America, as had already occurred in German-speaking Europe. By the year 2000 several English-language articles dealing with Sebald's work had been published. Ann Parry, a British expert on Holocaust literature, includes Sebald among the most important contemporary writers on the theme of the Shoah. She writes that he, along with Jean-François Lyotard, Emanuel Litvinov, Robert Harris, and Primo Levi, are the most serious representatives of the search for "an idiom for the unrepresentable."[49] According to Parry, Sebald has succeeded in demonstrating the tragedy of the Jews as deeply rooted in their "unassignability"—for her, the "peculiar power" of their unassignable otherness "is related also to the return of history experienced by the characters, the return of their repressed origins."[50] Yet Parry as a critic concentrates too exclusively on the Holocaust as the subject of *The Emigrants.* It is the sorrow of all history that wells up in Sebald's narratives, not just that of a particular group of sufferers. The tragedy of Ambros Adelwarth, though he was for years the companion of a Jew, is related less to his association with Jewishness than to the costs exacted, over the years, by his repression of his own homosexuality. Max Ferber, on the other hand, is a character who is at best marginally Jewish, because he was exiled from his homeland and family as a child. This is not to say he suffers any less because of his ethnicity, of course, but merely to point out that it was his mother, as shown in her memoir, who best knew what it was like to be Jewish in Germany before the Final Solution destroyed everything.

By far the most astute reading of Sebald's *The Emigrants* is that of Arthur Williams, who takes as his subject the multiple roles of the author—as narrator, autobiographical persona, reader, interpreter, and (in the case of Max Ferber's mother's memoir) ghostwriter. Williams emphasizes the complexity of Sebald's allusive textual fabric, the effect of which is "at once beguiling, unsettling, and compelling."[51] Williams is also careful to compare the original with the translation, noting shifts of emphasis, especially in the scene near the end of the book, when Sebald visits the neglected Jewish cemetery in Bad Kissingen. But Williams's keenest insight involves Sebald's "intratextuality," the way the text seems to communicate within itself, referring to the same or similar incidents, events, persons, characteristics, works of art, works of literature, and coincidences —at intervals throughout the book:

> The closed "author-text-reader" line of communication . . . is transformed here into a triangular set of relationships in which glances or identities exchanged between the first two are always intended to be glimpsed by the third. Once engaged, the reader's contemplation of almost any paragraph will lead ultimately to the furthest reaches of the book.[52]

Williams is convinced that the various attempts by critics to pin down the literary influences on Sebald are beside the point. The gray lady, with gray roses in her hat, who haunts Max Feber, for instance, may well be the Sulamith with ashen hair from Paul Celan's famous Auschwitz poem "Todesfuge" ("Death Fugue"); but then again, she wears a rose-studded, broad-brimmed hat one can hardly imagine belonging to Celan's Sulamith. As Williams sensibly argues, "such intertexts are always ultimately in the mind of the reader"—in *The Emigrants* alone, one can find traces of Thomas Mann, Ricarda Huch, Uwe Johnson, Heinrich Böll, not to mention the explicitly exploited image of Nabokov, the butterfly man.[53] The warp and woof of literary influences in Sebald also connects his work implicitly to lesser-known writers such as Gregor von Rezzori, the Romanian author whose autobiographical novel *Memoirs of an Anti-Semite* (1981) also treats the subject of Jewish life before the Holocaust. It resembles *The Emigrants* formally as well, divided as it is into five distinct sections that do not qualify as chapters per se, but represent parts of an ongoing first-person narrative. In spite of the profusion of literary allusions and identifiable influences, the overwhelming impression made on critics and readers by *The Emigrants* has been one of profound originality. In the years that followed its publication, *The Emigrants* became the seminal achievement against which Sebald's subsequent books were always measured.

CHAPTER 3

The Rings of Saturn

Signs of an Incomprehensible Order

The Aesthetics of Coincidence and Return

In examining Sebald's highly psychological prose, scholars have acknowledged his affinities with the many authors, primarily Austrian, who have preoccupied him in his scholarship. The list is a long one, and includes Kafka, Stifter, Schnitzler, Hofmannsthal, and Bernhard, but another kindred spirit has been consistently omitted, Sigmund Freud. *The Rings of Saturn* exhibits a striking affinity ✓ with Freud's aesthetics, though not in the way one might expect. For the most part, the sexual urge is mentioned rarely in Sebald's writing. It is true that he refers to Stendhal's sexual appetite and his syphilis in the novel *Vertigo.* And homosexuality is approached (mostly obliquely) here and there. But sexual attraction is mostly treated with discretion, and referred to as "yearning." When the sexual act is depicted in Sebald's books, it is typically because his narrators happen upon a couple in the throes of intercourse. The narrator remains a distanced witness to what seems simply yet another example of bizarre human behavior. Freud's influence, then, is evident not so much in the depiction of sexuality as in Sebald's use of the uncanny. Though this atmosphere of unsettling strangeness is not entirely missing from the more documentary style of *The Emigrants,* it is largely overshadowed in that book by the historical, the actual, and the elegiac, in keeping with its commemorative purpose. A marked sense of uncanniness returned with a vengeance in Sebald's third book, *The Rings of Saturn,* however. Contributing to the mood of uncanniness is a dreamlike, somnambulant quality to events. The narrator, a nameless wanderer, encounters strikingly odd coincidences, vaguely disturbing settings of various kinds, life-like hallucinations, and periods of catatonic disorientation. Moreover, dreams themselves impinge on a reality that is for Sebald already destabilized by the distinct impression that the borders between dream and reality are themselves unclear and uncertain.

Freud's essay "The Uncanny" locates the source of that "sense of helplessness experienced in some dream states" in the phenomenon of repetition.[1] As an example, Freud's description of a walk in an Italian town might as well have been written by Sebald:

As I was walking, one hot summer afternoon, through the deserted streets of a provincial town in Italy, which was unknown to me, I found myself in a quarter of whose character I could not long remain in doubt. Nothing but painted women were to be seen at the windows of the small houses, and I hastened to leave the narrow street at the next turning. But after having wandered about for a time without enquiring my way, I suddenly found myself back in the same street, where my presence was now beginning to excite attention. I hurried away once more, only to arrive by another *detour* at the same place yet a third time. Now, however, a feeling overcame me which I can only describe as uncanny, and I was glad enough to find myself back at the piazza I had left a short while before, without any further voyages of discovery.[2]

The narrator of *The Rings of Saturn* also becomes hopelessly lost, notably in chapter VII, only to find himself, suddenly and inexplicably, right back where he started. He is unable to reach a peculiar villa clearly visible just over a hill— he traverses the same paths over and over again, turning at the same forks, getting nowhere. He finally gives up and goes back the way he came. Freud describes this kind of disorientation:

Other situations which have in common with my adventure an unintended recurrence of the same situation, but which differ radically from it in other respects, also result in the same feeling of helplessness and of uncanniness. So, for instance, when caught in a mist perhaps, one has lost one's way in a mountain forest, every attempt to find the marked or familiar path may bring one back again and again to one and the same spot, which one can identify by some particular landmark. Or one may wander about in a dark, strange room, looking for the door or the electric switch, and collide time after time with the same piece of furniture.[3]

Returning to the same places again and again suggests a quality of mood that German literary scholars, in discussing the dark world view of influential twentieth-century European writers such as Kafka, call *Auswegslosigkeit*. The word means literally inescapability or "exit-less-ness." The rhetorical term for this state of immobilization or entrapment, aporia, refers to that most modern of conditions in which one is both helpless, as Freud suggests, and hopeless, as Sebald's narrators appear at first glance. In Sebald, the aporia of repetition is not confined to individual experience, however, but takes on a much larger dimension. Repetition is represented in Sebald as a global constant; it manifests itself variously in the form of conflagrations such as forest fires, species predation, violent storms, westward migration. Despite what some critics have claimed, Sebald's use of repetition in his fiction has little in common with Nietzsche's famous notion of unending recurrence, however. Sebald is a writer more interested in psychology and aesthetics than in the essentially ethical concept behind Nietzsche's idea of "eternal return." In the original Nietzschean text from which the term is taken, the reader is confronted with the subjunctive proposition of being required to repeat an individual life unendingly, the same life every time. It is an existentialist proposition, a conditional "what if?" Nietzsche would demand that one live life in such a manner that one's actions might be justified in recurring eternally.[4] Sebald's use of repetition, on the other hand, seems more closely related to his fascination with time. While it may appear that time is linear, moving "forward" and leaving the past "behind," Sebald suggests that time, if viewed somehow from the outside, is nonsequential. The perspective he toys with, most explicitly formulated in the novel *Austerlitz,* posits future events existing side by side with past events and events that are happening in the present. Viewed from this perspective, the global constants in Sebald are manifestations of a single ongoing event, combustion being one physico-chemical manifestation, while predation represents its zoological or social form. The most emblematic representative of this sort of natural recurrence in *The Rings of Saturn* is, however, not a process such as combustion, but a mindless self-replication of a particular species. It is the silkworm, discussed at length in the book's final chapter. Here again, Sebald's approach is to take a subject the reader is likely to know something about and expound on it in detail. Generation after generation, the silkworm repeats its remarkable metamorphoses. Every silkworm spins identical threads that in turn are woven into a fabric of exquisite uniformity, the basis for a centuries-old textile trade. In a sense nothing ever changes with the silkworm. Yet nothing is static, either; one is always at one stage or the other in the life cycle of this strange creature whose reproductive drive and chrysalis-spinning have been put to mankind's own purposes.

Sebald's repetitions exist on other, even stranger levels as well. In the realm of homo sapiens, perhaps the strangest level of all, Sebald dares to suggest that individual identities may not in fact be very individual. They are perhaps repetitions of each other, even simultaneous repetitions, as when the narrator feels himself merging with mind and body of the writer Michael Hamburger (183). That way lies madness, as we will discuss later, but the idea has a burgeoning Jungian logic to it, with its oblique hint at the possibility of collective consciousness. It is more evidence to support the case for Sebald's monistic universe.

A "Solitary Walker" Explores Suffolk

The Rings of Saturn, which appeared in German in 1995 and in English in 1998, was greeted with superlative accolades by critics who seemed unsure that any book could repeat the successes of *The Emigrants.* Even more than *The Emigrants, The*

Rings of Saturn defies description; it does not seem to fit into any conventional prose or fiction category. On the surface, it is a diary of a walking tour of Suffolk, and as such has precursors in Rousseau's *Daydreams of a Solitary Walker* (1782) and James Boswell's *Journal of a Tour to the Hebrides with Samuel Johnson* (1785). In some respects, especially its digressive style and frequent literary and historical references, it resembles Claudio Magris's rambling narrative of a journey through the heart of Central Europe, *Danube* (1986). In fact, Sebald seems to take his peripatetic cue from some of Magris's initial comments on the significance and function of travel. But despite the clear parallels and allusions to other writers, *The Rings of Saturn* is not merely a derivative work—though, to be sure, the nature of Sebald's originality is hard to pinpoint. Sebald's uniqueness is "buried under an unprepossessing, almost typical surface." [5] *The Rings of Saturn* is several things at once. It is his narrator's own story; it is an evocation of the lives and writings of literary figures and notable eccentrics connected with the region; it is an account and analysis of battles and natural disasters; and it is a braid of dazzling connections with Africa and the Far East, evoked by such phenomena as railroads, sugar, and silk. *The Rings of Saturn* is, as one reviewer expressed it, "a palimpsest of natural, human and literary history." [6]

The Rings of Saturn begins with the immobilized sensitive soul we invariably encounter in Sebald, this time a narrator who finds himself in a hospital in Norwich, unsure even of why he is there. As usual, the month and year is given: August 1992. The dog days have come around again. It is a year to the day after he began his walking tour of Norfolk and Suffolk, which occasioned in him both an inebriating sense of freedom and a "paralyzing horror" at the traces of destruction evident everywhere. [7] Thus, the reader is aware from the outset of Sebald's subject, namely ubiquitous destruction caused both by natural forces and by man. Once again it is Kafka, who is so influential for Sebald's fiction, who is present from the beginning. The hapless patient's hospital room clearly suggests, for those familiar with *The Metamorphosis* (1915), Gregor Samsa's bedroom, where he awakens one morning to find himself inexplicably transformed into a large, beetle-like insect. Gregor also doesn't know how he got into such a state or what it signifies. Like Gregor, the giant vermin struggling to the window for a look at gloomy Charlottenstrasse, the narrator of *The Rings of Saturn* must struggle to reach the wall of his hospital room for a look at the bleak urban landscape below. In fact, the narrator explicitly compares himself to "poor Gregor." This is hardly an auspicious beginning, of course, and the reader initially does not know if things are going to get better or worse. He watches an ambulance with its blue light drive through the streets, but can hear nothing. He is surrounded by a cocoon of silence.

Always eminently allusive, Sebald's complex flow of references, at the same time personal as well as literary, serves to introduce the central reference point of the book as a whole: the biography of Sir Thomas Browne. He is a kindred ✓ soul to Sebald, and, fittingly, the author of *Urn Burial,* a compelling essay on Roman interments in England. Browne, who was born on 19 October 1605 and died on his birthday seventy-seven years later, was born under the sign of Saturn, making him a kind of spiritual patron of Sebald's book. Browne's own excursions into the strange and perplexing—into realms of previously undisclosed meaning and permanent enigma—seem, in retrospect, to anticipate Sebald's. In his works, Browne delves deep, pursuing interconnections that are never readily apparent, and casting doubt on virtually anything that *is* readily apparent. So it is, Sebald tells us in a an unexpected segue, with the public autopsy of Aris Kindt, which Rembrandt painted and Thomas Browne [may have] attended during his medical studies in Holland. A copy of the painting *The Anatomy Lesson* is provided in large format, covering two pages. Closer examination of the image reveals a kind of counterfeit detail, as the author points out: the corpse has two right arms! Sebald wants us to see that, for all its exquisite representational artistry, there is nothing real about this painting at all—the poses are unnatural, the protocol for autopsies is clearly not being followed, and the exposed muscle of the left arm is copied from the standard anatomical manual of the time, which contained a steel engraving of the right arm. *Schein* —appearance—is not the same as reality—*Sein.* The most convincing representations can be false, which is why Sebald inevitably approaches everything obliquely.

In the stream of associations that follows, a great fog noted by Browne in November 1674 flows into the white mist escaping from an opened corpse, and from there into the more benign anaesthetic fog the narrator admittedly enjoys in the hospital. As in a film montage, each image appears immediately and fully formed, and contains the common element of the earlier ones, only within a new compositional frame. In his drugged state, the narrator believes a balloon is carrying him up among high mountains from which he is able to look down on the changing landscape beneath him. (Unbeknownst to most readers, many of the ✓ words used to describe the firmament above and the earth below are taken verbatim from the 1840 story "The Condor" by Adalbert Stifter, in which a young woman takes part in a balloon ride.) Finally, the sedated narrator, looking upward at the window, beholds an airliner's vapor trail high in the sky. The actual story of the journey can now begin.

Browne was insistent upon exploring the mysterious, the inexplicable. While he was convinced that order reigned (he was a devout Christian), he was also convinced of man's profound ignorance, and obsessed with the strange and unusual. In that his kinship with Sebald is most keen. What is to be made of the abnormalities of nature, when perfect order breaks down? What about nature's grotesqueries? What of the fabled monsters of the past? From Borges's *Book of Imaginary Beings* (1967) Sebald chooses a specific, though obscure, example attributed to the German author of the Baroque Period, Johann Jakob Christoffel von Grimmelshausen (1622–1776). In *Der abenteuerliche Simplizissimus Teutsch* (1669), his long picaresque novel set in the time of the Thirty Years' War, Grimmelshausen describes an episode in which the naive protagonist known as Simplicissimus comes upon a strange statue in the woods. The statue comes alive and transforms itself into a scribe who writes, "I am the Alpha and Omega," from the Book of Revelation, followed by twelve lines, pictured in the text, of coded instructions. The being then metamorphoses into various other creatures in a "continuous process of consuming and being consumed."[8] The associative thread rejoins Browne at this point, with the observation that in spite of the perpetuity of organic processes on earth, nothing endures, everything "descends into the dark." Sebald then elaborates at some length on Browne's ideas about the "iniquity of oblivion" into which everything eventually vanishes, addressing head-on the unpleasant truth of inevitable extinction. Browne's fascinations have in common with Sebald's the problem of order and disorder in nature, the meaning of time, and the need for mankind—and a small number of other species— to take leave of their dead by some form of ceremonial burial. But the fullness of the first chapter is only an introduction to the themes that will occupy the remaining nine. It is in the second chapter, in fact, that we first come across what seems to be the heart of the matter for Sebald: namely, the journey as a metaphor for our brief sojourn on earth. In the original German the subtitle of the book is "Eine englische Wallfahrt" ("An English pilgrimage"). By the end of the book Sebald's pilgrim will have reached his Jerusalem—one version of it, at least— and will have moved beyond it. The book is thus an associative, digressive, and allusive journey through East Anglia, in which the reader is introduced to people, past and present, and to a landscape that itself acts as a kind of character, with its own idiosyncratic presence and history.

Landscape as Setting and Character

Perhaps more than any of Sebald's other novels, *The Rings of Saturn* insists that place plays the role of a character. Somerleyton Hall, the narrator's first stop in his journey, is a physical presence with its own personality, although this becomes fully clear only after Sebald has brought its past to light on the way to Lowestoft. Before he embarks on a description of the house, the narrator has occasion to remark on the windmills that once dominated the landscape, an image that will appear again, fleetingly, but quite dramatically, later in the narrative. These are in essence the same sails, symbols of purity and serenity, that appeared in Dr. Selwyn's slide show of Crete in *The Emigrants*. Somerleyton Hall is a preserved relic of nineteenth-century industrial wealth in the form of a "dreamwork" mansion built by a self-made millionaire. The house is a remarkable creation, where interiors lead imperceptibly into exteriors, and artifice merges with natural growth. There is an illusion of complete harmony with nature. But Sebald is quick to dispel the illusion. The Argand gas that lit this pleasure palace so brilliantly at night was poisonous, and the intensity of its glare, while amazing to look at, was incompatible with the nocturnal surroundings. A nineteenth-century black-and-white drawing represents the scene, standing in contrast to the less than magical present condition of the place as described in the text. The house contains many a curio, however, and still holds a certain fascination, though there is something patently absurd about the vastness of its exotic collection of motley souvenirs and artifacts. The house is one grand eccentricity, an architectural complement to the idiosyncratic characters to whom Sebald is drawn.

The interconnectedness of all things is one of the guiding principles of Sebald's fiction, and here at a country house in Suffolk a connection with Germany becomes apparent, the first of several. A groundskeeper recalls the bombing missions that used to originate nearby, thousands of them, on their way to Schweinfurt, Hamburg, Munich, and Magdeburg. The gardener describes how, for a total of one thousand and nine days, the big machines lifted off and flew into the twilight. They used millions of gallons of fuel and dropped thousands of bombs. He remembers imagining the horror those bombs must have been inflicting, and he remembers learning the names of all the cities. When he served in the British occupation forces in Lüneburg in the fifties, he struggled to learn German so that he could read what it was really like during the air raids. He might as well have spared himself the effort. To his astonishment, he could find no reports. Sebald, here as well as in his scholarly study *Luftkrieg und Literatur,* expresses bafflement that in spite of the thundering devastation visited upon the Germans, the memory of it seems all but expunged from German life and discourse.

Mortality occupies the foreground in Sebald. In economically depressed Lowestoft, a hearse comes out of nowhere as if to complete the disheartening picture of the inevitable process of decline and death. The narrator is reminded of the story, unnamed, of the young man "from Tuttlingen" in Swabia who went to Amsterdam many years ago to make his fortune. The story, well-known among speakers of German, is from an anthology by Johann Peter Hebel called

Schatzkästlein des rheinischen Hausfreunds (1811, Treasury of a Rhineland family friend). In this short tale the young man, who cannot speak Dutch, encounters an elaborate and impressive funeral train. He is certain it must belong to a wealthy and important man, and he tries to ask whose funeral is taking place. "Kannitverstan" is the answer he receives. He assumes the response "kannitverstan" is the name of the dead man. Yet seeing the word in print, any German can recognize that it is simply the Dutch version of "kann nicht verstehen," meaning "[I] cannot understand." With this droll fable of earthly transience on his mind, the narrator moves on and visits a friend, Frederick Farrar. Frederick is a long-time resident of Lowestoft, and enjoys recounting episodes of its history; he drifts into a remembrance of one Francis Browne, a lawyer who cultivated flowers in his retirement and who, it turns out, died of terrible burns when his cigarette caught his dressing gown on fire. But Sebald does not end the chapter on such a morbid note. Instead, Frederick recalls the image of Francis as a child, playing his bugle "into the night in a Northamptonshire schoolyard in the summer of 1914," then the image of the illuminated pier pavillion where, as the common folk watched from the shore, from barges, and boats, "fashionable society swirled to the sound of the orchestra, seemingly borne aloft in a surge of light above the water."[9] Frederick's description of the "town like a mirage over water" is typical of Sebald's imagery—wistful, hallucinatory, and celebratory—and recalls Somerleyton Hall from a few pages earlier. It is important that the year is 1914, the year of deceptive calm before everything in Europe was irrevocably changed by the outbreak of the Great War. The concluding dream-image is of Frederick's family on the beach, resembling the exiled court of King James II on the shore at The Hague. This final allusive flourish resembles other hallucinations of historical figures (e.g., Dante, Catherine of Siena, Mad King Ludwig) that occur throughout Sebald's fiction. All these elements seem disparate but related, tied together by memory and the commonality of human experience over time.

The Many Faces of Annihilation

The Holocaust is represented in *The Rings of Saturn*, as it was in *The Emigrants*, from an exceedingly unconventional angle. In discussing an obituary of Major George Wyndham Le Strange, Sebald reveals that the local Suffolk eccentric was the commander of the regiment that liberated the Bergen-Belsen concentration camp in the spring of 1945. Sebald knows that the large photograph of naked corpses under the trees (the camp was located in the forest east of the picturesque German city of Celle) says more than words can. So Sebald simply shows us what Le Strange must have seen. Was the sight of all these naked dead, piled one upon the other like the corpses of so many discarded animals, perhaps the reason Le Strange paid his housekeeper, as the obituary tells us, to dine with him in silence every day? The documentary evidence Sebald employs is presented in such a way as to circumvent the problem of Holocaust representation. Rather than reimagining the death camps, as does Stephen Speilberg's well-known film *Schindler's List,* Sebald illustrates by pointing to outcomes and repercussions. He lets the picture of the corpses, obviously only a partial, even miniscule view of the full horror, speak for itself. Its very incompleteness suggests, moreover, the greater scope of the inconceivable tragedy. Le Strange's reclusion and rejection of the burdensome banalities of everyday speech is also meant to speak for itself; the meaning and effect of what he witnessed was beyond words, even to the point of repudiating language itself.

The phenomenon of mass killings comes in many forms. Sebald's spotlight falls on two additional examples, one factual and one scriptural. Herring are endlessly pursued by man and other predators, and Sebald indulges in a meticulous and almost lyrical description of the fish, little known for its striking beauty. The other example is found in Sebald's retelling of the strange story, taken from the Gospel of Mark, of Jesus casting out demons from the madman known as Legion. In this story, evil spirits are exorcized and made to enter a herd of a thousand swine, which in turn rush into the sea and drown. Though the connection is not drawn overtly, Sebald seems to be expressing, in a manner that intentionally avoids tendentiousness or moralizing, the metaphorical dimensions of the tragedy of mass murder. The biblical narrative has a perplexing quality; the tale takes for granted a baffling waste of life and livelihood. The swine die in an act that is not suicide but appears to be suicide. For no clear reason they are forced to participate in their own demise. The herring, on the other hand, are hunted for their flesh, and hunted relentlessly. The disregard for their lives is total; they have no right to exist except as a commodity. But Sebald's use of these mass killings is no less baffling than the story of Legion's exorcism. One is left to wonder what possible statement Sebald wishes to make by juxtaposing fish harvests and Holocaust victims, and linking them, moreover, with first-century demons, Jesus, and runaway swine? He does not say, of course, and there arises for some the suspicion that such apparently loose connections are not of great hidden significance but are instead false commonalities with little true significance. Herring, after all, are blindly instinctual. Swine are considered unclean according to the Jewish faith as well as Islam. Neither consideration is on the same level as Nazi genocide. Is it tasteless to lump together such qualitatively different phenomena? Whatever one's reaction, all of this "extermination business" will come full circle at the end of the book, when Sebald introduces the bizarre facts of Nazi silk manufacture, a little-known government project that was centered—coincidentally —in Celle, not far from Bergen-Belsen.

Sebald's considerable literary debt to Borges is acknowledged in a reference to the story "Tlön, Uqbar, Orbis Tertius" from the collection *Ficciones* (1956). This bizarre tale is mentioned more than once, the final time in what is simultaneously a verbatim repetition of the story's final lines as well as an implicit reference to yet another short story. (Such concealed meanings, planted for the astute reader, are a feature of Borges's work that Sebald emulates.) The Borges story describes an imaginary world, called Tlön, into which our own world is imperceptibly metamorphosing. The tale ends with the narrator expressing his indifference not only to this transformation, insisting that he will continue to work on a translation of Thomas Browne's *Urn Burial* (!), and furthermore, will write it in the manner of the Spanish satirist Francisco Gomez de Quevedo y Villegas (1580–1645). In a final flash of irony, Borges—*and* Sebald—aver that they intend never to publish the work. What is one to make of this literary sleight of hand? First, it should be pointed out that the Tlön metamorphosis begins with an allusion to a remark about mirrors. Sebald is clearly holding up a mirror to another text, and thereby taking intertextuality to its logical extreme in merging his own with Borges's. But he is also acting upon an ambition expressed in another Borges story from the same collection, "Pierre Menard, Author of Don Quixote." In "Pierre Menard," the protagonist of the same name is engaged in a seemingly self-contradictory attempt to write a book that has already been written, and in exactly the same words. "His admirable ambition," Borges writes, "was to produce pages which would coincide—word for word and line for line— with those of Miguel de Cervantes."[10]

The distortion of reality by representational, "realistic" art is, as we have noted, a major theme of *The Rings of Saturn*. In his travels along the coast, the narrator has occasion to ponder the great naval battles that took place just off shore. That such battles were nothing like the glorified paintings made by contemporaries or those who came after the fact is surely not a new observation, but Sebald goes to some length to demonstrate precisely why images from the past are counterfeit. The battles in this historical period would have been shrouded in an acrid smoke, concealing the action of combat from the view of those on shore. Though we can have no direct empirical knowledge of such battles, we can be sure that pictorial representations are distorted by various conventions, not the least of which are clarity and visibility. The painters and their patrons favored expressly dramatic composition. But these conventions do not so much interest Sebald in the text as the actuality, the reality, expunged by the images, images that "fail to convey any true impression of how it must have been to be on board one of these ships, already overloaded with equipment and men, when burning masts and sails began to fall or cannonballs smashed into the appallingly over-crowded decks."[11] As always, Sebald puts the available statistics into compelling human terms, noting that few cities on earth in those days had populations as high as the number of men annihilated in large sea-battles of this kind. It is hard to conceive the effort that went into building the ships themselves, most of them predestined to be destroyed. Here, alongside the notion of senselessly wasteful fratricide, the author introduces a theme that will be developed throughout the book: that of the enormity of certain environmental disruptions made by man. The denuding of forests in the Mediterranean region for shipbuilding and the smelting of metals is only one example among many. Many forests in Scotland and England were similarly destroyed. Sebald resumes his critique of senseless waste in general, and the prodigality of warship construction in particular, in his 1998 book of biographical essays, *Logis in einem Landhaus*. Quoting Hebel, he points out that only a single one of Napoleon's battleships would have required 1,000 large oak trees, 200,000 pounds of iron, rope in the amount of 104,000 pounds, 200,000 pounds of tar, and the entire ship, empty, would have weighed a staggering 5,000,000 pounds.[12]

Irrationality and destructiveness often join forces for calamitous effect. But in the end, annihilation is a process at work virtually everywhere and at all times, according to Sebald's aesthetics, which, as we will discuss in the final chapter, are based largely on the ideas of Walter Benjamin. It is no surprise, then, when the narrator, watching the sunset, imagines humanity as "but prone bodies, row upon row, as if leveled by the scythe of Saturn."[13] This is the second and final mention of Saturn in the book, a fact which brings to mind the question: Why the title? Is it just another postmodernist play with convention—a taunt to the average reader and a congratulatory signal to those savvy enough to appreciate the joke? It is neither. Sebald's style and imagery are intended to evoke, to sug-gest, to make references that can lead in several directions or exist on several lev-els. His prose is designed to pique the imagination and, accordingly, he leaves much for the reader to fill in. But in this way he opens rather than closes the doors of perception, to use Blake's famous phrase. Saturn in astrology is associ-ated with age and melancholia. In the quotation above, Saturn is portrayed much as the grim reaper, bringing death with his scythe. In one of two mottos at the beginning of the English edition (the German original has, in addition, a quota-tion from Milton's *Paradise Lost*), a *Brockhaus Enzyklopädie* entry is cited con-cerning the physical makeup of the rings of the planet Saturn. The key to understanding Sebald's allusion lies in the recognition that the origins of those awe-inspiring rings are origins posited by sentient beings who were not and could not have been present to witness their initiation. Nonetheless, according to modern ideas of planetary formation, immensely violent destructive forces were at work. The rings of Saturn are presumably the remnants of a moon destroyed by the great planet's draconian tidal effect. Transformations and transmutations as such fascinate Sebald, whether manifested in the degradation of an orbiting moon to a vast collection of rings, or in the endlessly repetitive life cycle of the silkworm from egg to caterpillar to moth. The change of one object or creature into another can be brought on by annihilation due to blindly destructive forces or by equally mindless procreative instinctual drive. But some critics have put another shade of meaning on the reference to Saturn. The writer Gareth Howell-Jones, for instance, offers the following interpretation, using a line from the book:

As Saturn is encircled by rings made up of the fragments of a former moon, so we revolve surrounded by the shards of a lost and broken-up world, 'our history which is but a long account of calamities.'[14]

But the "shards of a lost and broken-up world" often escape notice—their very existence can remain unacknowledged—unless someone knows where to look or is willing to take up the search. This is always Sebald's lesson about the past, and it is the reason he shows us, among other things, the naval battles and the great vessels of the seventeenth and eighteenth centuries: "For a brief time only these strange creatures sailed the seas, driven across the water on the winds of the world. They bore names like Stavoren, Resolution, Victory, Groot Hollandia and Olyfan. Then they were gone."[15] Nothing made by man will endure, yet the winds of the world will continue endlessly to circle the globe.

The reality of the past is always an unresolved paradox; it is both proximate and elusive. Sebald alternates between exposing misconceptions about the past and expressing doubt about our ability to know what went before. Even if we expunge historical inaccuracy, we are still a far cry from knowing how things really were. In irrefutable ways, history can be felt and seen in the present. In Southwold the narrator experiences the past in the Sailor's Reading Room. A photographic history of the First World War is the ostensible prompt for a lesson on the Balkans. Because of the repetition of atrocities and upheavals even into the late 1990s, the names Serbia, Bosnia, and Albania stand out. There is a picture of Archduke Franz Ferdinand's bloody, bullet-riddled tunic from 28 June 1914, the day of the assassination. In one of the most graphic, horrifying, and ultimately heartbreaking passages of the book, Sebald recalls—focusing on German complicity in the crimes during the Second World War—the ghoulish torment inflicted on Serbs by their Croatian captors. Women were rounded up to be worked to death in Germany, half the children were murdered in cold blood, and the other half sent to be raised in Croatian families. The passage is dominated by terrible ironies. For example, before Sebald came across the documentation of these atrocities he had been "feeling a sense of eternal peace."[16] More generally, one is struck that the people of the Balkans have the stamina or will to endure—and inflict—any more violence after so many years of repeated massacres and mutilations. One is struck by Serb and Croat disregard for the utter irreconcilability of New Testament teachings of forgiveness with the self-righteous maliciousness they share, while at the same time each side traditionally claims to represent Christendom. Finally, there is the small matter of the identity of the Wehrmacht soldier who signed the deportation orders for the Serbs. His name, unspoken in the text, is Kurt Waldheim, former Secretary General of the United Nations. In the sweeping conclusion to chapter IV, the space probe *Voyager II* approaches the outer limits of our solar system. The craft contains, "together with other memorabilia of mankind," a recorded message from the same Kurt Waldheim, in his capacity as Secretary General of the UN, greeting in the name of cosmic peace, "any extraterrestrials who may happen to share our universe."[17] It is an irony of universal proportions, quite literally, that the man chosen to speak on behalf of all humanity has been charged as an accomplice to murder and torture in one of the most morally destitute chapters of all of human history. He managed to conceal his past and rose to the highest position in the bureaucracy of the world peacekeeping body dedicated to the ideals of human rights.

The Life and Times of Teodor Josef Konrad Korzeniowski

The author Joseph Conrad is initially the subject of chapter V. This biographical digression is, like that on Sir Thomas Browne, modeled loosely on John Aubrey's *Brief Lives* (1698).[18] The transition to Conrad's biography is as mundane as the narrator's having fallen asleep in his recliner—no irony lost here—during a BBC documentary. Upon awakening, he is able to remember that the subject of the show was Roger Casement, whom Conrad considered the only man of integrity among all the Europeans he had encountered during his time in the Congo. The life of Casement is intertwined both with the history of the Congo and later with the failed Easter Uprising in Casement's home country of Ireland. This is not the last time in the book that Sebald will address the grisly injustices visited on the Irish by the "civilized" English in that troubled land; and indeed, the subject of the Congo brings out a barely restrained tone of outrage over the horrific atrocities committed by the Belgians there. Sebald notes the various ways in which impoverished and defenseless black men, women, and children were tormented and abused by these "cultured" Europeans led by a "noble" king. Like so many of history's doomed idealists, Casement has an Achilles' heel. Displayed in the text are pictures of a diary in which the Irishman (foolishly, in hindsight) chronicled his homosexual encounters. Sealed until 1994, this evidence was purportedly used by the British court to decide Casement's fate. He was executed as a traitor. The scrawled notes speak for themselves, and Sebald remarks only that "it was precisely Casement's homosexuality that sensitized him to the continuing oppression, exploitation, enslavement, and destruction . . . of those . . . farthest from the center of power."[19] Casement's fate thus reflects and underscores the tragic futility of Conrad's father's political engagement, described in the intervening pages dedicated to the life of the Polish author.

Joseph Conrad, as Josef Teodor Konrad Korzeniowski would later call himself, embarked on a life of travel inspired by French adventure stories. In this he resembles Sebald's other countless wanderers. Through Conrad, Sebald introduces the reader to a rich cast of characters whose connections stretch eastward to Austria and Turkey and westward to Lowestoft in England. Sebald is at his best when pursuing the threads that link various people and disparate places. Ironically, it was almost as an afterthought, while on shore leave in Lowestoft, that Conrad began to learn the English language. His future as a major novelist lay shrouded in the mists of time. But Sebald's interest in Conrad is not primarily literary, although the spirit of *Heart of Darkness* is very much present. Sebald concentrates on the factual, which is in this case stranger than the fictional. Belgian colonialism in Africa was more brutal than anyone except the harshest critics of the West might imagine, and Sebald traces the responsibility for Belgium's crimes straight to the top, to King Leopold, who was far more than a figurehead in his nation's colonial affairs. While natives were being worked to death in the Congo, at home in Belgium the profits of colonialism were being lavished on monuments and buildings of remarkable ugliness, according to Sebald, who also suggests the Belgian crimes sank into the very soul of the nation. The narrator recalls a visit to Brussels in the year 1964, during which he "came across more hunchbacks and lunatics than normally in a whole year."[20] Sebald's hyperbole here is not merely for rhetorical effect; no German makes an accusation of collective guilt lightly. Conrad, too, sensed the insidious effects of colonialism while himself visiting Brussels, where everyone he passed in the street seemed to him to harbor the dark secret of the Congo. As there is a always a hidden order of things in Sebald, one suspects a grim sense of justice at work, or bad kharma. Even Casement's failed efforts to expose Belgian, then British malfeasance, were not made in vain. They are remembered, if belatedly, by dogged historical detectives like Sebald.

The Bridge over the River Blyth

Astonishingly, a Suffolk walking tour with Sebald can connect one with not just Africa, but the Orient as well. He is intent on uncovering yet more astonishing facts buried just below the surface of contemporary life and retrievable only because a record was kept or, in this case, because the narrow-gauge railway train intended for the Emperor of China was never sent to its destination, but now passes over a bridge on the River Blyth. Sebald uses this image as the basis for his transition into Chinese history, its mythology of dragons, and, in particular, the strange Taiping movement, with its initial triumphs in the nineteenth century, at about the time the train was built, and its eventual mass suicides on an unprecedented scale. The spellbinding power of the exotic allows one to focus even more acutely on the bizarre nature of history, as Sebald demonstrates with a description of the Opium War and the deepening involvement of the colonial powers in China. The sorry tale of the Opium War is rife with mutual misunderstandings, and of course wanton destruction of priceless treasures, not to mention the senseless loss of countless lives. The narrator casts a cold, unblinking eye on human folly in all its shear presumptuousness and ignorance. The irony of "civilized" men wreaking so much havoc is always present, if only in the background. And there is, as with Sebald's treatment of Belgium, always the nagging sensation that the malformations and misfortunes of present-day Western society may be related somehow to the crimes of the past.

Returning to his English source, Sebald provides a cultural portrait of the nearby city of Dunwich, a now desolate place which has literally "gone under." The city, once one of the most prosperous ports in the Middle Ages, is now mostly underwater and dispersed. The last ruins fell into the sea in the early years of the twentieth century. Dunwich embodies a recurrent theme in Sebald's work: the "immense power of emptiness."[21] Nor is this the last time we shall hear of submerged cities or landscapes; Michael Hamburger's wife narrates a strange dream of an underwater journey later in the book, and the novel *Austerlitz* also includes a description the subaquatic world of a flooded village in Wales. And although it is admittedly an extreme example, the abandonment of the old town and the extension of Dunwich westward is representative of one of the fundamental patterns of human behavior. The slow advancement inland, away from the North Sea, goes on and on, ultimately crossing the Atlantic in the colonization of North America. Migration, as we have seen with annihilation, is a phenomenon that appears to be constant and universal. In America whole towns seem to move along the turnpikes, while in Brazil "whole provinces die down like fires" and move on, leaving behind a wasteland.[22] Sebald speculates that melancholy

Victorian poets favored Dunwich for the very reason that it was a lost cause, crumbling into the ocean. Here another East Anglian, Algernon Charles Swinburne, takes center stage, one of the strangest eccentrics yet encountered in Sebald. His tale is a tale of extreme creativity and extreme emotional fragility.

Erasure, Artifact, Identity

One could argue that not only do certain settings play the role of characters in the work of Sebald, global phenomena seem to do so as well. Processes of annihilation in various forms trigger Sebaldian musings, as does mass migration. As we have seen before, combustion is another universal phenomenon that Sebald ponders in *The Rings of Satun*. Combustion can of course be put to both destructive and constructive purposes, linking it to annihilation, but also to migration. Sebald returns to the topic in chapter VII. Advancing settlement of virgin territory requires burning, as does the production of agricultural implements and more sophisticated artifacts. It takes fire and heat to make weapons. The smelting of iron began in prehistoric times, and by the time Europeans became shipbuilders, many of the forests of the continent were doomed. All of Europe, from the Highlands of Scotland to the islands of Greece, was once covered in forests. "From the earliest times," the narrator remarks, "human civilization has been a strange luminescence growing more intense by the hour, of which no one can say how intense it will become and when it will begin to wane and fade away."[23] Fires are blazing all the time, whether in California, Italy, Australia, Southern France, or Spain, not to mention the almost constant conflagrations in parts of the tropics.

The scrubland of East Anglia was created by wanton burning. It is on such open scrubland that a scene of profound disorientation occurs. The narrator realizes he has backtracked and is caught in a maze of pathways. Despite repeated attempts, he cannot reach the only landmark discernable, a villa with a glass-domed observation tower. None of the signposts beside the diverging paths point him in the right direction. In a dream that occurs months after the experience, the tables are turned and he finds himself at the top of the world looking down. Above him is the unchanging wintry dome of stars. The landscape below him transmutes into an aggregate of images from previous chapters, while a military officer shines searchlights on the sky. A power plant glowers in the distance where herring once spawned and forests once grew in the sands of the Rhine delta. What Sebald creates in this mélange of images is the literary equivalent of a painting by Hieronymus Bosch.

The mystery of identity and the relationship of identity and memory preoccupy Sebald in all his fiction, but in *The Rings of Saturn* there is an especially vivid manifestation of this preoccupation. The narrator is in Middletown visiting his friend, the writer and translator Michael Hamburger, who is, like the character Max Ferber in *The Emigrants,* a Jewish refugee from Nazi persecution who came to England as a boy. Hamburger, unlike Ferber, was accompanied by his family. In his memoirs, as Sebald relates, Hamburger writes of a moment when he and his family realized the "monstrosity of changing countries under such inauspicious conditions."[24] His grandfather's parakeets, which had survived all the travails of the journey, are impounded by customs at Dover and disappear behind a screen never to be seen again. And like so many characters in Sebald who complain they remember very little, Michael chronicles at considerable length scenes from his childhood. He has the eye of a writer. But the loss of the parakeets, he believes, is the beginning of the loss of his original identity, a problem that will be taken up again and enlarged upon in the novel *Austerlitz.* By the same token, Michael is unsure to what extent the ruins of Berlin, which he saw in 1947, impose themselves on his memory of the city as a mere "blue-black background with a gray smudge in it, a slate pencil drawing, some unclear numbers, and some blurred letters in gothic script— β , $\mathcal{W}$, $\mathcal{J}$ —that have been half wiped away with a damp rag."[25] Memory, once again, is unreliable. Even immediate perception is unreliable; Michael often sees before him when he looks out over the marshes of Suffolk the road that leads out of Berlin to the Wannsee (the lake at which the Nazi leaders met to plan the Final Solution.) For both Hamburger and Sebald the question of personal identity is bound up the meaning of the act of writing, which both agree is a compulsion rather than a calling. But they question whether writing truly has significance and value, since it appears to be such a futile activity in the face of "the imponderables that govern our course through life."[26] Keen powers of observation are essential to the writer's craft, but the question arises: Is a writer a more perceptive person than most people, or just a person more prone to insanity?

Sebald is interested in whether identity is somehow fluid, something that can be shared. Michael notes that he shares, minus two days, a birthday with ill-starred poet Friedrich Hölderlin (1770–1843). There are numerous other coincidences and similarities, such as a name shared among Hamburger's forefathers and the count to whom Hölderlin's famous Patmos poem was dedicated, not to mention the date of the poet's birth being the same as the date inscribed on a water pump in Hamburger's front yard at Middleton. Hölderlin's genius probably would not have been possible without his spiritual proximity to madness. He was a dreamer who renamed himself, once his ineluctable descent into madness began, "Scardanelli." Is Michael mad to believe he is somehow one with Hölderlin? In a strange inversion of the question, the narrator begins to feel his own sensations of identity with Michael. Can it be that he in fact *is* Michael, or was once

Michael? The text displays pictures of the interiors of Michael Hamburger's cluttered house. Isn't this his own house? Aren't these in fact the narrator's things? To pursue such thoughts further would be madness, of course, and the narrator dismisses them as abruptly as he introduced them.

As with associations and allusions, one question leads to another in Sebald. The feeling of merging identity that the narrator experiences is based on coincidences and the repetition of coincidences. It turns out that Michael and the narrator were both were acquainted with—without the other knowing it—one Stanley Kerry. They both made the acquaintance of the shy professor of German twenty-two years apart—Michael in 1944 and the narrator in 1966—each when he was 22 years of age. The narrator cannot "slay the ghosts of repetition" that "more and more frequently" come to haunt him.[27] What is, he asks, the nature of this duplication that seems to occur and recur in life? Is it an "anticipation of the end," "a step into the void," or a kind of "disengagement" caused by "defect in programming," something like what occurs when a grammophone (Sebald's word) repeats a bar of music over and over again?[28]

The possibility that identity might not be what we think it is suggests that the nature of reality may be fundamentally different, or that there may be other realities or altered states. One of these is described when Michael's wife Anne recalls a dream in which she travels in a limousine that takes her into a beautiful dark forest. It is as if the car were traveling underwater but Anne can see vividly all the flora on the mountainside. It is varied and exotic. The ridge above is topped with palm trees that have fronds like those in some of Leonardo da Vinci's paintings. The scene is one of strange, exquisite beauty, such as she has not known since childhood. But the beauty of the recollected dream is shattered for the narrator as he waits for his taxi outside in the dark beside the "Hölderlin pump." A faint light is falling on the water in the well. A beetle of some kind is crossing on the surface, "rowing" as it were from one side to the other. The narrator provides no explanation for his reaction, but recalls that a shudder went to the core of his being. What is it about the sight of an insect at night that is so unsettling to the narrator? Not only is the aesthetic contrast between dream and reality hair-raising, but the moving water beetle underscores the notion that everything living, from the highest creatures to the lowest, is on the move, going somewhere. But where?

FitzGerald in Suffolk, A House in Ireland, Sails on the Shore

In Sebald the text reflects back on itself, thematic threads are taken up again and again, and thus a structure of repetition emerges within the digressive structure of anastomosis. For instance, a conversation in a hotel bar in Southwold redirects the narrator's attention to an earlier theme related to the East Anglian landscape, that of historical connections between England and The Netherlands. At the same time, the subject revives questions of the colonial past. In both countries, sugar production brought enormous wealth to numerous families, and the profits from the former slave economies of the Third World are still in circulation in England and Holland, having accrued, and continuing to accrue, interest many times over. Sebald points out that the Tate Gallery in London and the Mauritshuis in The Hague were both originally endowed by sugar dynasties—it seems that patronage of the arts legitimizes such fortunes gained by colonial exploitation.

Another "brief life" after the style of Aubrey is devoted to the writer Edward FitzGerald, who lived at his family estate of Boulge. Sebald is interested in him, naturally, for his extreme eccentricity, and much of chapter VIII is spent elaborating on his habits, friendships, and his inexorable decline. FitzGerald only ever finished one project, a rendering of the *Rubaiyat* by the Persian poet Omar Khayyam. In FitzGerald we find yet another example of the writer's tendency toward mental instability. His in some respects admirable self-assertion— he does nothing but what he wishes—is accompanied by a reclusive tendency, and once he loses his best friend that tendency becomes dominant. To be sure, it is astounding that he continued to move among society at all. One saving grace appears to have been his love of yachting. Here the term "German Ocean" occurs again—it had been used in chapter IV to describe the scene of naval battles between the Dutch and English fleets—to describe the North Sea. FitzGerald spends many a day sailing, even venturing to Holland to see a painting in The Hague. But traveling to London is a deplorable hardship for him, and as his health deteriorates he is capable of making only one trip per year, an arduous journey by train to visit the writer George Crabbe in Merton. In June 1883 he makes his last trip there, and dies the morning after arrival.

The FitzGerald family origins lie in Ireland—Edward's parents moved to England not long before his birth. Their Irish connection calls up an experience in an Irish country house, presumably Sebald's experience, worth noting for its strangeness and poignancy. The Ashbury family, whom Sebald met by coincidence, represents what happened to those families that, unlike the FitzGeralds, stayed behind in Ireland. The house is virtually empty of furniture, the floorboards are covered with dust, the curtains are gone, and the walls long ago stripped bare. Family members do not gather for meals or tea, but seem to roam about the house "like refugees who have come through dreadful ordeals and do not now dare to settle in the place where they have ended up."[29] It is a truly bizarre, self-contained, and aimless world. This is precisely the sort of subject matter Sebald turns his attention to when most would turn away—he even admits he was tempted to join the Ashburys in the colossal failure and hopelessness of their lives, a temptation to which he even regrets not yielding.

Theirs is an innocence that is essentially a state of living purposelessly and without apology for that purposelessness. The episode closes with Catherine Ashbury, one of the daughters, speaking distantly of the family's erstwhile plans to cultivate silkworms as a money-making endeavor. She is wearing a red dress with a red hat, and does not respond to his farewell. He recounts seeing her much later—either her double or a hallucination—in Berlin, playing a theatrical role in an avant-garde production of a play by J. M. R. Lenz (1751–1792), another of the German pantheon of writers who went mad. As if to complete the picture of feminine otherworldliness Catherine seems to embody, Sebald compares her to Saint Catherine of Siena, who, according to legend, took Christ as her bridegroom.

The German Ocean

The source of Sebald's idiosyncratic phrase "German Ocean" is revealed late in the book, once the narration of the walk in Suffolk is resumed. The town of Felixstowe has a little-known history as a holiday destination for German royalty in the nineteenth and early twentieth centuries. On the banks of the Deben River there was once a spa center called "German Ocean Mansions." The economic and cultural links being forged between Germany and Britain in this period were expected to last forever. But war undid all the Kaiser's plans for a new civilization joining the lands on the North Sea. "Whenever one is imagining a bright future," Sebald writes with an almost jocular pessimism, "disaster is just around the corner."[30] Sebald takes nearby Bawdsey Hall as emblematic for the period—it is an ugly combination of historical styles and represents unrestrained material ambition. When no one could afford to live in it anymore, Sebald reveals, it served for a time as a research center for the team of experts that developed radar. Countless other such large houses served, for a time at least, as schools, asylums, and old people's homes. This theme—the interchangeability of prisons, hospitals, boarding schools, refugee shelters—is one that will be developed more fully in the architectural commentaries in *Austerlitz*.

Ever the archival researcher, Sebald turns to the history of military installations in and around Orford, and describes the system of towers built when word of Napoleon's planned invasion reached England. Sebald recounts not only the French plans to tunnel under the Channel, but strange British experiments in preparation for a possible German invasion during the Second World War, documented in a government file that was kept secret for sixty years. Once made public, the file was bereft of references to anything unusual, though an entire company of British troops was said to have died in a test in which the seas off the coast were made to burn with petroleum piped underwater and set ablaze. Some maintained that the bodies found on the beach were actually Germans dressed in British uniforms. At Orfordness, an island visible from the town, complete secrecy was maintained for many years. The narrator visits the now declassified site and describes its emptiness and oppressive, desolate beauty. Severing ties with the mainland and setting foot on Orfordness makes him feel, paradoxically, "completely liberated and utterly despondent."[31] The island is a place of profound silence. Then something occurs that shocks him momentarily—a hare leaps up out of the grass just in front of him and bounds away. The incident is vivid in his memory, particularly the strangely human expression on the rabbit's face. Sebald's empathy comes to the fore here again; he imagines the poor creature cowering as he approached, afraid to move until it was almost too late.

The structures of the abandoned military site are for Sebald ruins with an almost sacramental aura. But they are relics of the cold war, not of an ancient civilization, and they put the narrator in the frame of mind of a survivor of some future catastrophe. Many of the buildings, or shells of buildings, overtly resemble temples, or even pagodas. A ferryman retrieves him at the appointed time, and as the sun sets he looks out at the towers and roofs of the town of Orford and experiences an odd sensation, as if it once had been his home. Perhaps it was, in fact, for he suddenly sees—is he hallucinating or does his memory stretch back to another time?—the sails of the windmills that once stood everywhere along the shoreline. History can be glimpsed again, because it is present constantly—as are the past and future. It is the conventional, "flowing" concept of time that is illusory.

The Jerusalem Temple, the Vicomte at Bungay, and the Hurricane

While many of Sebald's associations flow into each other, suggesting an allusive continuum, there are also deceptive disconnections. In chapter IX, it becomes apparent only after the narrator has traveled inland for some time that the temple-like structures on Orfordness were a preview of the next object of his scrutiny at his next destination. He soon arrives at Chestnut Tree Farm, where the Methodist lay-preacher Thomas Abrams has been working for more than twenty years on a scale model of the Temple at Jerusalem as it appeared at the beginning of the Common Era. Sebald's original differs somewhat from the English edition, in ✓ that a picture of the farmhouse is provided in the German text and the actual name of the model-builder is used: Alec Garrard. His farm is a silent, "drowsing" place, a place where meticulous work is proceeding almost imperceptibly on a project being done for no other reason than its own sake. It is the sort of place that fascinates Sebald. Abrams/Garrard discusses the reservations his friends and family held about his obsession with the pointless construction of the temple in his unheated barn, especially in light of his inattention to his own farm. On the other hand, visits from experts and lay people from all over the world have given his project a certain legitimacy. Not only must every miniature stone and column be made and painted by hand, but the growth of knowledge about antiquity and the ever changing directions of scholarly opinion require adjustments and rebuilding. Yet transience, not permanence, is the lesson taught by the model-builder's attempt to recreate the past and make time stand still. Abrams observes that "the actual Temple of Jerusalem only lasted a hundred years . . . perhaps this one will last a little longer."[32]

Again and again, aesthetic encounters of every ilk confront Sebald's narrators. They encounter exquisite gardens and splendid palaces, but also architecture and interior design of the most tasteless stamp. The worst decor is often found in places where travelers take shelter. In the town of Harleston, the narrator encounters another such hotel. In this case, his room at the Saracen's Head —in the German version, the Swan Hotel—is furnished with a pink bed that is attached to a large black, altar-like headboard. Everything seems to be at a tilt, and the narrator has the constant feeling the house is about to fall in. He is more than happy to leave in the morning and continue on his journey, ostensibly to see the church of Iketshall St. Margaret. Vicomte François-René de Chateaubriand (one of Sebald's favorite memoirists) had come here when the terrors of the Revolution were raging in France. He became acquainted with the vicar of the church of Iketshall St. Margaret, Reverend Ives, who lived in nearby Bungay with his wife and their daughter, Charlotte. Sebald conjures up the lengthy visits and the special bond that forms between Chateaubriand and Charlotte. They converse in French together, make music, and read books to each other, notably Torquato Tasso's *Jerusalem Delivered* (1581). Soon the Vicomte realizes that the companionship can go no further, that he must leave. Before he can say his farewells, however, marriage is proposed by the mother and Chateaubriand must admit he already has a wife back in France. Sebald again quotes verbatim, this time from Chateaubriand's recollections from "beyond the grave," *Mémoire d'outre-tombe* (1849–50). The passage that interests Sebald is the one in which the Vicomte reflects, years later, about choosing to accept the writer's calling over a life of pleasure and peace in rural Suffolk. His decision is to squander happiness knowingly for the sake of his talent; yet what will it really matter, he asks himself, that he chose one thing and not the other? Will anyone read what he wrote in the decades and centuries to come, much less understand it "in a world the very foundations of which have changed?"[33] Years after they parted they meet again and the fateful question arises as to whether he could rectify the mistakes of the past and rejoin Charlotte, living out the rest of his years in happy devotion. No, he knows for a certainty that he must devote himself to writing down the memories that overwhelm him frequently and unexpectedly. In words that could just as well be Sebald's own, Chateaubriand asks what we would be without memory—we need it to order our thoughts in a meaningful way, to preserve traces of the way things were. Yet there is a curse on those afflicted with the talent of a writer, for their vision is directed toward the past, which consumes them, and they become estranged from the experience of the present. Sebald quotes Chateaubriand's remark that he has become invisible, and that the world of the present is shrouded in mystery.

What follows is a sort of eulogy for the Vicomte, in which Sebald provides a digest of the Frenchman's remarkable travels and of the many historic events he witnessed. Sebald remembers the first time he read the twelve volumes of the *Mémoires,* starting with Chateaubriand's secluded childhood in Combourg. Sebald describes, in effect, a memory of a memoir. He does his readers an invaluable literary service, since Chateaubriand's voluminous memoir is little known outside the French-speaking world. In Chateaubriand's record of his development, childhood ends at the age of seventeen, the day the Vicomte's father sends him into the world to make his own way. He is given a hundred Louis d'or and told not to dishonor his name. The sad loneliness of his parents' country home is at an end, and a broad terrain opens up before him.

But Sebald will not allow the poignant but reassuring mood of autobiography to dominate the narrative. Chateaubriand's love of trees provides an occasion for a digression on yet another remarkable form of annihilation: the scourge of Dutch elm disease, the symptoms of which Sebald describes in unsettling detail. Sebald remembers the elm trees dying in his own garden in the summer of 1978. Invert the last two digits, he seems to be saying, and one gets 1987, the year a hurricane hit southeast England and finished off many of the hardwoods in the region. He remembers waking and looking out to see the forces of nature bending the crowns of trees almost to the ground. Moments later everything in the scene was gone, replaced by a "ghastly emptiness"—"a formless scene that seemed, as one watched, to merge into a vision of the underworld."[34] As the weather clears, the night sky is more brilliant than the narrator has seen since his childhood. But the destruction left by the storm is not temporary; Sebald shows how the initial effects of the disaster lead to long-term devastation. The nearby forest floor has been made barren by the clay deposited everywhere during the storm, the shade-loving plants have begun to die off in the glare of the sun, and the birds are gone, taking their songs with them. Despite man's technological domination of virtually all aspects of life, there is no standing up to nature's catastrophes, which can have permanent effects. Sebald, with his "historical metaphysics," is intent on reminding us how little life has changed in many respects, how little progress we have made.

The Culmination

In interpreting Sebald, it is difficult to avoid retracing his intricate narrative connections. Only by doing so does one recognize just how he manages to get where he is going. The final chapter of *The Rings of Saturn* begins with another reference to Sir Thomas Browne, but this time Sebald focuses his antiquarian eye on *Musaeum Clausum,* a compendium of mostly imaginary marvels that reminds one of the Borges bestiary mentioned in chapter I. The last of the numerous fantastic treasures mentioned is the bamboo cane used to bring the first silkworm eggs back from China during the reign of the Byzantine emperor Justianus. Sebald then launches into a treatise on the astonishing facts of the silkworm's life cycle. Just as the destructive beetle that carried Dutch elm disease was able to locate and infect every last elm in England, so the silkworm moth, in benign contrast, can find every white-fruited mulberry tree in Asia. The author provides, as one by now has come to expect, a historical account of silk-making (sericulture) in China, and a description of its clandestine spread—the Chinese did not readily relinquish their secrets—to Greece, then Italy, then France. Politics at the court of Henry IV complicated matters, but did not prevent the spread of sericulture in England, and it was not long before James I had laid out a mulberry orchard on the site where Buckingham Palace now stands. After the revocation of the Edict of Nantes in 1685, the Huguenots soon left France, and many of them settled in Norwich, Sebald's adopted hometown, then the second largest city in England. They brought sericulture to a city already steeped in the textile trade, and in the early years of the eighteenth century silk-making grew enormously.

Yet silk did not catch on everywhere. The Huguenots who went to Germany met with initial success in Frederick the Great's Prussia and in the Palatinate as well as in Bavaria. But the many German rulers involved were too despotic in their assignment of compulsory mulberry cultivation, and the costs imposed on villages (for supervisors and other bureaucrats) were more than burdensome. The prescribed duties and the despised costs were finally abolished, and the mulberry trees were felled for firewood. Sebald quotes from an Austrian manual published by Joseph von Hazzi in 1826, giving the reasons for the failure of silk in Germany and discussing the prospects for its revival under new conditions. Von Hazzi had hoped the introduction of silk-making as a cottage industry would not only add to domestic income by engaging women and children in productive labor, but strengthen the moral fiber of the nation by inculcating ideals of order, industry, and cleanliness. By coincidence, researching the documentary film on herring production that Sebald once saw as a child led him to another archival discovery. Although it is difficult to imagine, the Nazis had entertained notions similar to von Hazzi's, and had actively tried to reintroduce sericulture in the late 1930s. "Education Pamphlet F213/1939," a manual on silk production by one of the official promoters of the Reich Association for Silkworm Breeders, argues not only the merits of breeding silkworms, but, in keeping with fascist ideals of racial purity, mandates the extermination of inferior individuals in order to pre-empt the degeneration of the species. Here Sebald mentions for the first time the chilling fact that extermination has been an essential part of traditional sericulture for millennia. While the Asians, the Greeks, and the Italians put the larvae out in the sun or in a hot oven to die, the German sericulturalists of the Third Reich prescribed that they be suspended in baskets over seething cauldrons batch by batch, for three hours at a time, "until the entire killing business is completed."[35]

Thus, sericulture was attempted twice in Germany, once during the rise of nationalistic fervor in the first quarter of the nineteenth century, and once during the Third Reich's nationalistic revival. Further coincidences are the basis for the conclusion of the narrative. In the last two pages of the book Sebald brings what he calls his "notes" to an end, observing that it is Maundy Thursday, the 13th of April 1995. A series of remarkable anniversaries can be associated with the date, the author informs us. He produces a partial list that includes the premier performance of a great musical composition, a bloody massacre, and an act designed to foster tolerance and banish hatred and division: the declaration of the Edict of Nantes. On the same date fifty years before, British newspapers announced the fall of the city of Celle in northern Germany. The Red Army was advancing up the Danube. Thus, the fate of the narrator's homeland, a nation that had come close to conquering much of the world, was sealed. There is a personal coincidence as well, namely the death of the narrator's father-in-law in Coburg on that very day. Though the source is not mentioned explicitly, Sebald's next association is brought on by the reference to the city of Coburg, which was the home of Prince Albert, husband of Queen Victoria. Sebald remarks that Victoria's daughter-in-law, the Duchess of Teck—a German like Albert—was dressed in the finest black silk on the occasion of the queen's funeral. It came from one of the best silk houses in Norwich, and was manufactured just before the company closed down permanently. The final thread of the book, then, figuratively speaking, is a silken one. Sir Thomas Browne appears again—his father was a silk merchant—with an observation about funeral practices in Holland in his day. *The Rings of Saturn* closes with death as its theme, but also—remarkably, for modern European literature—with the presumption, or at least the possibility, of an afterlife.

Reception

Whereas in Germany Sebald's reputation as a novelist was already firmly established when *The Rings of Saturn* appeared, the book was regarded in Britain and the United States as Sebald's second remarkable masterpiece by many. Both books were noted for their uniqueness. And yet the two books share many stock Sebaldian features. As the British writer Blake Morrison put it, they have in common "an acute sense of place, a fascination with emigrés and eccentrics, a dislike of paragraphing, a uniquely seductive tone of voice."[36] Several critics have complained of the sometimes "tenuous links" that connect the various stations of Sebald's narrative, and those same critics are the ones who conclude that *The Emigrants* is the better, more compelling book.[37] Yet virtually no one denies the hypnotic effect of Sebald's prose and the fascination elicited by his kaleidoscopic continuum of associations. Absent in Sebald's prose for some critics is a certain resonance. David Auerbach does not find fault in this, although he, unlike most reviewers, finds Sebald difficult reading. "[Sebald] avoids moments of emotional intensity," Auerbach writes, "and when he portrays them, they are anything but personal."[38] In fact, the detachment of the narrative approach, not unlike that of Kafka's, seems to be an integral part of Sebald's authorial strategy, since he is obviously determined to look at everything anew, with the eyes of an extraterrestrial who is experiencing the susceptibilities of life on earth for the first time. The more serious criticism may be found in Andre Aciman's 1998 article, in which he assails the overly recursive nature of Sebald's style. "The problem is," writes Aciman, who is himself a professor and a novelist, "that Sebald's view of recursion, interesting as it genuinely is, is interesting as an idea only; it is conveyed intellectually, not aesthetically; it is not experienced, it is merely worded. Ultimately, it is drawn from the content of the author's life, not worked into the form of the book about that life."[39] The self-references, the literary references, the references to art and music, and the seemingly tangential digressions are indeed drawn from the author's life and researches—in this sense

Aciman is correct. But Sebald cannot be said to claim otherwise. He refers to the form of his writing repeatedly as "notes." He submits them for publication, then goes back to his writing. Whether the web Sebald weaves in *The Rings of Saturn* is reducible to "Shandyism"—self-conscious imitation of the eighteenth-century novelist Lawrence Sterne—is a judgment to be made by each reader on his own.[40] The *Times* critic Richard Eder does not concur, but sees *The Rings of Saturn* as a "darker, slower and more diffuse" book than *The Emigrants*—the latter novel possesses a "bright narrative energy" in the form, contradictorily, of a "dreamlike lament."[41] In contrast, *The Rings of Saturn* is a brooding "tidal surge instead of a series of eddies . . . lustrous and finally overwhelming."[42]

Most often in the months after *The Rings of Saturn* appeared in translation, reviewers' comments reaffirmed the strange allure of the book and its compelling power. The occasional tenuousness of Sebald's transitional technique was not deemed a decisive flaw. More than once Sebald was compared to Beckett, Borges, Conrad, Kafka, Nabokov, and Sir Thomas Browne. One American reviewer even saw in *The Rings of Saturn* an example of "purest Melville."[43] Among most critics in the English-speaking world, *The Rings of Saturn* served to confirm Sebald's stature as a European writer of major significance. James Wood, writing in *The New Republic,* spoke for many when he called Sebald "one of the most mysteriously sublime of contemporary writers" anywhere.[44] The stage was set for the appearance of Sebald's most mature and focused achievement, *Austerlitz*. But in the meantime *Vertigo,* his first novel, would be released in English.

CHAPTER 4

Vertigo

Return to the Beginning

The four-part novel *Vertigo,* which was not translated into English until Sebald's reputation was firmly established outside of Germany, stands at the beginning of Sebald's career as a writer of prose fiction, and demonstrates emphatically that some literary influences, notably Kafka and Stendhal, were with him from the start. From Kafka, Sebald draws inspiration for his narrative style—the deliberate pace, the sense of detail—as well as descriptive emphases that heighten the mood of foreboding, torpor, and entrapment, especially in the two middle portions of the book. The recurring leitmotiv, especially prevalent in the chapter "Dr. K.s Badereise nach Riva" ("Dr. K. Takes the Waters at Riva"), is Kafka's strange tale of a corpse condemned to wander the earth in search of the entrance to the underworld. The story "Der Jäger Gracchus" ("The Hunter Gracchus"), written in 1917, tells of a man who was killed during a hunt many years before, but somehow lost his way during his final journey to join the dead. From Stendhal, on the other hand, Sebald draws inspiration for his narrator's musings on the nature of memory and the act of recording those memories, as well as thoughts on the purpose of writing itself. Sebald's visual orientation and use of images evince an affinity with Stendhal's prolific use of drawings in *The Life of Henry Brulard.* (Stendhal wrote under several pseudonyms, and named even his autobiography for someone else—a monk he was said to resemble when he was a child.) Sebald identifies Stendhal in *Vertigo* only by his little-known given name, Henri Beyle, and makes him the protagonist of the first episode. In a similar fashion, Sebald makes Kafka a character in the third episode of the book.

The novel *Vertigo,* then, concerns itself in large measure with literature—the works, the lives of literary figures, and the act of writing. Because it concerns itself with these things, and because Sebald's narrators are always traveling, it is also a book that focuses on setting. Its venues are Italy and France, Austria and Italy, England and Germany, and its chronological benchmarks are 1813, the year of Napoleon's final defeat, and 1913, the year before the First World War altered European life forever. The seminal events of Stendhal's life, described in the first chapter, are associated with Napoleon's rise. Looming in the background of the third chapter is Kafka's astute appreciation for the moral inadequacy and cultural exhaustion of European civilization, though there is no sense of impending warfare in the spa town of Riva in the summer of 1913. But Sebald's narrative occupies more recent time as well; the narrator is our contemporary. As the second chapter demonstrates, *Vertigo* is in large part a personal tale about a troubled narrator, ostensibly fictional, who travels to Austria and Italy in 1980 and then returns to Italy again in 1987. In the final chapter we accompany the narrator on his return home to Germany some four decades after yet another terrible war—a war in which the moral inadequacy of Europe was demonstrated to be not just an insufficiency but bankruptcy pure and simple. Sebald's Bavarian hometown of Wertach is the setting for his autumnal ruminations on the world that has been lost.

Not only are two of the main characters in the book literary figures, but the language used—typical Sebaldian diction—is literary as well. Slang is avoided almost entirely. Wherever he can do so without seeming predictable, the author substitutes a dated word for a contemporary term. Some of the literariness is explicit and some of it calls little attention to itself. The novel's links and transitions are often predicated on overt references to literature, music, and art, but there are also unattributed, nearly verbatim quotations as well. At such junctures √ in the text, previous literature merges with the narrative in a quintessentially Sebaldian example of coincidence and repetition.

Part One: A Portrait of Marie-Henri Beyle

Sebald's fascination with Stendhal is in large part a fascination with Stendhal's ideas on memory as an essential and primary subject of serious writing. With his emphasis on memory Stendhal anticipates many authors, critics, and theorists in the twentieth century who focus on remembering as an act fundamental to literary creativity. Yet the notion is not as simple or straightforward as it might appear. In one of his reviews, Borges remarks:

> It is a general rule that novelists do not present a reality, but rather its recollection. They write about real or believable events that have been revised and arranged by memory. (This process, of course, has nothing to do with the verb tenses which are used.)[1]

Memory is active, not passive; it *arranges* events and impressions in the process of recollection. And by its very nature, Borges reminds us, memory is required during any telling or retelling, regardless of the grammatical tense employed. The key notion Sebald derives from Stendhal is that of the constitution of memories out of vivid and compelling mental images that may or may not be authentic, but rather are in fact composites shaped by subsequent accounts or drawn from other, often anachronistic memories. In recollecting a childhood accident, Stendhal explains what often happens when memories are created: "I can picture the event, but probably this isn't a direct memory of the mental image I formed of the affair a long way back at the time of the first accounts I was given of it."[2] Stendhal's metaphor for the memory of an event or time is the fresco. Yet it is in no way a perfect or complete work of art, but a fresco with gaps and holes. He constantly questions whether what he sees in the mind's eye is the same as what he saw at the time. Sebald, who follows Beyle/Stendhal on his march with Napoleon across the St. Bernard Pass in mid-May of 1800, illustrates his character's perception of memory's paradoxical vividness and uncertainty by the example of Beyle's recollection of a particular officer he later knew in civilian life. In his memory Belye sees "General Mamont . . . to the left of the track along which the column was moving, dressed in the royal- and sky-blue robes of a Councillor of State . . . this although [Beyle] is well aware that at that time Marmont must have been wearing his general's uniform and not the blue robes of state."[3] Among the reproductions of paintings and photographs, Sebald intersperses several of Beyle's drawings and handwriting samples, as Stendhal had himself done in the composition of his autobiography during 1835 and 1836. But as if to play a sly and subtle joke on the reader, Sebald leaves out the image that had originally undermined Beyle's certainty. It was an engraving titled "Prospetto d'Ivrea," which Beyle realizes upon redis-covering it among his old papers, has completely replaced his memory of the actual experience of viewing the town. He had seen the real Ivrea in the St. Bernard valley as the sun set in May of 1800—an event described in the first pages of the book. But in the strange world of mental images that fascinates Sebald, the mind can replace the real with images only *derived* from reality, thus displacing the first-hand with the twice-removed.

The uncertainty of what is real, even that which we think we know *to have been real,* is a mark of the inner turmoil that is so often Sebald's subject. It is not by coincidence that he chooses Stendhal for the first part of his book, nor is it by accident that the phenomenon of vertigo makes its first appearance early in the narrative. Psychology has applied Beyle's nom de plume to a condition known as the "Stendhal Syndrome," which refers to incapacitation due to sensory over-load. Sebald illustrates Beyle's experience of this syndrome at the second stage in his journey, at Marengo, where the decisive battle of Napoleon's first cam-paign took place. Returning to the site a year afterwards, the dissonance of his picture of the battle and the contemporaneous condition of the battlefield was too much for him. Though he himself had originally arrived at the battlefield too late to witness the event, he had heard "endless tellings and retellings, and he had himself pictured it in many and various shades and hues."[4] Sebald describes Beyle's reaction to what was now spread before him as he revisits the scene, which was a plain covered with the bones of 16,000 men and 4,000 horses:

> The difference between the images of the battle that he had in his head and what he now saw before him as evidence that the battle had in fact taken place occasioned in him a vertiginous sense of confusion and irritation such as he had never experienced before.[5]

Thus, a shabby war memorial in the form of a column aggravates the vertigo Beyle experiences. At this point in the text, a long vertical slice of a painting of the battle appears, under which, in the German edition, appear the last words of the paragraph, namely "wie ein Untergehender" (23). It is an eccentric visual joke of sorts; the image is formatted so that it begins on one page and ends on the next, drawing the reader's eyes down, then up, then down again—to a point where the words in German quite literally mean "like one going down." "One going down" can also mean "one who is doomed" in German, but the pun will not work in English, and is abandoned along with the formatting of the picture, which in the English edition simply covers the left third of page 18. Once again, not everything about the author's method works in both languages; such can be the trials of translating (and formatting) Sebald. Another similar visual prank is abandoned in the English version, in the passage where Sebald remarks on Beyle's unusually wide-set eyes. In the original, Sebald actually "interrupts" the text with a picture, substituting the portion of Stendhal's portrait showing his eyes for the word "Augen" ("eyes") on page 15, whereas the English restores the flow of the text and foregoes the overt interplay of text and image. (11) The translator has chosen severity over playfulness in such instances as these, an important decision for the cumulative tone of the English-language book.

What is gained in translation is the independent richness and elegance of Michael Hulse's version; but of course something is inevitably lost in the process of translation as well. Hulse's choice of diction tends to be consistently serious in tone. Where Sebald's German is playful, however, earnestness departs from the original. The overarching sense of irony in Sebald's *Vertigo* is suggested even by its German title, which is a play on words—a kind of punctuated pun—rather than the name of a medical condition that in turn conjures up associations with Hitchcock's suspense film of the same name. *Schwindel. Gefühle* is a recombination of the compound word *Schwindelgefühle* ("feelings of dizziness") using a period to divide the word into its component parts, whereby Sebald exposes an ambiguity in the German language (*Schwindel* can mean "dizziness" as well as "swindle" or "deception"). Even as he destabilizes the meaning of the title, Sebald maintains the association with the compound *Schwindelgefühle,* suggesting vertigo. Thus the title works on three levels at once, creating a promise of irony, ambiguity, and authorial "sleight-of-hand," where the English does not. It is also true that the word *Gefühle* ("feelings") standing on its own also promises a preoccupation with the emotional, the non-rational. To be sure, Sebald delivers on his promise from the beginning, as he proceeds to describe Beyle's experience of the "discreet madness" that is love, as indicated in the translator's title of the first section of *Vertigo.* Yet here again we encounter a variance between the German and the English. The original reads "Beyle, oder das merckwürdige Faktum der Liebe," in an orthography that belongs to the nineteenth rather than the twentieth century. A literal translation would read "Beyle, or the strange (curious) fact of love," suggesting that the very existence of love is bizarre, but stopping short of associating it, even discreetly, with madness. There are other occasional deviations from the original throughout the Hulse translation, though they usually represent a matter of shading rather than substance. Thus, "Lady Simonetta" gives the young Beyle a "pitying look" (13), where the German version reads "ironically sympathetic" ("ironisch-mitleidsvoll," 17). Stendhal's abiding concern for "what it is that undoes a writer" (15) is in German more forcefully put: "Woran geht ein Schriftsteller zugrunde?" (19), i.e., "what destroys a writer?" or "what causes a writer to fail?" There is a natural tendency in English to prefer understatement, but the German original is unambiguously direct.

The "feelings" (*Gefühle*) come hard and fast as the reader follows Beyle's travels in this miniature *Bildungsroman.* His imagination and emotions are, in a word, ignited by his experience of opera. Ironically, he does not encounter opera in the Parisian capital, but in the town of Ivrea during one of the Napoleonic campaigns. Cimarosa's *Il Matrimonio Segreto* is being performed. When he experiences the same opera later in Milan, the final thunderous applause seems to him like the "crackling caused by a tremendous conflagration," and he yearns to be consumed by that fire.[6] As the title of the opera suggests, Cimarosa's plot involves secret, but true love, legitimized by marriage but concealed from those around, who are plotting a marriage of convenience. Sebald explains nothing about the opera outright, but the implications are near to hand, with Beyle returning to the notion of secret loves again and again. He sings a tune of his own devising to the words, "I am her secret and intimate companion"—"Je suis le compagnon secret et familier."

Sebald's Beyle also gives us the first example of "swindle," as promised by the German title of the book, when he seeks the affections of a married woman,

Métilde Viscontini Dembowski in Milan. He becomes so obsessed with her that he even stoops to following her incognito. The contrivance fails miserably, yet he manages to come away with a plaster cast of her hand, which becomes a kind of fetish for him. Métilde, who is the unnamed object of his desire in his book *De l'Amour* (1822), never returned his affections. But there were many other women. Or were there? What can be said to be true about Beyle's claims about his paramours? The question itself points to Sebald's answer: "Who knows?" Did he really make the trip to Lake Garda with Mme. Gherardi, as described in *De l'Amour*? Did Mme. Gherardi really exist? At Riva the first enigmatic fore-shadowing of the coming chapter on Kafka occurs. Beyle and Mme Gherardi come upon a boat on the shore out of which two men in dark tunics with silver buttons remove a bier on which rests a corpse draped in frayed silk. Here the setting changes as the couple travels into the Alpine reaches of Austria, a region to which Sebald will return in the last part of the book. Discussions of the nature of love continue, drawn from Stendhal's account of the journey in *De l'Amour,* with Mme. Gherardi taking the sardonic, cynical, or melancholy point of view, thus stoking Beyle's own hopelessness about ever finding, then winning a woman of his own intellectual niveau. Undercutting the romanticism and the philosophizing is of course the lurid reality of Beyle's more prurient interests, which produced the syphilitic symptoms that plagued him all his adult life. It is his failing health that gradually comes to dominate his thoughts, and he becomes obsessed, uncharacteristically, with secrecy—rather than with love and lovers. Sebald shows us snatches of Beyle's cryptic records and longevity calculations, before closing the chapter with his collapse on a Paris street "on the evening of the 22nd of March, 1842, with the approach of spring already in the air," and his death the following morning.[7] The life of Henri Beyle was compulsive, even driven, but its strange passion and its proximity to events of historical importance render it extraordinary.

While Sebald stresses chronological notation as a means of reinforcing the persuasiveness of his historical and personal narratives, he at the same time undermines any real certainty. Sebald's questioning of the certainty of time is more than a form of temporal agnosticism; it is a source of irony. In *Vertigo,* even the notation of time is destabilized, freed from its moorings. A good example is Sebald's use of the republican calendar for his chapter on Beyle. He uses this system, which was adopted during the French Revolution in 1793, matter-of-factly, without explanation. According to the republican calendar, the year ended in late September with five holidays between 17 and 21 September. The autumn months were *Vendémiaire, Brumaire,* and *Frimaire;* the winter months were *Nivôse, Pluviôse;* and *Ventôse;* the spring months were *Germinal, Floréal,* and

Prairial; the summer months were *Messidor, Thermidor,* and *Fructidor.* By 1805, however, Napoleon had abolished the republican system. Ironically, it had counted the year of its inception as "Year One." Sebald drops it just as summarily, and proceeds to the next chapter.

In October of 1980 . . .

The next chapter, "All'estero" (Abroad), leaps forward to the year 1980 and changes perspective completely, employing the first person as its narrative voice. One may assume the narrator is Sebald himself, though one may hardly assume the story is meant as an autobiographical record in the conventional sense. Sebald begins as he often does, by locating the setting in space and time as if he were writing a diary: "I had traveled—it was in October of 1980—from England, where I had been living for nearly twenty-five years in a county that was almost always under gray, overcast skies, to Vienna, in the hopes that a change of place would help me get over an especially bad period in my life."[8] In Vienna, however, no resolution of his condition is forthcoming; rather he finds himself walking in circles, traversing the same urban territory over and over again. Incomprehensibly, his progress is confined within invisible and arbitrary borders, as if by some hidden force. When the narrator begins to hallucinate, glimpsing persons from his hometown who are long dead, along with the poet Dante, it is clear that we have fully entered the domain of vertigo for which the book was named. To be sure, the narrator pauses on the street due to his apprehension, which manifests itself in "nausea and dizziness," translated by Hulse as "a feeling of vertigo."[9] During his ten days in Vienna, the narrator visits none of the sights and speaks to no one but restaurant and hotel staff. He feeds the birds in a park, giving a white-headed blackbird the name of an imaginary creature, the "senafowl." Mentioned in the German version only, this bird is called in the original "der Senavogel" (45). In his disconsolate condition the narrator begins to collect miscellaneous useless things. Finally, on an evening when he has heard Austrian children singing, inexplicably, "Silent Night" and "Jingle Bells" in English, he falls into a deep sleep and awakes with the feeling that he has crossed a great body of water and is now stepping off a ferry onto some new land. He resolves to depart and travel that evening to Venice. He knows that in the meantime he must see one of the people he had intended to look up while in Vienna, the poet Ernst Herbeck.

Herbeck, whose work Sebald discussed in a scholarly article for one of his books on Austrian literature, *Die Beschreibung des Unglücks* (The description of melancholy), is no "ordinary" poet. He has been a mental patient since he was twenty years of age. They visit Burg Greifenstein, a medieval castle with a panoramic view of the Danube Valley below (the view as it once was, is pictured in the text). There is also a photograph, for comparison, of the new lock and dam below Burg Greifenstein. Memory, Sebald is reminding us, is no match for such profound alterations, and the sight of the straightened river "will soon extinguish the memory of what it once was."[10] Walking back to the train station, there occurs one of the bizarre but mundane scenes characteristic of Sebald. In this case the beauty of the autumn day is rent by the violent barking and lunging of a black dog behind a green iron gate. No one in the village of Kritzendorf is to be seen. The narrator feels terror, but Herbeck seems unshaken. The episode ends with a conversation in a gloomy bar, where the two men have fled from the traffic. Sebald introduces a quotation from a poem in order to illustrate the kind of writing Herbeck does. The humor comes through in translation, but not Herbeck's idiosyncratic spelling, which is like that of a child. Herbeck then writes a response to the narrator's description of the region where he lives in England, but as such it is only marginally related to what was actually said. "England, as is well known, is an island unto itself. If you want to go to England it takes an entire day. 30th October 1980 Ernst Herbeck."[11] In the figure of Herbeck we find traces of Kaspar Hauser, the mysterious foundling mentioned in *The Emigrants* —the schizophrenic poet has the same extraterrestrial perspective and the same uncompromising honesty, born of naïveté. As the two men say their farewells, Herbeck's gesture reminds the narrator of one who has traveled with a circus (as Kaspar once did).

Near Death in Venice

While in the train for Venice, for the first time in the book the narrator dreams. He sees an Alpine landscape, merging imperceptibly with the landscape around the Italian town of Este, as it appears in a painting by Tiepolo. There will be more references to Italian art, but for the time being the allusion is broken off by the train's arrival in the Venice terminal. In a nod to the impeccably dressed but moribund protagonist Gustav von Aschenbach in Thomas Mann's *Der Tod in Venedig* (1912; *Death in Venice,* 1925), the first thing the narrator does upon arrival is go to the barber.[12] Sebald evokes the uncanny atmosphere of Venice, the urban literary setting par excellence, with a few observations:

> As you enter the heart of the city, you cannot tell what you will see next or indeed who will see you the very next moment. Scarcely has someone made an appearance than he has quit the stage again by another exit. These brief exhibitions are of an almost theatrical obscenity and at the same time have an air of conspiracy about them, into which one is drawn unwittingly.[13]

Venice is more than a setting: it is itself a character, a being, a conspirator. As we might expect, Sebald refers to the literature of Venice, though he avoids explicit references to the more famous modern works about Venice, such as Mann's novel, or Daphne du Maurier's *Don't Look Now* (which was made into a movie with Douglas Sutherland). The two important literary figures in this section of "All'estero" are the Austrian playwright Franz Grillparzer (1791–1872), whose *Italian Diary* (1819) aptly and accurately describes the various sights worth seeing, according to Sebald, as well as the disappointment that invariably results when one finally sees them. Grillparzer also found not only the atmosphere of Venice, but the "Invisible Principle" that governed the place strange.[14] Particularly disconcerting for him was the administration of "justice" by the Council, which met in secret and acted with the utmost severity in many cases. The Italian writer and adventurist known as Casanova (1725–1798) was one of few historical personages to survive imprisonment in the Doge's Palace. He was confined there in the summer of 1755 and mulled over his escape for almost two years, as described in his autobiography, the twelve-volume *History of My Life*. Again, literature and life are conjoined in a characteristically Sebaldian way, as Casanova finds the key to his escape in reading Ludovico Ariosto's sixteenth-century epic about Charlemagne's paladin Roland, *Orlando Furioso*. A line that refers to the night between the end of October and the beginning of November is the omen he needs.[15] October 31 turns out to be the time the inquisitors would be away and, in their absence, his only remaining guard inebriated. He could make his break. But the coincidences do not end here. In composing these lines, Sebald checks his own calendar and finds that he was in Venice, reading about Casanova's escape on the very anniversary of it, the last day of October 1980. Thus concludes a passage that unites two of Sebald's abiding penchants: for coincidence and for biographical digression.

Another Sebaldian preoccupation, as we have seen, is with the religious capital of Jerusalem. One night in Venice the narrator encounters a man in a bar, Malachio, and agrees to take a midnight boat trip with him on the Grand Canal. The lights of the coastal refineries, the pall of white smoke rising from the municipal incinerator, and the huge, abandoned Stucky flour mill illuminated by the moon, all contribute to an eerie scene in which it is almost unavoidable to associate Malachio with Charon, the mythical ferryman to the underworld. He even brings up the Resurrection, and when he leaves the narrator on the dock his parting words are, "Next year in Jerusalem!"[16] Their common pilgrimage will continue, this kindred spirit seems to be suggesting. Sebald notes that Malachio once studied astrophysics at Cambridge and regards everything, not only the stars, from a great distance. In this he resembles Sebald's other extraterrestrial characters. In his interests, Malachio resembles the protagonist's friend Gerald Fitzpatrick in *Austerlitz,* who studies astrophysics at Cambridge and loves to pilot his Cessna through the night sky.

As in Sebald's other novels, the narrator is not immune to the immobilizing depression suffered by many of the characters. The silence that looms over Venice on All Saints' morning seems to signal the beginning of a depressive episode. It reminds the narrator of the invariably foggy mornings of the same day in his childhood in "W.," when his elders donned black and visited the graves of the departed. This mention of "W." (Wertach im Allgäu, where Sebald spent the first nine years of his life) is the first of several, culminating in a return to the town in the final section of the book. A feeling of emptiness soon overtakes the narrator in his hotel bed and he begins to feel that his life could end, that he is —to use an image that occurs again and again in Sebald—"already laid out for burial."[17] He dreams of St. Catherine. He dreams of the madmen in their hospital across the lagoon. He wonders why Malachio mentioned Jerusalem. Three days later he is finally able to rise and leave the room. The incapacitating bout of depression has come and gone.

Like Kafka before him, Sebald illustrates how the nightmarish qualities of some familiar and mundane experiences can be showcased convincingly, and everyday reality can be presented as horrifying in its absurdity. Thus, when Sebald attempts to buy a cup of cappuccino before departing the train terminal at Venice, he finds himself swept into a crowded, harried, inhospitable system that pits customer against customer and, in turn, customer against cafeteria employee. The indifferent cashiers tower imperiously above the fray, deigning to dispense receipts to whom they wish; these must then be redeemed from waiters looking down their noses from behind an elevated marble counter. Upon finally receiving his cup of coffee, the narrator feels the accomplishment is the supreme victory of his entire life, but in that moment encounters the gaze of the two young men who will shadow him for much of the rest of the story. In fact, he realizes they have already shadowed him—they were in the bar where he met Malachio, for example. The feeling grows that he is involved in "a dark web of intrigue," and sure enough, as dusk begins to settle on the arena in Verona, the two figures seem to be watching him from the shadows.

Aesthetic experience is always the opposing pole to dread in Sebald, and *Vertigo* contains its share of landscape descriptions and digressions on art. In "All'estero" much attention is paid to the frescoes of Antonio Pisano (1395–1455), also known as Pisanello. On his surfaces, which are somehow realistic without conveying a sense of depth, all creatures—flora, fauna, men, women, and angels— have an "equal and undiminished right to exist."[18] The equality of all beings is a firm conviction of Sebald's, as we have seen before and will see again. Sebald is also fascinated with the idea of eyes being windows to the soul, a notion to which he will return in *Austerlitz*. Here, too, images of eyes are integrated into the text. In one excerpt from the Pisanello fresco, St. George's eyes seem to show that he is anticipating the battle ahead. Sebald contrasts the sublime beauty of the painting with the kitsch of the spiritually withering restaurant decor he next encounters when looking for a meal. Just as Pisanello's art has a benevolent, even healing effect, bad art can have an agitating and malignant one.

Looming in the shadows of "All'estero," as the narrator learns by (apparent) coincidence is "Organizzazione Ludwig," a group claiming credit for the murder of a gypsy in 1977, a heroin addict a year later, and in the current year, 1980, a waiter. The possible motivation for these murders is not difficult to identify; the gypsy and the addict are on the margins of society, and such people are often the prey of right-wing extremists bent on "cleaning things up." One can assume the waiter may have been homosexual, and thus a member of a conspicuous target group. It is not easy to overlook the possible connection—unstated, as so often in Sebald—between Organizzazione Ludwig and the two men who have been following the narrator. If these men first saw the narrator in the bar where he met Malachio, another man (with whom he departed to take a moonlight boat ride) then perhaps they have assumed the narrator is homosexual too. Perhaps he is their next victim. Such questions are implied, one comes to realize, by the narrator's nameless dread. As he sits in the oppressively ugly restaurant contemplating the murderous Organizzazione Ludwig, this dread reaches a vertiginous crescendo. When the narrator notices on his bill that one of the owners of the restaurant is named Carlo Cadavero, the ghoulish coincidence is too much for him to take. He flees, boards a train, and heads north to Austria.

Seven Years Later

One technique Sebald used in both *The Emigrants* as well as *Vertigo* is to describe a visit or a journey or any period of time in the present tense, then revisit the same setting several years later. In "All'estero" Sebald returns to Italy again in 1987 to retrace his steps and "perhaps probe some of my blurry recollections from that dangerous time and record them."[19] In this section of the story the act of writing becomes a subject of his writing. The narrator describes himself sitting in a hotel bar, for instance, and the words seem to flow freely. Is he writing notes that will form the basis for the text before us? Is it something entirely different? Later the narrator reveals that he himself does not know, but that it might turn into a story about unsolved murders in northern Italy.

In Sebald's description of his narrator's return to Verona there occurs the first of several mentions of the year 1913, in connection with Kafka's diaries. It seems that "Dr. K." had taken a trip from Venice to Lake Garda that year. The question is perhaps inevitable: Is the narrator seeing the same lake, the same towns that Kafka saw? Contemplating his face in the mirror of the train station lavatory at Desenzano, the narrator sees a clue: *Il cacciatore* (the hunter) is written on the wall. He adds the enigmatic words *nella selva nera* ("in the black forest") before leaving to walk to the lake.[20] This reference points to the motif that has been subtly alluded to already, when a prone person looks as if laid out for burial. Kafka's protagonist in the story "The Hunter Gracchus"—an example of the "living dead"—is likewise placed on a funeral bier. This motif is central to the next section of *Vertigo,* where it is developed in detail.

Just as he did in the first chapter on Henri Beyle, Sebald explores the nature of identity in "All'estero." In one episode Sebald combines the notion of mistaken identity, the phenomenon of the doppelgänger, and an encounter with twins to hilarious effect. On a bus to Riva, the narrator sees two teenage boys, twins, who look remarkably like the young Kafka. After overcoming a feeling of vertigo as the bus descends toward a lake, the narrator attempts to converse in Italian with the boys, who comprehend nothing he says. Their parents, sitting behind the narrator, become increasingly suspicious of his addressing their sons, and suddenly it is unambiguously clear he has been mistaken for a pederast. It does not help that he explains the twins' similarity to Kafka, or that he requests a photo be sent—anonymously, for the sake of protecting their privacy—to his address in England. The scene ends with the narrator leaving the bus at the next stop, humiliated but nonetheless lamenting the lost opportunity to document a rare coincidence. Identity is also bound up with place—with nation, region, locality. In his hotel at Limone the narrator hears midnight German revelers "saying the most unsavory things."[21] He recognizes not only various dialects of his homeland among the loud voices, but his own village dialect amongst the loudest and unruliest. This moment of intense, solitary shame precedes the mysterious disappearance, in the night, of the documentary proof of his identity as a German citizen: his passport. The process of obtaining another illustrates the tenuousness of identity. A copy of the letter from the Italian police, vouching for the loss of the passport, and a copy of Sebald's new passport—eyes covered by a black strip—are the alleged "proof"of the narrator's identity.

The image of a circular labyrinth on the sign reading "LA PROSSIMA COINCI-DENZA" stands out in the Milan train station, providing a not-so-subtle clue to Sebald's obsession with coincidences. Are life's coincidences truly coincidental? Was it preordained that the narrator experience what he experiences in this scene? Suddenly two young men, talking to one another in an agitated fashion and evidently paying no attention to the narrator, bear down on him, collide with him, and attempt to pick his pocket. An even more unsettling encounter—because it involves no such identifiable threats—overtakes him the next day. Walking the streets of the city in the period before his train is scheduled to depart, the narrator takes refuge in the Milan Cathedral, but finds no comfort, only a growing sense of emptiness and dislocation. Suddenly he is not even certain where he is. Struggling with vertigo, he climbs to the topmost gallery of the marble edifice, which is notable among Gothic cathedrals for its breadth rather than its height. Looking down on the people in the square below, he realizes—hearing an Italian comment on the rising wind—that he is in Italy, yes, in Milan. Another bout of dizziness (*Schwindel*) begins to subside.

Up to this point in the narrative everyday reality has been intruded upon, but never fully absorbed by, the uncanny. However, for Sebald there are certain locations, as we shall find expressly described in *Austerlitz,* that seem to function as portals to another dimension. In *Vertigo* such a place is the Municipal Library of Verona. The narrator enters without regard to a notice stating the building is closed. The archivist, dressed in what could well be period attire, assists the narrator in researching newspapers for September and August 1913, the time when Kafka visited northern Italy. Advertisements for medical and dental services, highly outdated in their rhetoric and appearance, conjure up images of Veronese men and women from the past—these scenes are immediate and vivid but have the flickering black-and-white quality of silent motion pictures. It is as if the archive has become a "Magic Shadow-Show" and the past has come alive before the narrator's eyes. Sebald calls the visual episodes experienced by the narrator "revelations."[22] They conclude with the transformation of a picture of a lion—the trademark of a brand of mineral water—into an actual lion. The animal roars soundlessly, causing a pyramid of 10,000 gleaming water bottles to shatter into millions of crystal shards. Finally, the words on the printed page take on an auditory reality all their own. The English version of text, however, brings on this strange encounter in the Municipal Library without warning, while the German original explicitly prepares the reader by suggesting the notion of a "behind-the-scenes" manipulation of reality. When the narrator was trying to fall asleep in his miserable hotel room in Milan two days before, for instance, he used the words "the curtain of sleep descended on the stage" to describe his nodding off.[23] Sleep comes only when the director of the dream/play we call reality allows his characters to sleep.

Sebald takes up the thread of "Hunter Grachus" yet again, in preparation for the next chapter. An image returns to him, and he realizes he has seen it many times. It is the dark apparition of two men in dark tunics with silver buttons beside a corpse that has been laid out and covered with a large cloth with a floral pattern. Once again, Sebald does not attribute the scene to Kafka, but merely presents it as a recurring image, a preoccupation. The connection with Kafka is, however, suggested by Salvatore Altamura, a character who is waiting in a nearby café. Apparently he is known to the narrator, but Sebald—reticent again—refuses to explain. Salvatore is engrossed in a book by the novelist and essayist Leonardo Sciascia and relates to the narrator its story of a murder that took place, it so happens, during the year before Kafka's visit to Italy. A sensational trial followed a year later. The significance of the year 1913 here, as elsewhere in *Vertigo,* is summed up in Salvatore's observation that, "In that year everything was moving towards a single point, at which something would have to happen."[24] The German version adds a phrase the equivalent of which would read "no matter the cost"—a reminder that events eventually spiraled out of control, leading to the outbreak of war in August of 1914. But Salvatore, responding to an earlier conversation to which the reader has not been privy, is eager to discuss he outcome of yet another trial, that of the members of Organizzazione Ludwig, who had in the intervening years committed several more murders and arson attacks in Italy, Germany, and Austria. The more recent murders, including killings of two monks and a priest, had been described in a message from the murderers as punishment for those who had betrayed God. The young, adult male culprits, both intelligent scions of well-to-do families, were sentenced to thirty years in prison. Sebald thus brings the crime story at the heart of the tale to a conclusion, while Salvatore continues on with reflections on the state of opera today, a retelling of the conflagration that destroyed the Cairo opera house during a performance of Verdi's *Aida* in 1871, and a description of the image of a descending angel. In a postscript Sebald redirects the reader's attention to the figure of Kafka, the subject of the chapter to follow. Interconnectedness is clearly the guiding principle in the narrative, as the author explains that a copy of Austrian novelist Franz Werfel's *Verdi* (1924) came into his possession by a circuitous route. This book about the life of the composer of *Aida* was signed by its author and presented to Kafka shortly after its publication, which was shortly before his Kafka's death. A subsequent owner's bookplate (pictured in the text) completes the chain of Egyptian connections with an image of the pyramids of Giza. With these monuments of death Sebald prepares the way for a chapter on one of the most death-haunted authors who ever lived.

On the Trail of Dr. K.

Sebald takes many of the details of the third chapter, "Dr. K. Takes the Waters at Riva," directly from Kafka's diaries and letters, weaving them into a narrative ✓

that reflects the narrator's earlier visit to Venice and Lake Garda. Kafka's journey is initially a most mundane one; as the employee of an insurance company, Kafka is making a trip to a convention on rescue services and hygiene held in Vienna. Still, literary references and precedents are everywhere, starting with Kafka's first night in a Viennese hotel, the Matschakerhof, which he chooses because the dramatist Grillparzer often stayed there. It is also worth noting that Lake Garda, Kafka's ultimate destination, was one of Goethe's favorite sights during his journey to Italy. But it is Grillparzer who figures most prominently, if briefly, in an episode with homoerotic overtones.

The image of a descending angel recurs, this time in Kafka's hotel room in Trieste, first as a living being with white wings and violet vestments, then as a garishly painted ship's figurehead. The episode comes almost entirely verbatim from Kafka's diaries.[25] Among the visual documentation provided by Sebald is a sample of the letterhead of the Hotel Sandwirth, where Kafka stays in Venice.[26] One realizes that Kafka would have written letters on such stationery, including missives to his on-again-off-again fiancée, Felice Bauer. Sebald quotes from these as well. What is striking about both the diaries and letters, and what fascinates the painstaking observer Sebald, is how little Kafka wrote about what he saw and did in the places he visited. The Pisanello frescoes described earlier, for instance, were either ignored or made no impression on Kafka. He went to the cinema but there is no record of what he saw. Yet even when there seem to be no interconnections, Sebald finds connections. He describes a film that had been released during the month prior to Kafka's trip (on 12 August 1913, to be exact), in which something like the terrifying mirroring effect that haunts Kafka's dreams occurs. In D. Stellan Rye's *The Student of Prague,* the young Baldun, played by the famous silent film actor Paul Wegener, is seen practicing fencing in front of a large mirror (pictured in the text). Suddenly his reflection—that is to say, his doppelgänger—steps out of the frame. And a further coincidence, this one firm and definite, was that the opera *Aida* was being performed in Verona at the time Kafka was there, though we know this fact from the narrator's study of newspapers in the Municipal Library, not from Kafka himself. What we do know is that Kafka's journey continues to Desenzano, which the narrator visited in the previous chapter. One begins to wonder if Sebald is retracing Kafka's steps or the other way around, just as one wonders whether the two pictures of the assembled townspeople awaiting Kafka's arrival could possibly be authentic. Another missed connection underscores the tenuous link between image and reality, since the two photographs allegedly show a small group of Italians allegedly waiting to greet "the Deputy Secretary of the Prague Workers' Insurance Company," while he lies idly in the grass by the lake, as his actual letter tells us, "waiting for the steamer that was to take [him] to Gardone."[27]

Sebald takes pains to describe the atmosphere, so alien to the pace of modern life, of the sanatorium at Riva where Kafka spends three weeks taking various "hydropathic" treatments. What interests Sebald is Kafka's love interest in the course of his therapy. Sebald depicts what the reader realizes must be the kind of non-attached relationship Kafka would like to have with Felice. It is without commitment or any sort of exchange, whether in the form of pictures or a single written word. Both their dispositions are buoyed by their love affair that is not a love affair. Sebald describes them on boat rides together, enjoying scenery that seems to be "an album with mountains drawn on an empty page by a sensitive dilettante as a remembrance for the lady to whom the album belongs" —words taken nearly verbatim from Robert Walser's short story "Kleist in ✓ Thun."[28] But the girl must presently depart, choking back tears, and soon a pall falls over the mood of the place when an elderly bachelor commits suicide. At this point Sebald introduces another image from the story "Hunter Gracchus." For Kafka, he writes, a further darkness fell over those "beautiful and appalling" days at Riva in the ensuing three years, and by the first half of 1917, the "contours of a barque appeared out of the shadows, with masts of inconceivable height draped in dark sails."[29] During this period, the Great War is raging, of course, but the meaning of the vessel is personal, and associated with Kafka's worsening tuberculosis. In "Hunter Gracchus," which is on one level an allegory of the dying process (Kafka's tuberculosis was localized in the throat, gradually asphyxiating him), a dark, foreboding vessel—the page includes a photograph of a gloomy, blurred sailing ship—brings the dead hunter, doomed to wander the world in search of an entrance to the underworld, to dock at Riva. Sebald's text intersects and almost merges with Kafka's at this point. In Kafka's story, the mayor of Riva—by a strange coincidence, also named Salvatore—greets the living corpse after it has been brought ashore by the two men in dark tunics and silver buttons described before. Thus, the fragmentary references coalesce, and the allusion to Kafka's story comes into focus. Sebald retells the tale, from the huntsman's origins in the Black Forest ("nella selva nera") to his death and present homelessness, for which no sure reason is known. By way of interpretation, Sebald suggests the meaning of the huntsman's ceaseless journey "lies in a penitence for a longing for love," and cites another of Kafka's letters to Felice, in which, according to Sebald, he reveals that he experiences that longing only where there is "seemingly, and in the natural and lawful order of things, nothing to be enjoyed."[30] And here the narrative returns for the last time to the issue of homosexuality. In the aforementioned letter, Sebald tells us, Kafka confessed his fascination with a homely bookstore clerk.[31] Sebald's words become Kafka's as he asks Felice if she can understand his feelings on a recent evening after closing hours, when he followed a stiff, big-boned, broad-shouldered, no longer youthful man down the street. Kafka's pleasure is all the more intense because his aching desire must remain hidden from the world—men are inaccessible, women are not. As enigmatic as the story of Hunter Gracchus is, another plausible reading of the text finds in it an expression of the kind of helplessness, loneliness, and inability to connect with the living that accompanies the suppression of an unconventional sexual orientation. The hunter's final gesture in the story— the placing of his hand on Salvatore's knee—represents, in Sebald's retelling, both an unconscious expression of homoerotic longing, and a confirmation of the hunter's resignation, that is to say, his rejection of the mayor's offer of safe harbor in Riva. Kafka's story "The Hunter Gracchus" illustrates a vision of personal exile that is complete; the true identity of Gracchus, who has been dead already for hundreds of years, is not known by anyone, cannot be found by anyone, and he could not be helped by anyone, even if he were found and his identity revealed. It is no mere coincidence that the word Gracchus, which means grackle or blackbird, corresponds to the word Kafka in Czech. In the same letter quoted by Sebald there is a reference to a photograph of Felice Bauer's niece "Muzzi." In Kafka's description of the little girl's "fearful gaze" before the camera we sense a reflection of Kafka's own terrors, "terrors of love," as Sebald suggests, terrors such as no love could have ever overcome.[32] The chapter thus ends in a gesture of empathy for the tragic solitude of Dr. K.

[Sebald's] Return to W[ertach]

The fourth chapter of *Vertigo*, "Il ritorno in patria" (Return to the fatherland) is a description of the Sebaldian narrator's return to his home village in Germany during the month of November in 1987. He leaves Verona and travels to "W."— the letter is a literary convention typical of nineteenth-century European prose fiction—where he revisits the setting of his early childhood. But the effort at anonymity is merely a token gesture, given the dust jacket's explicit mention of Wertach im Allgäu as Sebald's birthplace. The mood of danger and foreboding dissipates almost immediately, although the narrator continues to note the bizarreness around him, such as the early morning assembly, seemingly out of nowhere, of a group of homeless drinkers around a case of beer in the Innsbruck train terminal. Sebald's special brand of humor is at work in this minor episode, transforming a mundane urban occurrence into a complex interplay of urgent philosophical assertions and theatrical conventions known only to the initiated. As so often happens in Sebald, a seemingly insignificant feature or object is suddenly imbued with meaning that is weighty and insistent, but inexpressible. In the case of the narrator's bus trip into the mountains around Wertach, it is the sight of a dozen hens in the middle of a wet green field. The little collection of flightless birds, having ventured so far out into the open, is somehow profoundly moving to him.

Sebald's fondness for names becomes apparent during the journey—the closer he gets to home, the more frequently he lists the proper names of the passing villages, lakes, mountains, and valleys. His descriptive powers take center stage as he recreates his walk down through the dark, spruce-lined gorge towards his village. The mood is distinctly elegiac; this part of the narrative is a paean to forgotten purity and wonder. The path Sebald takes is also the one taken by the Italian artist Tiepolo, who painted the magnificent ceiling frescoes in the prince-bishop's palace at Würzburg two hundred miles to the north. Art is never far from nature, as Sebald is reminded when he enters the chapel at Krummenbach, which he remembers from his childhood. Its paintings of the stations of the cross are far more crude than anything Tiepolo ever painted, yet they retain a certain power due to the intensity of the emotions expressed and, more specifically, the explicitness of the violence depicted. There is also, paradoxically, a perfect inner tranquility to the paintings. This portion of "Il ritorno in patria" contains another of Sebald's trademark cascades of associations, seemingly disparate yet interconnected by a sense of place or by history. Nearby is a small cemetery containing a tribute to the boy-soldiers who died in the last skirmish fought in the area, at Enge Plätt, in April 1945. The tragic futility of their resistance need not be pointed out; it is left unspoken. The memory of seeing gypsies on the way to the nearby public swimming pool calls up a description of a photo album kept by Sebald's father during the war. There is no overt recrimination for the Nazi treatment of the Roma population, only a snapshot taken by his father of a gypsy mother with her baby. In the picture she can be seen standing next to several other people behind barbed wire, and she is smiling. The caption states simply the German word for gypsies: "Zigeuner." Again, what is left unspoken—her fate at the hands of the Nazis—is more important than what is said. And Sebald reflects, since his mother always picked him up and held him whenever she passed the gypsy encampment on the way to the pool, that they, the gypsies, were both normal and alien simultaneously. But he always wondered how they managed to survive, then return, and why they chose the miserable place they did to set up camp. In *Austerlitz* a similar note is struck when the protagonist learns of a forgotten childhood book that portrays the lives of various animals across the season. His former nanny recalls his fascination with the ability of squirrels to find the nuts they buried a season ago, despite their concealment in the wintry snow of the present.

One of the lessons of "Il ritorno in patria" is, predictably, that one simply cannot go home again. It is not the same home; everything has changed. Sebald has been away, living in England, for more than twenty years. His descriptions of the way things once were find little resonance with the Wertach of 1987. Engelwirt Inn, where the weekly feature films and accompanying newsreels were shown during his childhood, still exists. But the place's significance goes beyond weekend films and occasional performances in the function room; it was at one time the residence of the Sebald family. Once inside, everything comes back to him— the decor, the books his father bought but never read, the bone china tea service in the armoire—and he reconstructs the physical surroundings of his youth as well as the cast of characters of the town.

One wouldn't expect a remote German village to provide a platform for a discussion of art, but Sebald is tracing origins in this part of *Vertigo,* and the origins of his own interest in art lie here. Besides the frescoes in the parish church, a regional artist's murals and frescoes were virtually the only art with which the narrator was familiar until the age of seven or eight. But this artist's murals (several are pictured in the text) do not delight as much as overwhelm him. In a similar fashion, the many local pathways he remembers from childhood are not comforting, but leave him dispirited, even though they remind him also of his grandfather, the kindly companion of his youth. Sebald's skepticism about the solidity of identity is repeated here in a most personal way. The remark of an old acquaintance causes the narrator to realize that his own appearance and gait resemble that of his grandfather. This is another example of the phenomenon of repetition Sebald finds irresistible. But repetition is not the focus of the story as a whole. The primary theme is loss—loss of relatives, loss of the security of childhood, loss of friends, and the loss of one's health in the course of aging.

In this, the last chapter of *Vertigo,* Sebald describes quiet village scenes, eccentric personalities, and the curiosities that intrigued him as a child. One such curiosity, pictured on two full pages, is a remarkable drawing from an old atlas. It depicts the length and shape of the world's rivers vertically, each with the river's mouth at the top, from the longest on the left to the shortest on the right. At the bottom of the page, running in the opposite direction, are the mountains of the world, with the highest on the right and the lowest on the left. This atlas was the one thing he was allowed to examine on visits with his grandfather to Mathild Ambrose, the elder of two sisters who were destined to die on the same day (*Austerlitz* contains a similar coincidence). The episode is worth examining, because the point Sebald is making is that revisiting the past can yield epiphanies, clear up misconceptions, and draw connections previously unnoticed. The narrator recalls that Mathild always forbade him to go upstairs, where her "gray *chausseur*" lives. He formed his own childish ideas of what a "gray *chausseur*" might be. When the sisters' nephew Lukas shows the narrator the attic years later—a place full of "tokens of the slow disintegration of all material forms"—

he soon comes upon a ghostly gray figure that had been concealed by a blinding shaft of light.[33] The uncanny apparition turns out to be a tailor's dummy dressed in a gray uniform—it is Mathild's gray *chausseur*. The uniform, which was that of the Austrian irregulars who fought against the French in 1800, points back to the first chapter of the book, in which Henri Beyle comes upon the battlefield at Morengo. The bones of one of Lukas's ancestors on the other side of his family would have been among those of the thousands of horses and men killed there.

Sebald makes sure the Hunter Grachus motif appears in this part of the novel as well, reflecting back on previous references and resuming a thread that unites all four chapters of the book. The strange figure of Hans Schlag presumably represents Sebald's first experience seeing a corpse, the source of the image, oft repeated in Sebald, of people laid out as if for burial. But the figure is also associated with sexual intercourse in this version of the "Hunter Grachus" story, since the narrator comes upon him and the innkeeper's daughter Romana copulating in an outbuilding. The scene resembles in many details a scene of copulation in Peter Weiss's novel *The Shadow of the Body of the Coachman,* and several German critics and scholars have suggested it is another of Sebald's "quotations" from other works, especially because the couple appears to merge into one separate indivisible entity in both renditions.[34] There is humor in the otherwise startlingly prurient incident as well; the narrator exchanges glances in the dark with Schlag's patiently waiting dog. The hunter's sordid conquest of Romana has its consequences, however—that very night Romana's father flies into a rage and destroys all the fittings and the furnishings. Within twenty-four hours Schlag is dead from a fall from a footbridge. As the physician Dr. Piazolo examines the body, his pocketwatch plays a bar of Mozart's melody to the poem "Üb' immer Treu und Redlichkeit." The words by the eighteenth-century poet Ludwig Hölty (1748–1776), though Sebald does not quote them, assume in their Sebaldian absence a dark irony in view of the way Schlag lived his life. In English the first verse reads: "Always be upright and loyal / until you are laid in your grave. / And never turn for an instant / from the path God has chosen for you."[35]

Home, this chapter seems to be insisting, may be lost, but the attempt to retrieve it is a natural human longing. Having lived in voluntary exile, one is destined to remain both a stranger and, to some degree at least, an intimate. *Vertigo* in this last chapter functions as a statement of Sebald's estrangement from his homeland. Even the physical landscape, Sebald writes, had always seemed "unbegreiflich" ("incomprehensible"; the translator uses the word "alien") for as long as he could remember, most especially because of its pervasive orderliness.[36] The country is tidied up and straightened out to the last square inch, creating an almost sinister mood of tranquilized restraint. Though he is himself

German, the narrator has been away so long that he feels himself a stranger now —an outsider looking in—and notices the things only foreigners would notice about Germany. All the detached houses, for instance, have fences and walls around them, no matter how small the property they occupy. This is just one example of the carefully delineated and maintained borders and limits everywhere. Sebald also notices the ubiquitous grayish white of the stucco covering virtually every structure, creating an oppressive sense of drab uniformity. The hurrying automobiles seem more numerous than people. Coupled with the silence of the fellow passengers in his train compartment, the subdued quality of everything in the German landscape makes Sebald wonder if mankind hadn't already "made way for another species" or if we aren't now living "in some form of imprisonment"—the translator uses the perhaps more plausible expression "under a kind of curfew."[37] The translator here also omits an authorial intervention that sets some ironic distance between the narrator and his foregoing "conjectures." But on page 288 of the German original the narrator remarks that such thoughts were not going through his mind then at all. Then, in both versions, the sentence occurs: "The expression 'the territory of southwest Germany' was repeating itself constantly in my head as I looked out the window at the passing landscape that had been so thoroughly segmented and so completely utilized."[38] In the German version Sebald is stressing once again the editorial function that adds to and revises memory. His thoughts on Germany are thus really afterthoughts he injects as he composes a description of his actual experience. The whole digression on the German mania for order has a hint of ironic resignation about it as well, as if simultaneously acknowledging that such criticisms of German orderliness have been made many times before, often by the Germans themselves, and yet nothing ever changes. A national character cannot be unlearned; meticulousness and industriousness cannot be transformed into insouciance and indolence.

As illustrated by elaborate hallucinations involving the English bride of the "Winter King" of Bohemia (Friedrich V of the Palatinate, who served briefly as king of Bohemia during the Thirty Years' War) and the Great Fire of London, history is always alive to the aesthetic consciousness. This is a theme that would later be developed explicitly in *The Rings of Saturn* as well. For that book's narrator, too, who witnesses the hundreds of white sails of the no longer extant windmills on the East Anglian coast, there is no distinction between past and present. In *Vertigo* there is no distinction between past and future either—the German version ends with the date 2013, printed below the last line, thereby casting the time of its composition into a fictional future. It also reminds the reader of the book's chronology, beginning with the period thirteen years before Napoleon's defeat in 1813, and leaping ahead to Kafka's visit to Italy in 1913, then ending in the year "13" a century after that, in the new millennium. Sebald suggests numerous implications with such references. As we have noted, 1913 is for Sebald clearly *the* watershed year in modern European history. The nationalism that emerged during the Age of Napoleon reached its irrational extreme with the outbreak of the Great War in the summer of 1914. The Second World War, which looms mostly in the background of "Il ritorno in patria," is simply the most recent in that series of calamities we call history. Like the Great Fire of London, such calamities are often followed by "a silent rain of ash"—in this case, as Sebald tells us, paraphrasing Pepys, "westward, to Windsor Park and beyond."[39]

Reception

This novel, which launched Sebald's literary career in Germany as a writer of fiction, did not appear in English translation until 1999, almost a decade after its publication in Germany in 1990. As Anthony Lane has suggested, nothing more than the strategies of publishers were at work—the marketplace was deemed more hospitable for Sebald's English-language premier with the second novel, *The Emigrants*. *The Emigrants* was a book with "graver concerns" in some respects than *Vertigo*.[40] Its relation to the Holocaust, for the most part implicit, was nonetheless enough to earn it the label of Holocaust literature. Whatever the reason, or combination of reasons, there was a long delay in publishing *Vertigo*, a work that contains all the hallmarks of Sebald's recursive, allusive style, interweaving seemingly unrelated literary, personal, and historical strands. As with *The Rings of Saturn*, its subject matter is, to a large extent, literature and literary figures. And as with all Sebald's books, the past sometimes seems to blend with the present, just as the text sometimes merges with other literary texts. In any case, the dilatory progress of *Vertigo* on the way to publication in English was, as one critic put it, "gratifyingly true to the world of Sebald, where nothing can be trusted to cleave to its proper place."[41]

German reviewers on the whole followed the lead of Hans Magnus Enzensberger, whose reputation as a poet and novelist in his own right lent credence to his celebration of Sebald as a major new talent. But it was acknowledged that Sebald stood quite apart from the mainstream literary scene, "splendidly having nothing to do with our German present," as the critic Andreas Isenschmied put it in the *Die Zeit* (21 September 1990). He calls Sebald's suggestive "network of images" both "enticing and puzzling," yet admits the style often "smacks of art-for-art's-sake." Still, the total effect is captivating. Other German commentators— Jörg Drews, Martin Meyer, and Franz Loquai, for example—were equally taken in by Sebald's fully formed literary voice, which seemed to come from another place and time.[42] The slyly playful, enigmatic side of the book—its teetering on the border between ingenious deception and laconic description—is a "swindle" these critics recognize and welcome. A few, like the Austrian poet Antonio Fian, saw in Sebald a purveyor of secondary literature disguised as fiction—its appeal among the critics being based in snobbery and elitism.[43] The pleasure in reading Sebald, according to Fian, is merely the pleasure of recognizing the explicit and veiled literary references and congratulating oneself for having done so. Sebald elicits this complaint—that he is a "critic's writer"—from a small but vocal minority.

One of the earliest reviews of the English-language version was Anita Brookner's "Pursued Across Europe by Ghost's of Unease," which appeared late in 1999 in *The Spectator*. In this review she calls Sebald's narrative journey a "descent into unverifiability, presented within a framework that implies a rigid purpose," and suggests that this uncertainty, inherent in even our most vivid memories and impressions, "is responsible for the strange admixture of biography and autobiography with which Sebald's name will always be associated."[44] Brookner is not the first to highlight the unease that seems to be increased rather than dissipated by illustrations. Yet her verdict is nothing if not positive—she considers reading Sebald a genuinely novel, unique, affecting experience. For the English-language audience as a whole, however, Susan Sontag's review is perhaps the most influential, given her stature as a writer and cultural critic. Unlike Joyce Hackett (also a novelist and critic), Sontag expresses no reservations that the two previously released novels are stronger, more successful works. She insists, rather, that *Vertigo* must be taken on its own terms as a book whose subject is, more than the others, "the narrator's own afflicted consciousness."[45] Sontag notes that the elevated diction and elegiac tone in much of Sebald's work is alien to modern prose, especially in the case of postwar German literature, with its mindfulness of "how congenial the grandiosity of past art and literature, particularly that of German romanticism, proved to the work of totalitarian myth-making."[46] To elegize the German past, as Sebald does his childhood in "Il ritorno in patria," and to speak in the cultivated idiom of bygone days, perhaps one must do so from a permanent domicile abroad. Sontag is also aware of the voices that can be heard in Sebald's work. There is the whimsy of Jean Paul, the intimacy of Robert Walser, the philosophical-linguistic skepticism of Hugo von Hofmannsthal in "The Letter of Lord Chandos," and the jaded sophistication of Franz Grillparzer's travel diaries. To be sure, travel provides the narrative with a steady engine of advancement, as it does in all Sebald's novels. The narrator:

> . . . travels about, registering evidence of the mortality of nature, recoiling from the ravages of modernity, musing over the secrets of obscure lives.

On some mission of investigation, triggered by a memory or news from a world irretrievably lost, he remembers, evokes, hallucinates, grieves.[47]

Despite the destructive processes that Sebald sees at work, inescapably, everywhere, his oeuvre is predicated on the power of remembering. It celebrates—and here Sontag quotes a line from *The Rings of Saturn*—"the mysterious survival of the written word."[48]

Joyce Hackett's review appeared in the summer 2000 issue of the *Boston Review,* and was also laudatory. She emphasizes the "multiple images of failed escape" in *Vertigo,* as most concisely and at the same time suggestively represented by the figure of "The Hunter Gracchus." She also notes, as does Sontag, Sebald's use of silence, the unsaid, in his prose: "His is a language of silence, in which meaning surfaces in the negative space between juxtapositions, repetitions, variations, and ruptures."[49] She rightly connects this recognition of the "message" of silence with Wittgenstein's admonition, at the end of the *Tractatus,* to remain silent about that which one cannot speak. The idea is not attributable to Wittgenstein alone, however—Heidegger's literary criticism also contains references to the meaning of the unsaid in poetry. Hackett sees in *Vertigo* a four-part musical structure like that of *The Emigrants,* but considers Sebald's first book in the end "more abstruse and less tight."[50]

The summer of 2000 also saw a lengthy, positive review of *Vertigo* by Tim Parks in *The New York Review of Books.* Parks emphasizes the strong element of comedy in Sebald's strategies of narrative destabilization—the concrete becomes elusive, and "the narrative momentum is dispersed in a delta as impenetrable as it is fertile."[51] Parks also recognizes the essential—and mystery-laden—role of coincidence and repetition in Sebald's narrative technique. Another long review in another major periodical was written by the critic Pico Iyer and appeared in the October issue of *Harper's Magazine.* It too is an admiring essay, remarking that, "even in translation, [Sebald's prose] rises to a pitch of antique sonorousness, even majesty, that makes almost everything else we read seem small and charges the most unremarkable of scenes with the imminence of something larger."[52] The question is, what *is* the something larger? For, as Iyer also maintains, Sebald does not spare us the emptiness at the bottom of all intensity, the ineluctable dwindling of all things into nothingness, the merciless destructiveness of storms, fires, and wars. "It may be customary to talk of a fashioner of exquisite prose as 'writing like an angel,'" Iyer observes, "but in the case of Sebald—doing nothing to make us feel at home, seated alone on a bench at twilight, presenting his back to us—it might be truer to say that he writes like a ghost."[53]

CHAPTER 5

Austerlitz

The Mechanisms of Erasure and the Struggle to Recall

The novel *Austerlitz,* first published in Germany in early 2001, is Sebald's profoundest and most comprehensive treatment of the relationship of identity and exile. It is a meandering exploration of one man's consciousness and its mechanisms for coping with loss—loss of family, loss of a past, and, finally, loss of one's most intimate and defining possession: one's native language. In the course of the novel, Sebald reveals that the eponymous protagonist of the novel was raised in Wales under the name of Dafydd Elias. In late adolescence Elias learns that he was actually born not in Britain but in what was then Czechoslovakia, the son of parents he hardly remembers at all. The narrative of his early childhood is the product of a kind of historical archeology, and evolves as the protagonist's researches deepen his knowledge of what was taken from him: namely, his first four and a half years of childhood in Prague. The results of his reconstruction of the past, an effort begun late in his life, are revealed in lengthy conversations carried on during chance encounters with the nameless narrator of the book. The boy, whose original name was Jacques Austerlitz, was evacuated to England —sent on his way by his Jewish mother who could not leave—and was put in a foster family once he arrived in Britain. He was one of scores of chaperoned passengers in an organized *Kindertransport* that left Czechoslovakia just before the beginning of the Second World War. This rescue action undoubtedly spared his life, but it also closed the door on his past, and exiled him permanently from his homeland and family.

The narrative in *Austerlitz* is a complicated interplay of authorial narration and the protagonist's own narration of his quest to find out who he really is, a quest that itself represents an interplay—an interplay of archival research, interviews, and apparent coincidences. And there are the numerous analytical digressions for which Sebald is known, mostly on Austerlitz's field of interest, which is architectural history. The narrator first encounters Austerlitz by coincidence in the late 1960s during travels in Belgium. Their initial conversations are concerned not with personal matters but with a common interest in history and architecture. Only much later, after a decades-long hiatus, does the narrator begin to learn the details of Austerlitz's life. This time the narrator encounters his erstwhile interlocutor in London rather than Belgium, and Austerlitz begins to tell a story which unfolds as an unrestrained retracing of origins and identity.

In this book Sebald explores the power of erasure, focusing on the example of one man's extinguished memory of childhood. But he is also concerned with a broader subject. There are certain forces, Sebald constantly reminds us, that are bent on neutralizing all historical consciousness; they are continually wiping the slate clean, as if the experience of living—of having lived—means nothing. Sebald refers not just to the effects of the passing of time, or the physical forces that eventually bury all civilizations, but to a blind force at work in contemporary culture. It erases all evidence regardless of its historical significance, its moral content, or the absence of either. Contemporary Europe, as the site of collaborative atrocities throughout the twentieth century, provides countless examples of this antihistorical force at work smothering the truth about the past. In the final pages of *Austerlitz,* a man called Henri Lemoine, an old acquaintance of the protagonist, makes the observation that modern life seems increasingly bent on putting an end to everything that has a vital connection with the past. His remarks are part of a scathing critique of the enormous, hideous, and dysfunctional Bibliothéque Nationale, a building that seems to be, in almost every imaginable way, the opposite of what a library should be. But the monstrous legacy of France's "pharaoh-like" former president (François Mitterrand) has an even darker side, if one applies Sebald's investigative methods. It so happens that the desolate property on which the library stands was once the site of an important link in the great chain of meticulously organized efforts by the Nazis to persecute and destroy the Jews of Europe. A huge warehouse once stood there, in which all possessions taken from the Jews of Paris—from furniture to silverware to clothing to works of art—were stored, sorted, itemized by category, rated by quality and condition, carefully packed in boxes, and finally dispersed to Germany, where they remain, conveniently unaccounted for, to this day. The stocks and bonds, not to mention the real estate, Lemoine adds, are to this day still in the hands of the city of Paris and the nation of France. Thus, the great statesman's "monument to himself" is sullied at its very foundation, just as French history during wartime is more accurately characterized not by *résistance* but by collaboration with the Nazis—Sebald touches on several examples, such as the French police raid in July of 1942, in which over three thousand Parisian Jews, the last to be interned, were captured and taken away.

Reconstructing history with its startling realities and painful repercussions—as well as its benign attachments and emotions—constitutes in *Austerlitz,* as it does in the other novels, the raison d'être of Sebald's fiction. He combats the erasure of history on the collective level as well as the individual, for example, in the denial of the Holocaust, or in the suppression of the effects of bombarding Germany's cities, or in the refusal to acknowledge the brutality of Belgian colonialism. In the individual experience of Jacques Austerlitz, however, we find what is perhaps the most insidious, if oblique, infliction of harm achieved by the actions of the Nazis. The case of Austerlitz is the case of a larceny; but what the Nazis take from him is not his life or property but his essential personhood, and though this crime is merely the indirect result of the organized persecution of the Jews, it is nonetheless real and devastating. One wonders how many other *Kindertransport* biographies resemble that of Austerlitz, who experienced in the intervening months and years a near totality of erasure. Astonishingly, this erasure was self-imposed, carried out by his own psychological mechanisms of repression. Sebald conveys the mental anguish suffered by Austerlitz in his own words, applying Thomas Bernhard's technique of simply allowing the protagonist to speak openly and at his own pace. What he recounts is a reconstructive odyssey in search of himself.

The Return to Belgium

In *The Rings of Saturn* the setting for part of the action—if one can speak of "action" in Sebald's highly contemplative fiction—was Belgium, and the novel *Austerlitz* also partly takes place in several of the country's cities and towns. In *The Rings of Saturn* Belgium was presented in a thoroughly unflattering light, as a country whose surfeit of hideous monuments, lunatics, and humpbacks was proof of its imperialist crimes in Africa. Sebald's fictional narrator in *Austerlitz* is a student at a university in England when he first meets Austerlitz on a visit to Belgium. The book announces its temporal and spatial setting at the outset, as do all Sebald's tales; but unlike the others, it does not place the narrator in a specific month and year but in a space of years—the second half of the 1960s. And as is customary in Sebald's prose, certainty is almost immediately undermined, in spite of the preciseness of the author's language. Thus the introductory lines are inconclusive—"In the second half of the 1960s, I traveled repeatedly from England to Belgium, partly for study purposes, partly for other reasons never entirely clear to me"—and they also echo the evasive conciseness of von Rezzori, whose *Memoirs of an Anti-Semite* includes a chapter that begins with the words "In 1957, for reasons and under circumstances I won't go into now."[1] In *Austerlitz,* the narrator has no real idea why he traveled so often to Belgium or what might have drawn him there, but the attraction is evidently shared by the title character for similarly uncertain reasons. The source of the Sebald-like narrator's compulsion to return to Belgium is and will remain a mystery, though the mystery of the lure of Belgium for the character Austerlitz will gradually be revealed. It is in any case the mood of mystery that dominates the foreground almost immediately as the book begins—the narrator is overtaken by a sense of unease on his approach by train to the city of Antwerp, a destination about which he knows nothing at all but the name. It is a radiantly beautiful summer day, but the strange appearance of the pointed turrets along both sides of the tracks combines with the enveloping darkness, as the train moves downward into the terminal, to heighten the narrator's dread and distress. Though he doesn't make the explicit connection, it is clear that his descent into darkness represents a descent into an unknown world, with the obvious parallel of a mythological descent into the underworld. Such descents, with their accompanying sense of foreboding, recur several times in *Austerlitz:* in the Liverpool Street Station in London, on an approach to Prague from Terezin, on arriving by motorcade in Marienbad, and in the labyrinthine stairways and underpasses of the Gare d'Austerlitz in Paris.

A dominant metaphor for the book is provided by the newly-built Nocturama, not far from the railroad terminal. This special section of the Antwerp Zoo contains a replica of jungle terrain darkened so as to encourage activity that normally occurs at night. The nocturnal animals inside become gradually visible as one's eyes adjust to the artificial darkness. Here Sebald produces excerpts from photographs of eyes—an owl's and a monkey's, one above the other, and beneath them two sets of human eyes staring ahead at—or beyond—the reader. These pictures are ostensibly provided to illustrate the narrator's assertion that the fixed, searching gaze of the nocturnal animals resembles the look on the faces of certain artists and philosophers. This odd comparison juxtaposes two vastly different kinds of intelligence, yet a startling commonality is apparent in the pictures, as both sets of pairs of eyes seem to be trying, "by means of unsparingly honest observation and pure thought, to penetrate the darkness surrounding us all."[2] The memories of this "false world" the narrator encounters in Antwerp merge and combine with scenes from the waiting room of the train terminal, to which he returns that same day. He relates how—again, as if foreordained—his entry into the station the second time, from the street this time, coincides with the sudden fall of darkness. As he enters from the street, the sun is simultaneously sinking below the skyline, so that as he walks into the *salle des pas perdus* the shadows swallow the few waiting passengers in a gloom that the narrator now expressly compares to that of the underworld.[3] In his memory the Nocturama is alternately superimposed on the dark interior of the train station and vice versa, but in the end the image that dominates his memory is that of the silent, motionless travelers seated in the cavernous hall like the last remaining members of a race that has been overrun and dispersed, or whose culture has collapsed of its own accord. The same sorrowful expressions that one perceives on the confined nocturnal animals are seen on their faces.

By now it is clear that Sebald's fourth novel is yet another travelogue, dominated, like *Vertigo* and *The Rings of Saturn,* by feelings of uprootedness and unease, and filled with vague foreboding. A perfectly pedestrian and mundane experience in a European train station becomes the catalyst for a mood that is nothing less than gothic, with the paradoxical difference that no really gothic outcome seems to be forthcoming. In fact, Sebald turns the reader's gaze suddenly and completely away from the gothic twilight, focusing on one of the travelers in the hall, who seems to appear out of nowhere. It is the title character of the book, Austerlitz, a youthful older man drawing sketches of the surrounding architecture. He is the only traveler engaged in an activity of any kind. The others merely stare ahead and sit motionless under the regal ceiling of King Leopold's capacious terminal. Austerlitz's clothes are outmoded and somewhat frayed, but his appearance is dominated not by his sartorial shabbiness but by a shock of wavy blond hair such as the narrator remembers seeing only once before, in Fritz Lang's 1924 silent film *Die Nibelungen,* in which a similar coiffure is sported by the actor who plays the hero of the medieval German epic. Though the allusion is for most readers a relatively obscure one, the irony of a solitary eccentric resembling the hero Siegfried will be lost on few. His rucksack contains an old camera he occasionally uses to photograph the building's details, though the ambient light is clearly insufficient. It is the same camera he will be using when they meet again in 1996, when their conversation finally turns to Austerlitz's life history. In the meantime they will encounter each other, ostensibly by coincidence, again and again in their respective travels, discussing matters of architecture and history, but sharing nothing of their personal lives.

Photography occupies a central position in the protagonist's life—he is a collector of pictures of doors, gates, domes, and windows—as well as in the appearance of the book's characteristically Sebaldian text, which is accompanied by numerous photographic illustrations. The dust jacket itself showcases a photograph—the title picture of the young boy in a white satin cavalier's costume. The image constitutes the actual beginning of the book, just as a picture of the tree in the cemetery constitutes the beginning of the text of *The Emigrants.* The photograph of the boy is thus itself an integral part of the narrative, posing its own question: Is the child in the picture Austerlitz as a child, and if so, under what conditions was the photograph made? Of equal importance is photography's function as a reproductive and aesthetic process; it is essential to understanding Sebald's means of telling the tale of the protagonist's strange and tormented life. A central metaphor for one of the mechanisms of memory, and in turn for Sebald's technique of unveiling his story of Austerlitz, is provided by the moment when Dafydd Elias witnesses, in the photographic laboratory at boarding school, images taking shape on a developing print. He is fascinated as he watches the black and grey "shadows of reality, arising . . . out of nothingness, as memories do that come in the middle of the night, the kind that darken again quickly if you try to possess them, like a print left too long in the developing fluid."[4] Such is the impression left by Sebald's descriptive technique, as well; the author creates the illusion that he permits the shapes and shades of episode after episode to emerge into view—he reveals and relates, but appears not to fabulate.

A Boyhood in Wales

Sebald uses the conceit of the "false world" from the beginning of *Austerlitz,* but it is only in retrospect that the reader realizes to what extent Austerlitz's description of his childhood is a description of a world that was also false. It was a counterfeit childhood, an experience that had not been meant to be. The Nocturama in Antwerp sets the tone for this and subsequent examples of deceptive realities. They exist both in benign forms—the world of the theater, for instance—as well as in the form of grotesque distortions of reality, such as the use to which the Nazis put the fortress at Breendonk. Moreover, the deformed, false universe of the Holocaust is the cause of Austerlitz's removal to an unforeseen world where he does not really belong. Only in childhood's fleeting moments of half-sleep does he catch an occasional glimpse of the figure that must be his mother, or a smiling father putting on his hat. But Austerlitz cannot hold the moment, and he concludes, as children often do, that he himself is responsible for the ill that has befallen him, and that his present exile is his own fault. He himself is the unwitting cause of his exile to another, alien universe. Austerlitz's childhood is not mentioned, however, until the forty-fourth page of the novel. The first encounters between Austerlitz and the narrator, which take place in several different Belgian cities, are concerned with other topics. They are opportunities for the author to introduce several themes that will become increasingly important in the course of the novel, such as the futility of fortified cities, particularly those of the late seventeenth century, the walls of which form the shape of eight-pointed and twelve-pointed stars. These follies continued to be built and expanded long after they had been proven obsolete. In a logic that contradicted actual experience, the twelve-pointed star was considered perfect for its intended function of defense against siege. Domes, particularly the domes of railroad terminals, also hold a fascination for Sebald. The dome is a shape for which mankind seems to have a universal proclivity. Another architectural theme in *Austerlitz* is the reutilization of structures, especially outmoded structures. The Nazis used the obsolete forts at Breendonk in Belgium, Terezin in Czechoslovakia, and Kaunas in Lithuania for their vilest purposes. This reuse always stands in stark contrast to the current condition of the buildings, which appear far less formidable than one would expect given their histories as Nazi torture chambers. Today, except for their function as museums, they appear merely as grim abandoned relics. Yet another theme that recurs in *Austerlitz* is the similarity of places of punishment and places of healing. Finally, Sebald, through the voice of the protagonist, points to the barely concealed traces of pain left in abandoned sites of torment: the concentration camps, the mental hospitals, the train stations where the Jews began their final journey. There is a human cost to every building; in the Antwerp train station Austerlitz remarks in French that the tall mirrors that line the hall were manufactured by men working in toxic fumes, inhaling mercury and cyanide vapors.

The French language has an important role in the novel. The common language of the encounters between Austerlitz and the narrator is French to begin with. The narrator is impressed with the clarity and precision of his use of the language, but notices, when the two take a ferry to England together, an odd discomfort that Austerlitz seems to feel when he switches to English. This is the first hint that Austerlitz is not altogether at one with himself. This shy academic, who has devoted himself for years to a massive, unachievable book project, has the same "look of horror" on his face, the narrator tells us, that one sees in some photographs of the philosopher Ludwig Wittgenstein, who also traveled with his few possessions in a rucksack.[5] Some of the keys to Austerlitz's personality are to be found in the narrator's comparison with Wittgenstein, who was also "disconsolate, . . . imprisoned in both the clarity of his logical thinking as well as the confusion of his emotions."[6] A more concise description of Austerlitz's person is not forthcoming from Sebald, however—the features of his character are meant to come together for the reader as a result of Austerlitz's own telling of his story. The central problem, which some critics have failed to realize, is that his personality defies description—Austerlitz's self cannot, by its very nature, be pinned down. His emotional life has been deformed and damaged by his experience. At the core of the main character's identity is thus an emptiness that resists filling, despite his quietly heroic attempt to find his mother, his father, and to recall his earliest memories.

Roughly thirty years since their first meeting, after an unintentional estrangement that began in 1975, the two main characters—Austerlitz and the narrator— meet again. This meeting represents a turning point in the book. Austerlitz, whose monologic initiatives always began formerly in medias res, picking up where he last left off, declares himself now ready to tell a listener his own personal story. Presumably something has happened in his life to bring about this turn to intimacy and revelation. And by now it is also abundantly clear that both men are kindred spirits. Each is a man without a country. Austerlitz is a man in search of the facts of his own exile, while the narrator is a German living in England. Over the years of their acquaintance, the narrator has also shown a certain loyalty, sent him letters periodically, and endured long periods in which he received no response. In addition, their chance meeting in the Great Eastern Hotel in London has a certain internal logic, according to Austerlitz. He does not elaborate, but nothing is accidental in Sebald, an author who constantly provides hints and clues as he tells what is in large measure a detective story—a story about a vague, forgotten crime hidden by the pall of intervening years. It is no accident, for instance, that the ophthalmologist whom the narrator consults during his visit to London is a Czech, and that the encounter with Austerlitz takes place in a hotel in Liverpool Street. The nearby railroad terminal plays a major role later in the story, as does the Czech city of Prague. But for the time being the narrative turns exclusively to Dafydd Elias's boyhood in Bala, a small rural township in Wales.

The novel attempts to answer the question of what happened to Austerlitz in the years before he became Dafydd Elias of Bala, Wales. What happened in the years that were erased? It is significant that one of the boy's strongest recollections of his boyhood home in Wales is of shut doors. Several of the upstairs rooms in the big, isolated house were locked and their doors never opened. Shuttered or closed windows and doors are potent symbols throughout the novel, always suggesting barred passage, concealment, or inaccessibility rather than the possibility of progress. Conversely, seeing a house in which all the windows are wide open evokes in Austerlitz an overwhelming sense of liberation. The childhood home Austerlitz remembers was his foster home, the residence of a Calvinist clergyman, Emyr Elias, and his wife Gwendolyn. The house was a place of virtually total silence and complete orderliness, in which the dour couple lived behind closed windows, closed curtains, amidst only the sparest furniture. Sunday sermons were fiery, threatening orations on sin and the inevitability of punishment, after which, ironically, Elias's mood would invariably lighten and his spirits lift for a few hours. Gwendolyn was cold and distant, occupied with household chores and checking to see that things were in their proper places. She also has a compulsion to powder herself with talcum, which she does so frequently that her dressing table, bedroom, and most of the top floor frequently become covered in a fine layer of white. Austerlitz relates how the memory of this ubiquitous white dust recently came to him upon reading "a Russian writer's memoir" (actually Nabokov's *Speak, Memory*) in which the author's grandmother, who also powders herself inordinately, sleeps with the window open and awakes one morning to find herself and her room covered in snow. But memory is not consistent or logical—Nabokov's grandmother resembles Gwendolyn in nothing but the obsession with talcum. Lying on a sofa eating candies, she represents rather the insouciant, self-indulgent opposite of the Welsh preacher's stern wife. Sadly, Dafydd Elias glimpses Gwendolyn's emotional side only once, in a brief accidental encounter. She has been crying, but why? The young Dafydd doesn't ask and his foster mother doesn't tell.

In the course of the narration of his early years it becomes clear that the boy's young mind copes with his strange everyday reality by both repressing the past and actively searching for the meaning of events he knew had to be concealed just beneath the surface of things. He is certain there is more, somewhere, somehow. The possibility of dual or multiple realities is a theme that is more pronounced in *Austerlitz* than in any of Sebald's other books, and the life of the title character expresses this theme virtually from the beginning. Though he possesses only the most meager shreds of memory from his earlier childhood elsewhere, he both accepts unquestioningly his situation and knows for certain that he is living in an alien house with strange people; he also knows that he is being called by a name that is not his own. Later in the novel, when the facts are finally made known, it will be clear just how completely different the personalities of the players on this strange Welsh stage were from his true parents. But there is for him yet another reality, one that occupies the boy's imagination and seems to exist side by side with the everyday world. One day the clergyman Elias tells him that beneath the manmade lake at Vyrnwy, the village where he himself grew up —Llandwddyn—lies buried. When the boy sees the family album with photographs of Elias, his village, and various members of his family, he imagines that Elias has left them behind, the sole survivor of the flood, and that the others are still below, going about their subaquatic lives. The only difference is that this is a silent world, and the inhabitants are unable to speak. This is a lost world much like the lost world—subconscious rather than subaquatic—of Austerlitz's earliest years in his true homeland.

Another kind of world parallels and even intersects with the everyday world in the boy's early years: the world of the dead, as described by Evan the cobbler. He describes, in Gaelic, how the dead, who are somewhat diminished in size from their lifetime dimensions, lead a mostly solitary existence, but sometimes travel in small single-file processions. The boy senses the nearby presence of this hidden world—concealed, yet proximate, like the repressed memories of his own origins. Later in the novel the adult Jacques expresses the conviction that this sensation has become more rather than less intense, that "the border between the living and the dead is more permeable than we think."[7] Such processions of the dead are also thematically related to Sebald's fascination with the image of the desert caravan. For Sebald, the caravan is emblematic of the human predicament—the living are always on the move, always trudging toward some vaguely conceived destination, but just as in the story told in the film about Kaspar Hauser, related in *The Emigrants,* they do not know if they will reach it or what will happen when they do. All they know is that the "real" story will begin there. Such uncertainty is of course completely alien to the moralistic spirit of the Elias household, in which all the answers are known and no one trudges anywhere, except perhaps to the next village. The biblical literature to which the boy is exposed at home provides the first of several images in *Austerlitz* of exiles on the move; the first is that of the children of Israel wandering in the wasteland of the Sinai. The story of these exiles exerts a strong appeal for the lonely boy for reasons we are left to deduce. The Promised Land toward which they are trudging is a formulation of his unexpressed desire to be in another, more welcoming world. An engraving that shows Moses's encampment in the mountains is provided in the text, covering two full pages (56–57), and one can almost make out the anachronistic train tracks the boy believes he sees in the right bottom corner. The camp itself is a model of orderliness and self-sufficiency, seeming to demonstrate that one can, if one prepares and plans ahead, make the best of things even in an outcast state. One can pitch one's tent and make a home despite one's homelessness. But the illustration also has unmistakable associations with a more recent kind of camp, and this similarity is strengthened by the presence in the picture of high fences, a rising plume of smoke, and rows of identical temporary dwellings. The depiction of the camp is clearly meant to illustrate order, hope, and strength of purpose, but for the contemporary beholder it possesses an uncanny similarity to the concentration camps of the Holocaust—it resembles an idealized mountaintop Auschwitz.

The boy's childhood can best be described as static. Even the war seems to have no real relevance among the isolation of the small Welsh town and its people. Things change only when, at the age of twelve, Dafydd Elias is sent to boarding school in the autumn of 1946. Not unlike Max Ferber's experience in an English school in *The Emigrants,* the atmosphere at Stower Grange borders on the carnivalistic, with the most powerful and the most clever boys in charge, making a mockery of the faculty's claim to authority. What the weaker boys regard as a prison, however, is for Dafydd Elias a place of emancipation. There he is freed from the dreariness of Bala. In fact, the Bala of his younger days is no more. On his return trips during the holidays he finds Gwendolyn increasingly incapacitated by depression and physical decline. It is as if she and her husband are the unwitting victims of some degenerative process against which even their austere and uncompromising faith has no power, and with her death begins the sequel to her tragedy, the grieving minister's descent into madness. His commitment to an asylum in 1949 is the occasion for the startling and befuddling revelation that, although the boy will receive a stipend for study at a university, he must take his qualifying examinations under a name he has never been called— Jacques Austerlitz. He is not, after all, Dafydd Elias. His foster parents, as Mr. Penrith-Smith calls Emyr and Gwendolyn Elias, had intended to explain his origins to him and possibly to adopt him before his departure from secondary school. Thus the "false reality" of his childhood is formally confirmed.

A New Name

Jacques was a name known to Dafydd from a familiar French children's song, but the surname Austerlitz was one he had never heard.[8] That very year, however, the curriculum in history required discussion of the Napoleonic Wars, and Austerlitz soon learns in detail about the battle that bears his name. The true rarity of the surname Austerlitz becomes clear to him only much later, when, as an adult, he searches telephone books for another person or persons with the same name. By odd coincidence he hears on the radio a description of the life of the dancer Fred Astaire, whose surname was actually Austerlitz before he took a stage name. Still later, a neighbor informs Austerlitz that his surname appears in the diaries of Kafka. But at the time he was told his real name, Austerlitz knew not even these things, and felt all the more isolated and alone. Help in this difficult period comes in the form of two waxing friendships, one with the brilliant history teacher André Hilary, in whom Austerlitz confides, the other with the schoolmate Gerald Fitzpatrick, whom the older and stronger Austerlitz takes under his wing. He is rewarded with invitations to join Gerald and his family at their country house near Barmouth at the mouth of the Mawddach River. The Andromeda Lodge is set on a hillside overlooking the valley and the distant seacoast, and the grounds are the home of a multitude of exotic plants and white tropical birds. These cockatoos awaken in Austerlitz a sense of relatedness to the animal world—yet another favorite theme in Sebald. Here at the Fitzpatrick home, Austerlitz learns that even moths and butterflies have conscious lives, even fears and joys. What Sebald suggests with such passages is simultaneously the need for our empathy with all beings as well as the interrelated oneness of nature. These holiday visits at Andromeda Lodge are among the happiest, most idyllic in Austerlitz's life. It seems to be a place outside of time. The house is full of books and collections of various kinds. The only dark side to this "timeless" existence in his memory is the figure of Uncle Evelyn, who is plagued by a disease known in Germany as Bechterev's disease (ankylosing spondylitis), in which the spine becomes increasingly rigid. In his unfurnished chamber, the parsimonious and prematurely old man shuffles about constantly in a vain attempt to slow the progress of the disease. He is a figure very much like some of the sick shut-ins described by Bernhard in his novel *Gargoyles*. The sick and dying, Austerlitz remarks later, stand outside of time, just as the dead do; time is nothing but an invention of the mind. The question of the nature of time is a central concern for both narrators, Austerlitz and Sebald, in the course of the book. One of their conversations on the subject takes place at the Royal Observatory in Greenwich. Time does not flow, Austerlitz insists, but exists as a kind of eternal present, with all past and future moments existing side by side. Sebald returns to this idea later, but at the end of the visit to Greenwich he also calls such sweeping speculation into question with sly humor, by making a point of noting the time (3:30 in the afternoon) when they left the observatory. A nearby country house called Iver Grove provides the setting for a further digression on the topic of places seemingly frozen in time—not only does the old mansion represent a bygone day, but a billiard room sealed off in 1951 by a false wall seems like an emblem of immobilized time. The room implicitly recalls the locked rooms of Austerlitz's childhood. Explicitly, it is connected to the owner's unhappy childhood experience of being sent away to a boarding school—the man explains how, when he inherited the house and reopened the room in 1957, it evoked in him such anger that, before he realized what he was doing, he found himself out in the courtyard firing his rifle at the clock tower's face. In typical Sebaldian fashion, such incidents are related without explanation, but clearly the new owner of Iver Grove wanted to destroy time. His boarding school years were years stolen from him. Significantly, the dubious nature of the conventional conceptualization of time as linear and forward-moving is introduced early in the book, the reader will recall, when the narrator and Austerlitz observe the huge clock in the entrance hall to the Antwerp station. Its movements have an unsettling power of negation:

> During the pauses in our conversation we both noticed what an endless length of time went by before another minute had passed, and how alarming seemed the movement of that hand, which resembled an executioner's sword, even though we were expecting it every time it jerked forward, slicing off the next one-sixtieth of an hour from the future and coming to a halt with such a menacing quiver that one's heart almost stopped.[9]

Whether one prefers the more poetic "sword of justice" for *Richtschwert* or the more literal "executioner's sword," the passage retains a sinister power. This seminal sentence, surging forward on a tide of precisely described emotion and physical detail, culminates in a typically Sebaldian note of hyperbole. As one critic has written, "This arch-Sebaldian description, detailed and precise, resonant and ominous, announces themes that run through everything he writes: transience, neglect, decay, menace."[10] In the final analysis, it masterfully illustrates Sebald's point: there is something perversely violative about measuring time as a progression, as a process in which the meaning of the present is constantly being lost to oblivion.

The experience at Iver Grove reminds Austerlitz of his frequent feelings of being "cut off" (*abgetrennt*) or completely isolated—as well as the sensation that there is no ground beneath one's feet. It is presumably the date 1957 that reinvokes Austerlitz's memories of Andromeda Lodge; for Sebald—true to form —resists a conventional, logical transition. Associations, not considerations of structure, move the story forward. In 1957 Austerlitz went to the house near Barmouth for the last time, to attend the funeral of Gerald's great uncle Evelyn and his uncle Alphonso, who died, by an improbable coincidence, within twenty-four hours of one another. Here further associations begin to flow into one another: a recently viewed watercolor by Turner resembles the scene of the funeral but is in fact a picture of a scene at Lake Geneva titled *Funeral at Lausanne*. Turner himself had been in Wales, Sebald reveals, at the mouth of the Mawddach on a journey in 1798, when he was the same age as Austerlitz was at the time of the elder Fitzpatrick's funeral. The connections do not end there, however. A further association is formed by Austerlitz's and Gerald's visit to Lake Geneva—a favored setting in Sebald's books—in 1966. The friendship with Gerald is the closest Austerlitz ever comes to an intimate relationship with another male, that is, until he gets to know the narrator. But Gerald is not just a secondary character; rather he is an alter ego of sorts, a person at ease with himself and capable of enjoying the world around him with an immediacy that is denied Austerlitz. He becomes a pilot and an astronomer. His death, foreshadowed in the pages devoted to Andromeda Lodge, will prompt a decline in Austerlitz's mental condition, an experience of grief—though Austerlitz does not acknowledge it as such—that drags him to the depths of depression. The expanding network of associations reaches fruition in an exquisite image that is itself a metaphor for the impressionism of Sebald's associative technique. Austerlitz remembers afternoons playing badminton with Gerald's mother, Adela, in the empty ballroom at Andromeda Lodge:

> We watched, until they disappeared, the images cast on the opposite wall by the beams of light entering almost horizontally through the branches of the hawthorn tree just outside the high arched window. The pale patterns appearing in steady succession on the illuminated surface were mute and

scattered, and hardly lasted longer than the moment of their inception. Yet there existed here, captured in these incessantly merging and re-emerging webs of shadow and sunlight, images of mountain landscapes with glaciers, high plateaus, deserts, islands in the ocean, fields of flowers, undulating grain fields, archipelagoes, coral reefs, atolls, whole forests bent down by raging storms, and drifting smoke.[11]

It is the mute beauty, but also the mysteriousness of these recombinatory images that captivates Adela and Jacques. How or why is it that these images are so perfect, intricate, and at the same time ephemeral? Moreover, their magic is indifferent, displayed irrespective of the presence of an audience. And one knows all the while that the moment will pass, the sun will set, and the narrative must cover other ground. In the end associations alone are not enough; the mind also requires a larger narrative context. This the author provides in the form of the narrator's almost pastoral series of visits, which allow the main character to tell his story impeded only by the strictures of time and circumstance. But as in everyday life there are interruptions, uncertainties, dead ends. The mundane, the ordinary, and the understated provide the starting points for each new beginning in the telling of Austerlitz's tale.

But Where . . . Shall I Resume My Story?

Much of Austerlitz's story is the story of depression, the toll it takes on him, and his gradual recovery. His real problems began when he took early retirement from teaching at the Courtault Institute in 1991 to pursue his architectural interests and escape the mindlessness of British reforms in higher education fostered by the Tory government. (Here Sebald's own sentiments are clearly present; he has acknowledged in interviews the Thatcher government's meddling in British universities as an impetus for his own efforts in fiction and poetry in the late 1980s and early 1990s.)[12] Austerlitz, like Sebald, finds the act of writing extremely difficult. And as his mental illness worsened, he noted that reading too became more and more difficult. Language, he tells the narrator, is like an ancient city, but it is covered in fog and nothing is clearly recognizable. If we are brutally honest about the efficacy of language in really making sense of the world, we must admit that we are groping about us in a hopeless darkness. As his pessimism overwhelms him in the months after his retirement, Austerlitz becomes increasingly isolated, and spends his nights walking the streets of London. These walks become occasions for the kind of meandering historical digressions that Sebald pursued in *The Rings of Saturn*. He hallucinates, imagining people in period dress returning from the past. To Austerlitz it seemed during this time that the dead, whom he more and more often glimpsed passing on the street, were returning from their long absence. Here too the notion of repetition occurs, raising the specter of eternal return. But the eternity to which Austerlitz's phantoms are condemned is not a realm of greater understanding and enlightenment, but an afterlife in which the dead must repeat tasks that the living can only regard as bafflingly senseless. It is in this uncanny connection that a figure emerges in the half-light of the subway station, a man in a white turban who continually sweeps rubbish from the floor onto a piece of cardboard.

This scene is worthy of discussion for its bizarre imaginative power. Following the man with the turban, Austerlitz finds himself compelled, after some hesitation, to enter the long-abandoned Ladies Waiting Room, a relic of the Victorian era. He passes through a heavy curtain designed to retain the room's heat and keep out the cold. What ensues is one of the most fantastic scenes in Sebaldry. Stairways, bridges, and colonnades rise upward toward a distant dome that seems to be the ancient ancestor of all domes. The vision is of a dream-like ziggurat such as M. C. Escher depicted in his drawings, or an infinite atrium such as Borges described in short stories such as "The Library of Babel." What is one to make of this strange ruin? It is another "false universe," as Austerlitz himself seems to realize in the moment he perceives it, populated by prisoners ambling in the distance? The rotunda is broken, with birds nesting in the eaves, and moss growing here and there. Three figures appear—a lady, a clergyman, and the child they have come to collect—and Austerlitz realizes this station is the very place he arrived as a young child in 1939. This is Austerlitz's first "premonition of the past," as one might term Sebald's paradoxical inversion of time in such scenes of recognition as these. Austerlitz beholds an image of himself as a child sitting on a bench, clutching his rucksack, and he realizes the truth: "I have not lived my life as myself," he tells the narrator, "or perhaps I am only now being born, so to speak, on the eve of my death."[13] The central question of his childhood is at this point in the novel manifestly clear: Why did the Elias couple take him in at all? The mental breakdown that soon follows this realization is the first of two.

Prague

As we have noted before, Sebald's narratives advance largely on the basis of associations or mundane occurrences such as coincidences. As always there is the suspicion that these associations and coincidences are in fact part of a hidden order of things. Thus, a conversation on the radio between two women talking about the once little-known transports of Czech and German Jewish children to England in the months before the Second World War strikes a chord with the protagonist. His flashback is immediate and total: Austerlitz sees himself in a crowd of children waiting on a Dutch quay for the ferry to take him to England; he sees the name of the ferry (ironically, "PRAGUE"); he sees the chaperone, who, he realizes, has since appeared to him in dreams. From here on there is no turning back from his journey into the past. With this imagery, Sebald shows us once again a scene that comes into being suddenly and fully-formed, like the shapes and shadows of a photographic print once the developing fluid has done its work. Just as those shapes and shadows are invisible up to that fateful moment in the darkroom, so too memory can be indelibly marked in the mind, though dormant and invisible until the time comes for its reemergence. Such memories, because they lack a contextual relationship to other memories, inhabit a mute and inactive realm of Austerlitz's unconscious. They are phenomena that seem to exist outside of time. In this they resemble other fictional elements in Sebald: the returning dead in their period dress, the chronically ill waiting to die, and the spaces such as Iver Grove or the strange, vaulted labyrinth in the Liverpool Street Station, where time stands still. When Austerlitz arrives in Prague to begin his search for his origins, it is precisely the impression of timelessness that overcomes him. The city seems to stand apart from what has been happening all around it. And there is good reason for Austerlitz's impression; Prague is one of the few major central European cities to escape bombardment during the Second World War. In the ensuing years it was neglected by its Communist rulers, who devoted their limited resources to industry, weaponry, and worker housing.

The trip to Prague occasions the use in the text of a new group of photographs to illustrate the sense that time is standing still; we see the interior of the State Archive (resembling both an opera house and a prison), the doorkeeper's table with its primitive telephone, an eight-pointed star mosaic, and an art nouveau staircase in the apartment house where Austerlitz once lived with his family. Here the narrative becomes a detective story, though a limited one, since there are only a few addresses that can be paired with the name Austerlitz in 1939. At the address one Agata Austerlitzova resides Vera Rusanova, Austerlitz's former nanny. Here the narrative resumes the style of a memoir and the reader realizes it has taken on a tripartite structure, with Sebald's narrator narrating Vera's story through Austerlitz. This is a technique used to great effect in *Wittgensteins Neffe* (1982; translated as *Wittgenstein's Nephew,* 1989) by Thomas Bernhard. In tone, Vera's memoir resembles that of Max Ferber's mother in *The Emigrants*. It is a description of the daily cares and joys of a way of life that is on the edge of destruction. The compositional problem of a presumed language barrier between Austerlitz and his former nanny is solved by Sebald's device of linking Vera and Agata Austerlitz through a common francophilia, made plausible by Austerlitz's name Jacques. As Vera describes their life together before the war, she falls into Czech, which up to now has been alien to Austerlitz. But Vera's domestic descriptions and the intimate familiarity of her voice prompt a resurgence of his native ability in the language, and he even begins to recall episodes and people on his own. This passage underscores the centrality of language for identity. When Sebald describes, in the words of Austerlitz, the process of mental decline, it is language itself that becomes intractable as one's condition deteriorates—Austerlitz's linguistic paralysis seems the delayed result of the abrupt severance of his primal connection with his native tongue. In Prague, the nearly all-consuming nature of Austerlitz's erasure of memory is most keenly evident. The trauma of separation, although submissively absorbed when it occurred—what else could a four-and-a-half-year-old do?—left its permanent mark. But as in the case of figures like Ambros Adelwarth and Paul Bereyter in *The Emigrants,* the effects of the injury are not fully felt until much later in life. In *Austerlitz,* the traumatic effects are not felt until the distractions of study and career are cleared away, exposing the emptiness of his disconnected, dislocated existence. This was the secret he would not and could not reveal to the woman who once loved him, Marie de Verneuil.

Rediscovering One's Mother

The narrative seems to circle, rather than directly approach, the figure of Agata Austerlitzova as if to emphasize not so much the elusiveness of her identity— there is in fact much Austerlitz *can* know, now that he has found Vera—as the irretrievability of her person. The first time Austerlitz saw his mother perform, Vera tells him, she was performing the role of Olympia. When he visits the theater the next day, Austerlitz photographs the interior of the opera house, and while doing so glimpses a sky-blue shoe under the curtain. Later Vera confirms that his mother wore blue shoes when she played Olympia. Unabashedly literary in all his works, Sebald leaves it to the reader to know (or to discover) that the character Olympia is from the Offenbach opera *Tales of Hoffmann.* Her story is the that of a beautiful woman who is in reality an automaton devised by her father, Spalanzani. The infatuated protagonist, relying on a pair of glasses provided by Spalanzani's collaborator, cannot see her for what she is until he attempts to dance with her and her mechanisms go awry. At the same time the collaborator, Coppelius, realizes he has been cheated out of his share of the expected proceeds from Olympia's performances. He destroys her and she cannot be put back together again. Coincidentally—and Sebald makes no mention of this—the name of the banking house on which Spalanzani drew his worthless check to Coppelius, is none other than Elias. A further literary association is the enigmatic blue shoe, though it will be recognized only by those familiar with the writings of Hugo von Hofmannsthal. In his story "Andreas," the eponymous ✓ protagonist recalls witnessing his first theatrical performance as a child. While the orchestra finished warming up, he caught sight of a lovely sky-blue shoe just under the stage curtain. As the curtain rose, he beheld to his sheer delight a princess in blue and silver. The delight was even greater when the curtain descended again and only the shoe could be seen.[14]

Olympia cannot be restored, just as Agata Austerlitzova's identity ultimately cannot be put back together again. Clearly the impossible mission of the book, however, is to do just this, for it is the only way to begin to put Austerlitz's own identity back together. The effort will inevitably be incomplete, but it must be undertaken. Vera remembers how mesmerized Jacques had been by his mother on the stage. But he had also been afraid she might not return from that fantastic realm of make-believe. It is a sad irony that Austerlitz had feared, even before his exile, losing his mother to some "other world." Vera returns to the subject of the theater again later in the book, when she shows Austerlitz photographs, including the one with the little blond boy dressed in the white satin costume of a cavalier. A small version appears in the text, embedded in the passage in which Vera explains that Austerlitz had been a page at a masked ball in February of 1939, carrying the train of the Queen of Roses. In perhaps the most poignant moment in the book, the four-year-old boy's searching expression seems to demand that the adult Austerlitz "grant him his due," that he, the adult, should go back in time and act to prevent the tragedy that was about to befall him when the picture was taken.[15]

Though the unhappy future awaiting the child Austerlitz is belied by the serenity of the moment that is captured on film, Sebald carefully avoids sentimentalizing the picture. The innocence of the child's face and the radiance of his white satin outfit combine to create an angelic quality, but the picture is not entirely remarkable—it has the familiar quality of a photograph from a family album. The familiar appeal of childhood pictures consists largely in the innocence, but also the ignorance, they capture—such photographs are made before the cares and burdens of adulthood have overtaken their subjects, before accidents or illness have taken their toll. The ignorance of the future so painfully obvious in childhood photographs is universal; it is common to those who will one day become model citizens as well as those who will become ne'er-do-wells, murderers, or thieves. Austerlitz happens to be a victim, but the uncomfortable truth is that his picture is not dissimilar to childhood photographs of those who in effect victimized him. The fact of the matter is that it could be any costumed child. It is worth noting that history has preserved several disarmingly innocent-looking pictures of the *Führer* himself in typical childhood poses and dress of the period.[16] Just as we have repeatedly seen the deceptive power of memory in Sebald, so too photographic reproductions of "reality" can conceal or distort the truth. And as Sebald makes a point of stating in one of the book's first descriptions of the thorough-going and efficient cruelty of the Germans during the Second World War, the perpetrators were more often family men than monsters. The SS guards at Breendonk Fortress, he asserts, like those at Auschwitz and Theresienstadt, "were heads of households and good sons from Vilsbiburg and Fuhlsbüttel, from the Black Forest and the Münster Plain."[17]

The passage concerning the image of the little blond page offers another key to appreciating Sebald's fascination with old photographs. Vera says she senses something stirring in such forgotten photographs. It is as if pictures such as these emit little sighs of despair, as if the pictures themselves are possessed of memory and can recall "how we once were—those of us still living as well as those who went before."[18] The relationship of the living to the dead is at the heart of the mystery of the haunting power of old photographs. This passage also contains one of Sebald's most explicit descriptions of that relationship: "To me it seems more and more as if time did not exist at all, only various interlocking spaces in a kind of higher stereometry, between which the living and the dead can move back and forth as they like."[19] Despite appearances to the contrary, then, the dead and the living inhabit the same timeless world and can move in and out of each other's dimensions. As if in passing, Sebald mentions Ibsen's last play—its title, unnamed in the text, is *When We Dead Awaken*. Extending the metaphor of the living dead further still, Austerlitz suggests an even more unsettling inversion: it is not the dead who may be glimpsed as ghosts only under certain "atmospheric conditions," but those of us who are still living. To the dead who have gone before them, the living—when they are perceptible at all—seem unreal and insubstantial. In his own experience, Austerlitz has always known he was somehow absent from life, and this feeling is all the more intense as he regards the picture of himself as a child.

One feature of the German language for which there is no corresponding grammatical form is the subjunctive mood for indirect speech, often referred to as the special subjunctive. This form occurs occasionally throughout Sebald, but is most common in passages such as Sebald's narration of Austerlitz's retelling of Vera's narrative. The special subjunctive is one device that renders German a stylistically more subtle medium, in that the verb is inflected in such a way as to distinguish it from the ordinary present or past, distancing the narrator from the question of veracity of the content of reported speech. The special subjunctive emphasizes that the words reported by the narrator are the speaker's words and his or hers alone. When Vera reports Agata's realization of just what it meant to be prohibited, as a Jew, from visiting parks and the banks of the Vlatva, for example, the German, "Sie setzte hinzu, daß sie erst jetzt wirklich verstehe, wie schön es ist, sorglos auf einem Flußdampfer an der Reling zu stehen" (247), actually leaves some doubt whether she *really* fully understood the significance of such restrictions; whereas the English must be rendered something like "she added that she only now truly understood how wonderful it is to stand by the railing of a river steamer without a care in the world" (172). The use of the special subjective is even more striking when Vera speaks of Agata's expression of hope for reuniting her family in Paris: "Andererseits . . . sprach Vera davon, daß sich jetzt . . . gewiß auch für sie ein Ausweg eröffnen werde" (249). This construction is more clearly noncommital than the English rendering: "Agata spoke about the possibility that a way for her too to leave would soon be found" (173). It is all too clear, of course, that only Agata's child Jacques would escape.

Her Final Destination

One of the lessons of *Austerlitz* is the extent to which the Nazis planned their methods of persecution and torment down to the last detail. Their cruelty was masterminded for efficiency and thoroughness. The Jews of Prague were required to participate in their own degradation by carefully following long lists of instructions, and they were finally summoned to appear at an appointed place to be confined, then sent on by train to an unknown fate. They were sent first to the prison camp at Theresienstadt, which served most of the time as a distribution point. But for a period it served as a "model" concentration camp designed to deceive the International Red Cross. Thus, Theresienstadt represents the most counterfeit of all the counterfeit worlds explored in *Austerlitz*. Sebald's description of present-day Theresienstadt (Terezin) is accompanied by photographs of the dilapidated buildings in the town. A series of images of closed doors and windows illustrates the narrator's impression that these sealed openings—the reader is reminded of the bricked-up window and the locked doors of Austerlitz's foster home in Wales—"obstruct access to a darkness never penetrated."[20] The fortress itself is the embodiment of the architectural design that has haunted Austerlitz since he visited the fortress prison at Breendonk—the eight-pointed star, which is identical, in Kafkaesque nightmares, to his own dark inner prison. But why does Sebald preface his descriptions of the hyper-organized machinery of extermination at Theresienstadt with a detailed description of items in the windows of a darkened curiosity shop? More than one critic has called into question

Sebald's good taste in suggesting that such things as collectible porcelain, staghorn buttons, and a Japanese fan share hidden connections with the annihilation of millions in the Holocaust.[21] The unlikely mention of Casanova, who wrote his memoirs while living at nearby Dux, strikes some as a gratuitous literary reference, but is in fact part of a dream sequence and as such not without its own internal logic. In any case, Sebald was singularly unconcerned about charges that he indulged in gratuitous allusions. His choice of photographs—often highly arbitrary—bears this out. The dust jacket of the German version of *Austerlitz* boasts that Sebald is one of Germany's most independently-minded authors. His antiquarian interest in the miscellaneous contents of the shop, which caught his eye because it was one of the largest buildings in a virtually empty town, is vintage Sebald. In addition, Sebald's numerous references to the grotesque fastidiousness of German efforts to catalogue household items confiscated from the Jews points to the significance of such trinkets, mementos, and treasures for the lives of their former owners, and, in a strange way, for their dutiful tormentors. Surely the displays, cabinets, and shelves at the Antikos Bazar include at least a few Jewish possessions from the 1930s, such as the little squirrel—*veverka* in Czech—that conjures up a childhood memory in Austerlitz. Vera confirms that as a young boy Austerlitz had been especially fascinated by a book about the changing seasons, and that he had often asked how the squirrels know where to find the nuts they have stored, when all the world is covered in snow.

The nearby spa at Marienbad also plays a major part in *Austerlitz*. It was a favorite destination of Agata and her husband, Austerlitz's father Maximillian. When Austerlitz as a grown man visited Marienbad, in the company of the woman mentioned before, Marie de Verneuil, it was twenty years earlier, 1972, and he didn't know about his past. He could not have known he had been there as a boy. The place exerts a strange, oppressive power over Austerlitz for reasons of which he is unaware. The hotel in Marienbad is another expression of Sebaldian gothic such as we have encountered in *The Emigrants* and *The Rings of Saturn*: the large, antiquated house with an inner life of its own. The concierge and his elderly bellhops are tired, slow-moving, almost inert. Their fatigue is made more conspicuous by the grey uniforms they wear. All of Marie's efforts to penetrate the psychological barriers around Austerlitz—and she is the first person ever to try to do this—are doomed to failure. In fact, doom is the prevailing mood of their entire time at Marienbad. Doves and other birds sometimes symbolize doom or aimless stasis in Sebald, and such is the case here. Austerlitz cannot shake himself free of the image of a decrepit aviary seen on an excursion to Königswart—the doves, cooing in their niches above the corpses of their brethren and the hardened layers of decades of excrement, seem just as prone to dementia as people are. A nervous breakdown, we already know, lies in wait for

Austerlitz. And in retrospect, the reasons for Austerlitz's unease and feelings of extreme isolation in Mariendbad are clear: the place reminds him, though he does not know it, of his former self and his hidden past.

The Return to England

The notion of places possessing character—or of objects possessing a form of consciousness, as we saw in the case of Vera and her photographs—is not an idle thought in Sebald. Prisons and other buildings seem to have a kind of personality, towns and cities can exert spiritual power over people, and things can communicate secrets. When Austerlitz departs Prague, for instance, an iron support column on a train platform in Pilsen seems to remember him, not the other way around. Did he see the same column in 1939 on the way to England? The object seems to "bear witness to what he himself no longer can know."[22] Sebald uses the occasion of Austerlitz's trip through Germany to comment on the strangeness of contemporary Germany when viewed by an outsider, especially an outsider conscious of its suppressed history. Stopping in Nuremberg, Austerlitz has one of those Sebaldian moments of "extraterrestrial" perspective, when he becomes caught up in a surging, but eerily silent throng of Saturday shoppers dressed all in shades of grey, green, and brown. Later he is told that this happens every Saturday—silent shoppers simultaneously surge through the pedestrian zones all over Germany. Exhausted by the struggle against the tide, he sits down to rest, and an elderly woman in a Tyrolean hat, mistaking his rucksack for that of a homeless person, hands him a coin. But there is much more to Austerlitz's German experience than such grim, Kafkaesque humor. Whereas in Marienbad twenty years before he had not been able to comprehend the meaning of his surroundings, the train ride through German is an epiphany. He realizes that the deep, nameless forests through which he is traveling are the same ones that haunted his dreams when he was a boy in Wales. He realizes he has dreamed of the trip and a twin brother in the train compartment with him. In the dream world's symbolic manipulation of persons, images, and events, this twin brother is none other than a companion self to Austerlitz. It is also a self that is dead from neglect by the end of the journey. Austerlitz realizes now, retracing the train trip through Germany, that his mind was trying to tell him what had happened to him. In one of the book's saddest (and most trenchant) expressions of Austerlitz's fate as a child, the lifeless body of the boy in the dream is seen lying in the netting beneath the luggage rack with the other things.[23]

One would think the many revelations and recollections awakened by the trip to Prague and the return to England by way of Germany would have a salutary effect. As we have said, *Austerlitz* is largely a book about depression, and

Sebald means to be realistic and clinical. So it is that Austerlitz's confrontation with the past does not lead to emancipation but to a second breakdown. At home in London he suffers the effects of his years of suppressed anxiety, effects that evidently could not have been successfully treated in the aftermath of his first collapse. A feeling of complete abandonment and personal erasure overcome him. After recovery, he is able to turn again to the subject of his mother, as he tells the narrator. Details from H. G. Adler's voluminous work on the ghetto at Theresienstadt mark the resumption of Austerlitz's search for Agata. From Adler, Austerlitz learns how a counterfeit world, a Potemkin village, was created to convince the International Red Cross that the Jewish inmates were being treated well. Shops were set up, as was a lending library, and there were even concerts and plays. The first production performed in the new Theresienstadt was Jacques Offenbach's opera *The Tales of Hoffmann,* a favorite of Agata's as we already know from remarks made by Vera. Believing he might be able to see a glimpse of his mother in the "documentary" film made by the Germans *Der Führer Schenkt den Juden eine Stadt* (The Führer gives the Jews a city), he obtains a copy and screens it. While Olympia, the role played by his mother in the opera, does not appear, there are excerpts from the performances of the Cancan from *La Vie Parisienne* and Mendelssohn's *A Midsummer Night's Dream.* Austerlitz tells himself he sees his mother, however, briefly in a scene in a café, and as a sales clerk in a fashion accessories shop. But he is even more certain she is in the audience at the premier performance of a work composed in Theresienstadt by the composer Pavel Haas. Sebald shows us the still frame of a young, some-what thin woman sitting just behind an elderly man. This image, obtained only by showing the film in slow motion—a surreal experience in itself—can be com-pared to a picture obtained from the Theater Archive on Austerlitz's second visit to Prague and displayed on page 253. There can be little doubt they are the same person, and Vera confirms the identity. Almost in passing, she mentions that Agata loved to visit the park at Liboc, where Archduke Ferdinand had built a summer residence. The foundations of this palace are laid out—and here we finally encounter what is possibly the source of the archetypal form that recurs throughout the book—in the shape of a star. Thus, Sebald imbues the rather abstract discussions of traditional fortifications that appeared early in the book with a highly personal meaning.

The Paris Epilogue

As fiction is often more vividly real than present reality, so the past is more invit-ing than contemporary reality. The Paris of September 1996 is a hot, dry, smoggy, and altogether unromantic place when Austerlitz and the narrator meet again there toward the end of the book. The protagonist, having found evidence of his mother, is now looking for signs of what happened to his father, Maximillian Aychenwald, who as a political activist fled Prague at the time of the Nazi takeover and was known to have gone to Paris. When Austerlitz studied in Paris in 1958, he knew nothing about his father, of course. Austerlitz recalls a number of things about that year, especially his relationship with Marie de Verneuil. But one episode is worth noting for its evocative intensity. One day, walking between the Gare d'Austerlitz and the Quai d'Austerlitz (!), Marie and Jacques come upon a small circus. They enter in time to witness a scene that captivates Austerlitz, though he doesn't understand why. Its significance seems purely formal or symbolic; its meaning is ineffable, non-verbal. The lights are lowered and stars appear on the darkened tent ceiling above. After a few moments of suspense, a troop of players in "oriental" garb marches in with musical instruments— a magician, a beautiful woman, and three beautiful children with black hair, the last of whom carries a lantern and is followed by a white goose. The little procession, like a tiny caravan from the Caucasus or Turkey (the last of several images of caravans in the book) begins its strange music, which seems to Austerlitz part Welsh folk song from his childhood, part waltz, part funeral dirge. They march slowly, keeping each foot momentarily aloft with every step forward, much like a ceremonial guard. (The translator must give a periphrastic translation of the compact German *letztes Geleit*.) The goose stands motionless in the middle as long as the music is played, as if fully aware of "its own lot in life, and the fate of the little company of players to which it belong[s]."[24] The scene is striking in itself, but one also wonders if Austerlitz might not have witnessed just such a circus performance when he was a child in Prague, with his mother and father beside him.

There is much that we don't see, Sebald reminds us again and again, because we are not looking. Personalities like Austerlitz have a heightened sensitivity, however. He can see, for instance, his father walking toward him in the Gare d'Austerlitz, the station where he would have departed for the concentration camp at Gurs in 1942. But Austerlitz himself is also capable of overlooking features of the present that connect us with the past. A door in the wall next to his house in London stands open one day, and he discovers inside a Jewish cemetery. A caretaker, a small, elderly woman, is working among the headstones. The narrator, too, makes new discoveries about people, places, and things, returning to Antwerp to visit the Nocturama and to Breendonk to see the fortress. Literary to the end, Sebald's conclusion flows together with a memoir by the literary scholar Dan Jacobson, whose grandfather was Rabbi Yisrael Yehoshua Melamed, known as Heshel. The book was a gift from Austerlitz. Its connection with Austerlitz's experience is multifaceted. Not only did many of Jacobson's family die in the Holocaust, but there is also a Breendonk-like fortress in his mother's hometown of Kaunaus, Lithuania, which German troops occupied and used for incarceration and torture. *Austerlitz* ends with the narrator finishing chapter 15 of *Hershel's Kingdom,* then making his way on foot to the town of Mechelen, where he arrives as night is falling.[25] Sebald was determined not to permit the erasure by time of the stories he encountered in his own lifetime, whether they are represented by composite characters such as Austerlitz—created from the stories of the *Kindertransport*—or by historical figures in Jacobson's (or Simon's, or Améry's) writings. Though the narrator doesn't tell us so, by walking to Mechelen he is retracing the steps of the Jews, but in reverse—Mechelen was the point of departure for every shipment of Belgian Jews destined for the death camps of Eastern Europe.

Reception

As late as summer 1998, Sebald was in the midst of putting the finishing touches on literary historical essays for non-fiction books, and was unsure of what his next project would be. It was a surprise to many, then, when a thick new book called *Austerlitz* appeared early in 2001. It was clear that there was little new about the stylistic techniques at work in the book, but its unifying concept represented a more overtly holistic ambition—the reconstruction of one remarkable identity, from the remnants of a lost childhood. Austerlitz, unlike the broken men and women of *The Emigrants* is a victim who seems hardly aware of his victimhood until his true name is revealed to him and the effects of his exile begin to make themselves known. Who were his parents, their friends, his family? The task is clear: every possible shard must be found so as to piece together as much of the broken vessel as can be done.

The *Süddeutsche Zeitung* greeted the appearance of *Austerlitz* with enthusiasm, one of the first German newspapers to comment on the novel, on 24 February 2001. Roughly a month later, the critic Wieland Freund, writing in the 23 March 2001 issue of the *Rheinischer Merkur,* asserted that *Austerlitz* is Sebald's most non-biographical work yet. According to Freund, the main character Austerlitz is more clearly a creation of fiction than any other Sebaldian character. In an interview with *Der Spiegel* magazine, Sebald confirmed that he based the character Austerlitz on at least two distinct persons, a man and a woman.[26] Freund also remarks, rightly, that the narrative method, in which a narrator "re-narrates" at length the narration of another, stems from the Austrian writer

Thomas Bernhard. Sebald has made it his own by assuaging the stinging Bern-
hardian contempt, limiting the diatribes, and heightening the empathy that is,
paradoxically, inherent in Bernhard's often savagely scathing work. Bernhard has
a legitimate successor in Sebald. In a review for Austrian television, the critic Gerald Heidegger also compares Sebald to Bernhard, calling *Austerlitz,* "a tremendous
piece of writing."[27]

Not everyone was so deferential. The weekly cultural newspaper *Die Zeit,*
which had mostly praised Sebald's work in the past, pronounced *Austerlitz,*
in contradistinction to Freund's opinion, a "non-novel," and "a literary bastard
child," in its issue of 5 April 2001, and asserted that the character Austerlitz was,
like all the others in Sebald, half-fiction, half-real. In this review the influential
critic Iris Radisch deems *Austerlitz* the product of a "virtuoso of the card catalogue, a ventriloquist, a raconteur, and an archivist."[28] She is not taken in by the
hypnotizing style about which other critics have spoken. In fact, Radisch sees
nothing but pretension and bad taste, especially when the protagonist visits
Terezin and lingers over the hodgepodge of antiques and curiosities in the
Antikos Bazar. She blames Sebald for falling under the spell of that "theorist of
collectibles" Walter Benjamin.[29] Naïveté, especially feigned or aesthetic naïveté,
has no place at Theresienstadt, she insists. And though one might argue that
Radisch neglects to consider the profound effects of Austerlitz's traumatization
by the Nazis, the fact remains that Sebald leaves himself open to the kind of criticism Radisch and others have made. According to this line of thought, Sebald's
archival approach to exploring hidden correspondences breaks down before the
monstrousness of the Holocaust; it is not up to the task, and is better suited for
digressions into historical territory of less consequence. If everything were
equally "unfathomable," as Sebald seems to suggest, then no one event or catastrophe would be of greater or lesser significance than any other; the mass killing
of herring would be equivalent to the extermination of the Jews. Finally, according to Radisch, Sebald's effort to "liberate" the past through his combinatory play
of images, emotions, scenes, and clues, is ultimately nothing but "superstition."[30]

It is regrettable that *Austerlitz* has aroused in some readers suspicions that
the Final Solution is being relativized in its pages, because the novel is in effect
a lengthy *hommage* to the writer Jean Améry. Améry's experiences in numerous ✓
concentration camps, including Auschwitz and Fort Breendonk, are recorded in
the book *At the Mind's Limits* (1966), to which Sebald refers in *Austerlitz*. After
the war, Améry spent the rest of his life in Belgium and refused to use his
Austrian given name, Hans Mayer, preferring the French equivalent of Hans,
Johannes, and an anagram of his surname in the form of Améry. He became
well known in the 1960s and 1970s through his essays and lectures as a moral

spokesman for those who experienced the horror of the Holocaust. He refused to succumb to the deleterious effects of his imprisonment in the death camps, and took his own life in 1978, before his health failed. Sebald's sympathy for Améry and other victims of degradation at the hands of the Nazis is indisputable, no matter what judgments one wishes to make about his literary techniques. It should also be noted that the publication of *Austerlitz* came within a year of the release of one of the most moving documentary films every made on the subject of childhood exile, *Into the Arms of Strangers: Stories of the Kindertransport* (2000), directed by Mark Jonathan Harris. The film traces the personal histories of Czech, German, and Austrian children, who, like Jacques Austerlitz, were taken away to England in an effort to save them from what lay ahead for the Jews. It is a serious, sad subject that the film explores, as does Sebald's *Austerlitz*. Both do so with care, respect, and sensitivity. By the same token, Sebald is well aware that aesthetic manipulation of the historical period in question invariably invites skepticism and suspicion. In an interview in the spring of 2001 he said, "My thoughts [on this problem] were that the writings of German non-Jewish authors on the subject of the persecution and attempted destruction of the Jewish people are generally inaccessible, and are in large measure embarrassing usurpations."[31] In other words, so little justice had been done to the theme of the Holocaust and its effects that there seemed to be ample room for an honest and responsible attempt to give voice to individual pain. Sebald seeks to do the opposite of relativizing; he seeks instead to endow everything with its proper significance. All beings suffer. As in the case of the lost moth, forlornly clinging to a bedroom wall at Andromeda Lodge, we in no way belittle the suffering of the one by acknowledging the suffering of another. All the subjects of remembering have their own validity in *Austerlitz*. In the words of Peter Craven, "Sebald refuses to admit that any memory can be so trivial or intolerable that it cannot become the subject of art."[32]

Austerlitz appeared in the United States in October 2001, in the aftermath of the horrific terrorist attacks of September 11. One of the first Americans to review the book, Daniel Mendelsohn, writing in the magazine *New York,* saw at once the connection between the subject of *Austerlitz* and the recent experience of mass terror:

> To the victims of mass terror, and to their contemporaries, falls the painful duty of recording what happened, of counting the murdered and missing; to those who come afterward, and to their descendants, belongs the perhaps more complicated responsibility of remembering to commemorate the dead. Can victimhood—or guilt—be collective and inherited? How far does the bloodstained past reach into the present?[33]

Like other critics before him, Mendelsohn recognizes that Sebald's method is in large part the pursuit of clues to a crime story—in *Austerlitz* the scene of the crime is Europe itself. Whatever its current condition and appearance, Terezin was once the site of the Theresienstadt concentration camp, the Mitterrand Library rests on the site of a huge warehouse for the collection of property confiscated from Jews. Paradoxically, however, most of the clues seem on the surface neither connected to the Holocaust nor to each other; they are Turner water colors, unkempt Jewish cemeteries from the previous century, star-shaped fortresses, boarded windows, porcelain figurines in a Czech curiosity shop, cupolas, and macaws and moths on an estate in Wales, to name but a few. "The breadth of Sebald's fascinations with concrete things," writes Mendelsohn, "is merely the visible symbol of the breadth of his moral and historical imagination."[34] Mendelsohn also recognizes the problem of representation discussed earlier: How can one find a compelling way to speak about what is, in all its horror and complexity, unspeakable? In the title character Mendlsohn sees the perfect naive protagonist. His repression and ignorance of his own identity have made him "shamefully unwilling to learn about the holocaust in general," a form of denial that leaves the reader alone with the knowledge of boxcars full of people whose destinations and destinies were the concentration camps of Eastern Europe—it is this denial that invites the author to approach the ghastly subject in the first place.[35] As Austerlitz learns the details of what happened, he recognizes, as the world did in the aftermath of 11 September, that some crimes truly defy comprehension.

Whereas Sebald's first three English-language books were published initially in Britain, appearing in the United States after a period of months, *Austerlitz* was published on both sides of the Atlantic virtually simultaneously. Its appearance had been greatly anticipated in the press; an excerpt had appeared in the *New Yorker* on 3 September 2001. On the same day *Newsweek* magazine heralded the publication of *Austerlitz* as "the literary event of the fall." *Austerlitz* had already been celebrated as a major new novel in the London *Guardian* when *Washington Post* critic Michael Dirda published the first major American review, in which he described the "crepuscular, autumnal world" of this and Sebald's other "original and exhilarating" creations.[36] Michiko Kakutani's review in the *New York Times* complained of the "gratuitous device of the narrator," but otherwise praised the book for its "harrowing emotional power reminiscent of that found in *The Emigrants*."[37] The critic Richard Eder, writing in the *New York Times Review of Books* compares *Austerlitz* somewhat less favorably to Sebald's other novels, suggesting that the new book lacks their "paradoxical lightness, [and] buoyant variety."[38] The connections Sebald draws are, as we have come to expect, extraordinary, Eder admits, but despite the richness, brilliance, and emotional power, its lingering, unrestrained focus can make it at times a plodding, ponderous book.[39] This lack of restraint, as well as the almost complete absence of paragraphing, are features of the prose style of Sebald's literary model, Thomas Bernhard, whose relentlessly allusive novels read like rambling, long-winded effusions. The most negative criticism of *Austerlitz* is that Sebald's style unsuited to the protagonist's too conventional story of grown man in search of his forgotten origins and a place to belong. According to the writer Benjamin Markovits, Sebald fails to convey a true sense of Austerlitz as a character, despite all the self-discovery that goes on.[40] The frustrating absence of a center around which characterization might have been built—were Sebald intent on characterization, which he is not—is of course at the heart Austerlitz's tragedy. In many of Sebald's protagonists, damage manifests itself for the first time only years later, organically, and often eventually overwhelms the characters, as in the case of Paul Bereyter and Ambros Adelwarth in *The Emigrants*. The emotional impotence of Austerlitz, demonstrated so painfully in the episode with Marie de Verneuil in Marienbad, is a symptom of the hollowness of his identity. Still, the book ends not in Austerlitz's succumbing, but in his refusal to give up the search. He has rescued the memory of his mother from oblivion and would like to do the same for his father, but for Markovits, this rescue provides little sense of triumph. The memories merely fill a gap and the true shock of a split self is not effectively depicted.[41] Yet Sebald seems to be aiming at something quite different from what Markovits would require. Sebald's method is to convey the telling of the story by the victim himself, which occurs mostly in chance meetings at different stages in the process of discovery. The very problem of Austerlitz's suppressed past emerges well into the narrative, as such a condition might well in real life. This is the story of the patient piecing together of various clues. It requires archival work and interviews. The writer Gabriele Annan, who also reviewed *The Emigrants,* explains that Sebald's authorial posture is not so much that of a constructor of narratives as a contemplative facilitator of narrative progress:

> [Sebald] is one of the most gripping writers imaginable. It's not the story so much that takes hold of the reader: it's the descriptions and the meditations, which can be hallucinatory in their effect. This is true of all his books, but in *Austerlitz* the proportion of rumination and evocation to narrative is larger than ever.[42]

For the novelist and critic John Banville, Sebald's descriptions can be breathtakingly beautiful and profoundly affecting: "The moment, toward the close of the book, when we are finally shown a photograph of a woman who is almost surely

Agata, is one of the most moving moments that a reader is likely to encounter in modern literature."[43] And for the majority of critics the same is true; the power of Sebald's prose to evoke emotion has not waned in his fourth novel. This is a remarkable feat, considering the delicate and difficult nature of its subject matter. Sebald was, after all, an outsider, a German gentile born in the last year of the war, writing about the misfortunes of a Jewish victim of Nazi persecution. If the book occasionally "plods" under the weight of its ruminations, it is nonetheless recognizable, according to most critics, as one of the major literary accomplishments of the new century. Its cumulative effect is not resolution, however, because Austerlitz's pilgrimage can lead only into a further regress of words and images. But such is the nature of any attempt at the historical reconstruction of past lives, especially the lives of an orphan like Austerlitz and his forgotten family.

Major British and American newspapers published obituaries within twenty-four hours after Sebald's death on 14 December 2001, but it would be two to three days before German newspapers took note of his passing. The critic Thomas Medicus, writing for the *Frankfurter Rundschau,* commented on the dilatory German response, and suggested that Sebald's significance had been more keenly appreciated in the English-speaking world, where his highly eccentric, "European" style of contemplative association was welcomed for its originality.[44] The grave loss for contemporary literature was generally acknowledged, however, both in German-speaking Europe and the English-speaking countries. With time, appreciation for Sebald's willfully unconventional, digressive, sometimes baffling prose may well grow in his native land. His death will surely redirect attention to his oeuvre. For British and American readers, who first learned about Sebald when they read the astonishing masterpiece, *The Emigrants,* the passing of this elusive and alluring German novelist is a deeply-felt tragedy. To them, he seems to have vanished as suddenly and inexplicably as he appeared.

CHAPTER 6

A Plangent Parting

With Sebald's sudden and untimely death at the age of fifty-seven, a remarkable literary career came to an end. As many of the obituaries pointed out, Sebald was just beginning to attract the wider audience he deserved; he seemed poised to ascend the final steps to the pinnacle of his literary career. In the wake of critical acclaim and limited but not inconsiderable market success, he had signed a contract for *Austerlitz* and future books with Hamish Hamilton (Penguin) in Britain and Random House in the United States. These contracts superceded his agreements with the smaller presses that had published his previous books: Harvill in London and New Directions in New York. He was beginning to receive the financial as well as critical recognition he deserved as a major contemporary talent. But while the originality of his fiction has been readily and generally recognized, the task of locating Sebald's work in the context of contemporary German literature remains problematic. Sebald does not seem to belong to the same tradition that produced the country's two modern Nobel laureates, Heinrich Böll and Günter Grass. Nonetheless, one would think that a writer such as Sebald, who makes as many references to other writers and texts as he does, might more easily find a definable place in literary history. Yet it is precisely the scale and eclecticism of his allusions and quotations that make the contextualization of Sebald so difficult. Here was a writer who drew on a daunting knowledge of four national literatures—German, British, French, and Italian— for much of his inspiration. Here was an outsider in several senses of the word. Sebald was, after all, a latecomer to fiction writing; he did not live in the country he initially wrote for, he composed in staid, intentionally archaic diction, and he mostly ignored matters of characterization and plot. At least two supportable assertions can be made about Sebald's place in German literature, however: In his interest in subject matter he owes much to the documentary theater of the 1960s in Germany, which dealt openly with the Holocaust and its repercussions. In narrative style he owes much to Thomas Bernhard, an influence especially apparent in Sebald's last novel, *Austerlitz*. With the latter observation we come full circle, however, because Bernhard too was an outsider in his native country.

Furthermore, the Austrian's disregard for the conventions of fiction earned him a special, if isolated, place in the canon of German literature. Thus, even if one considers Sebald to be Bernhard's successor in German and European literature, it must be admitted that he has less, not more, in common with the majority of serious contemporary German writers. He certainly has little in common with British and American writers, as numerous critics have attested. What, then, accounts for Sebald's idiosyncratic separateness? What main principles served to guide him as a novelist? We may begin where Sebald always ends up, contemplating the writer and the act of writing.

The Writer as Tireless Observer

When Henri Beyle looks at himself in the mirror in the novel *Vertigo* and asks, "What is a writer's undoing?" he is responding to his own sudden realization that he has allowed himself to be absorbed into the affairs of the world. Intent on full participation in the rituals of military life, and—more importantly— social life, he has purchased the dress uniform of his regiment. Seeing himself in the mirror he realizes that the uniform makes his figure more masculine, concealing the somewhat girlish features of his body. But the question of what "undoes" a writer implies another realization as well. Above all, writing requires detachment. It is essential that writers, whose work by its very nature aims at objectification, must be observers more than they must be actors in the world. Writers are "undone" when they succumb to the distractions of the active life, when they participate too fully, thus losing the distance from experience that is essential for contemplation and composition. Therein lies a central paradox. Writers must also know life, too, in order to create literary artifacts of depth and authenticity. This does not necessarily mean that one must have experienced everything one writes about in order to write compellingly. One doesn't have to have seen combat, for instance, to write compellingly about war. But a writer must be willing to find out about the experience of others in war, and use that knowledge effectively and persuasively. Sebald, always the collector, employs historical writings, documentation, interviews, journalism, autobiographical writings, and fiction in the construction of his narratives, which for the most part reflect—perhaps the better word is refract—the experiences of others. The detachment of the serious writer—his or her ability to listen and observe— is thus fundamental to Sebald's work. It in no way precludes his sympathizing with his subjects, though his tone in treating biographies is one of emotional restraint. This restraint is perhaps most clearly and consistently present in the descriptions of the protagonist's experiences in *Austerlitz*. As the true depths of the tragedy of Jacques Austerlitz's life begin to dawn on the reader, the effect is all the more gripping because the narrative "never raises its voice."[1]

One can gain considerable insight into the origins of Sebald's approach to literature by examining his scholarly books, articles, and essays. First, he had an abiding interest in Jewish authors and their relation to society. His publishing career began in 1969 with a monograph on the German-Jewish writer Carl Sternheim, followed a decade later by a book on another Jewish writer, Alfred Döblin. He then turned his attention to various Austrian writers of the nineteenth and twentieth centuries, as well as the radical theater in German-speaking Europe during the 1970s and 1980s. As a scholar and teacher of European literature, however, Sebald is steeped in the texts, some quite obscure, of a much broader range of writers, Latin American as well as European. It should come as no surprise that these serve as "pre-texts" for his fiction, and many of these, though by no means all, the author seems to expect his readers to recognize.[2] Sebald's non-academic prose, then, represents a natural extension of his many years of literary scholarship as well as reading for pleasure. His poetry and fiction writing emerged in the context of middle age and a growing dissatisfaction with the tenor of academic work in Britain. He found himself wanting to do something entirely new. By the same token, he regarded the struggle to write as precisely that—a struggle, a toilsome act, a labor of great difficulty, one which, moreover, mostly goes wrong, requiring revision upon revision. Sebald is interested in writers who feel the need to constantly revise, like the Austrian Adalbert Stifter, the Swiss Robert Walser, or the Englishman Edward FitzGerald. And, like the painter Max Ferber in *The Emigrants,* they perceive their work as inherently imperfect, as a work in progress. Sebald's narrator expresses something of this incessant drive to "get it right" late in the same book:

> It was an extremely arduous task [composing the story of Max Ferber], which consumed hours and days, often without any progress at all, often regressing rather than proceeding. I was plagued by a scrupulousness that was closing in on me and threatening to paralyze me completely. This scrupulousness applied not only to the subject of my narrative, which I wasn't sure I could do justice to, but to the whole questionable business of writing. I had covered hundreds of pages with my scribblings in pen and pencil, and most of what I had written was crossed through, rejected out of hand, or obscured by revisions. Even the "final" version I was able to salvage out of the mess seemed to me an utter failure, a patchwork of shreds.[3]

This is undoubtedly another example of occasional hyperbole in Sebald, but it illustrates the point that perfection is always receding from one's grasp, even as one moves on to new projects and leaves the old behind. This is the common thread Sebald sees in the lives of many of the writers he has studied. It is also a thread he weaves into his own narrators' narratives.

Favored Subjects: Expatriates and Mental Patients

Though much of Sebald's professional literary research has focused on the social conditions in which writers pursue their work, he repeatedly returns to subjective, psychological issues. He is particularly interested in the link between artistic talent and depression. Part of the "problematic" nature of the authors to whom Sebald is drawn is their common tendency to melancholia. They find themselves groping about in the darkness, in a state of profoundest solitude. Often the depression immobilizes them completely. But while one might think that writing about depressive personalities would itself be a depressing topic, the subject provides for Sebald a source of encouragement and even inspiration. For the creative act is often is an act of resistance for the artist. The odds of recovery are not necessarily in the artist's favor, nor is there necessarily a triumph on the horizon. A hallmark of Sebald's documentary fiction, derived at least in part from his scholarship, is that—true to life—most conditions do not improve in the long term. Still, to confront depression squarely, as many Austrian writers especially have done in and through their work, remains an act of resistance and thus an affirmation of the value of life. Sebald first suggested this thesis of resistance in his book of essays on Austrian literature, *Die Beschreibung des Unglücks,* in 1985, four years before his first novel. "Melancholia, the contemplation of unhappiness as it is occurring, has nothing in common with the desire to die," writes Sebald, "and at the level of art in particular its function is anything but reactive or reactionary. . . . The description of unhappiness carries with it the possibility of overcoming that unhappiness."[4] The originality of Sebald's approach to literature can best be appreciated by considering his studies of writers whose mental illness becomes so severe that they are completely debilitated, requiring hospitalization. In the course of responding to their private diaries as well as their oeuvre, Sebald explores analytically their private suffering and its relation to their work in much the same way that he reconstructs, in aesthetic form, the suffering and decline of the four depressive characters in *The Emigrants.* Sebald is always conscious that these subjects are outsiders, people on the margins of society. As such, they have a unique perspective worthy of exploration. The perspective of the schizophrenic poet Ernst Herbeck, for instance, has a remarkable freshness, something like that of the foundling, Kaspar Hauser. Ernst Herbeck's poetry warranted inclusion not only in an episode of the novel *Vertigo,* but in an article in *Die Beschreibung des Unglücks* as well. In his article on Herbeck, Sebald also addresses the impotence of conventional literary criticism to deal with the vivid immediacy of the author's imagination—Herbeck's poetry arises from the odd collaboration of imaginative power and the symptoms of linguistic disintegration. Admittedly, Herbeck's condition does not allow for the extended concentration necessary for sustained literary work, but his periods of reduced psychotic stimulation can produce, as Sebald demonstrates, startlingly original and empathetic combinations in diction. A schizophrenic is impeded not in his poetic imagination or ability, but primarily in his social and discursive skills. The compulsion to write is even more unrestrained in the schizophrenic than among most writers, because for someone like Herbeck the finished product is of no concern at all. He writes purely in response to experiences and events, not with a finished product (a book or a poem intended for a readership) in mind.

A different, initially less severe, case is that of Robert Walser (1876–1936), as described in Sebald's volume of essays on Swiss and Alemannic authors, *Logis in einem Landhaus.* As the English critic Michael Butler has observed, not just Walser, but all of the writers discussed in this book, including Johann Peter Hebel, Gottfried Keller, Eduard Mörike, and Jean-Jacques Rousseau, are in a state of exile—sometimes literally, but always in spirit. They live their "imaginative lives at a tangent to social reality."[5] It goes without saying that Sebald shares something of this experience of exile himself, of being an outsider even when at home, and that the "spiritual affinities" that draw him to these writers suggest "the sources of his own inspiration as a creator of fiction."[6] The essay on Robert Walser (the briefest among all the essays) is in some ways the most interesting, not nearly so much for the extreme nature of Walser's condition and his inexorable decline as for its insight into Sebald the writer. It leaves "the professional Germanist firmly in the background."[7] Sebald's interpretation definitely stresses Walser's eccentricity and isolation; but Sebald sees in his record of mental deterioration a heroic attempt at resisting the disease that had him so firmly in its grasp. Walser's struggle against depression stands in the foreground, and overshadows the eventual victory of melancholia or the final triumph of death. The aesthetic response that comes out of Walser's struggle to defeat his disease is the compulsion to create for the sake of creating. The end product is not nearly as important as the process of creating. And Walser continued to create almost to the end. Even the seeming impotence of the asylum inmate, able to cope with his condition only to the extent that he composed "micrograms" from everyday life, takes on larger meaning. "Against the approaching barbarism of fascist grandiosity," Butler concludes, "Walser's concentration on the miniature, the unconsidered trifles of everyday life, represents a deeply humanist gesture."[8] When Sebald demonstrates, through photographs, the physical similarity between Walser and his own grandfather, this humanism assumes a deeply personal relevance.

The solitary world of the literary artist seems especially prone to collapse, and German literature has a strong tradition—though perhaps no stronger than any other literature—of sensitive literary artists who suffered mental illness and nervous breakdowns. Perhaps the most famous—besides Nietzsche, whose insanity was induced by syphilis—was the aforementioned Friedrich Hölderlin, ✓ a sophisticated, accomplished poet who went insane and lived the last decades of his life largely confined to a tower in Tübingen. Another well-known German writer who went insane, mentioned previously in connection with *The Rings of Saturn*, was J. M. R. Lenz (1751–1792). A fictionalized account of Lenz's descent into madness by Georg Büchner is an early example of German literature on psychosis. Lenz becomes deranged and is put under the care of a Swiss pastor who makes a determined effort to help until he realizes he can do no more; in the end, Lenz must be sent home to his relatives. Büchner's well-known novella appeared posthumously in 1839, bearing the simple title *Lenz,* a word that also means "springtime" in German. But there is nothing of springtime in the book—not even a figurative springtime—and Büchner's masterful nature descriptions exist in stark contrast to the chaos of the protagonist's emotions and thoughts. Büchner's approach to the subject is almost clinical (he had studied medicine at Giessen and Strassburg), anticipating the kind of writing that emerged as naturalism in the late nineteenth century. Büchner suppresses nothing for the sake of the reader's comfort, and the result is dark but fascinating study of mental illness, resembling in its realistic technique and bizarre subject a story by another writer in Sebald's repertoire, Alfred Döblin. In "Die Ermordung einer Butterblume" (The murder of the buttercup, 1913), Döblin describes, with remarkable clarity and ingenious use of detail, the delusions of a senile old man taking a walk in a park. The character believes himself threatened by a harmless flower, defends himself with his walking cane, and is consumed by guilt when the "bloodied" flower dies. Whereas the delusions are unrelenting in Döblin's story, *Lenz* ends with a certain relief, as the subdued title character sits in the coach, restrained, waiting for his journey home to begin. As with many of Sebald's narrators and characters, Büchner's character Lenz finds himself swallowed up by a profound emptiness.

Beauty and Transience

The title of Sebald's book *Logis in einem Landhaus* stems from the first line of Robert Walser's story "Kleist in Thun," in which he describes Heinrich von

Kleist's sojourn at the town of the same name in Switzerland. In Walser's story, Kleist experiences the same rare feeling of tranquility that Sebald describes for Rousseau in the second chapter of *Logis;* in both instances, these writers find solace by a Swiss lake. Throughout Sebald's works alpine lakes provide lyrically beautiful backdrops for various meditations and confessions of longing. These lakeside sojourns are also occasions for some of his most admired descriptive passages. But beauty and tranquility exist in contradistinction to their opposites, as Sebald's prose continually demonstrates. In the case of Rousseau on the Isle of St. Peter on Lake Biel, Sebald contrasts the thoughtlessness and crude indifference of modern tourism with the probing discrimination of eighteenth-century sensibility, while also commenting critically on the meaning of such landscapes for Rousseau's works, and, by implication, for his own. They are brilliantly clear landscapes like that at the beginning of Rousseau's novel of education *Julie ou la nouvelle Héloise* (1761). Sebald describes such scenes as "somehow supernatural, in which one forgets everything, even oneself, and soon one doesn't even know where one is."[9] The brilliance and purity of lakes surrounded by mountains are for Sebald the supreme expression of natural beauty, so overwhelmingly powerful in effect on the perceiver that individual existence dissolves into thin air. This oblivion of the self through the aesthetic or "metaphysical" experience of nature is described in Sebald's essay on the Austrian writer Gerhard Roth:

> The metaphysical experience of a view from the heights originates in a profound fascination, in which our relationship to the world is reversed. In looking we sense that we are being looked at, and that we are not here to comprehend the universe, but rather to be comprehended by the universe.[10]

In a similar vein, the faces in Sebald's photographs often seem to be probing the beholder, rather than vice-versa, especially when the eyes in the pictures meet those of the reader. There is a verbal description of the power of the visual in the final paragraph of *The Emigrants*—Sebald describes being addled by the unrelenting gaze of three Jewish women in a photograph form the Lodz ghetto. This reversal of the roles of the perceiving and the perceived represents Sebald's response to the ideas of Maurice Merleau-Ponty and others.[11] Sebald expresses the idea more emphatically in *Austerlitz,* in a scene in Prague when Vera insists photographs have memories of their own and that she can hear their "sighs of despair." (182) In fact, Sebald's choice of pictures is part of his method of composition, influencing the progress of the narrative. He studies images at length and writes "towards" them as well as "away from" them.[12]

Sebald never lingers long over scenes of sublime beauty, however. It is the very briefness of the experience that endows the beholder with the sense of the eternal, as Austerlitz observes upon recalling fleeting afternoon shadows at Andromeda Lodge (95). Often Sebald turns away abruptly from the lyric experience of nature to the uglier side of reality, which usually entails the human inhabitation (and often violation) of the natural environment. To linger too long, or to make the description of beauty the primary purpose of writing, is to risk creating a literature of almost "hermetic" stasis.[13] In any case, verbal landscape painting, like the romanticized landscapes of nineteenth-century painters and engravers, has its origins in a certain disingenuousness, first emerging in a period of feverish industrialization and disregard for the environment:

> The poeticization of nature expresses a view of the landscape that suggests that nature can be painlessly accommodated to the civilization that subdues it. What remains problematic is that nature is only "beautiful" from the standpoint of civilized man. Descriptions of nature first appear and develop as the world is opened to commercialization.[14]

This is another of the paradoxes that Sebald will not let his audience shake off. While admiration and respect for nature have doubtless been common emotions since the dawn of human consciousness, the verbal expression of natural beauty as we know it is a product of European civilization's disengagement from nature. It is also the product of a futile wish, as Sebald has commented in regard to Adalbert Stifter's prose: the wish to depict a world of "eternalized beauty."[15]

In another article on Stifter, we find several insights pertinent to Sebald's art, including an analysis of the relation of transience and photography. Sebald contrasts verbal description with photography, noting that the former fosters mindfulness, whereas the latter encourages forgetting—a perfect explanation for Sebald's use of a description of a photograph at the end of *The Emigrants* rather than the photograph itself. He continues:

> Photographs are the mementos of a world that is in the grips of a process of destruction, a world that is disappearing, whereas painted or verbally described scenes have a life ahead of them in the future; they document a consciousness that is concerned with the continuance of life.[16]

Thus we are reminded once again that at the core of Sebald's aesthetics is the knowledge that the passing of time will ultimately erase everything.

History and Truth

Admittedly, for many writers the compulsion to write exists irrespective of any concern for history's ineluctable process of erasure. They are compelled to leave behind some form of record of their life, regardless of whether it can be expected to last and for how long. At the heart of the human desire to memorialize and to elegize is the recognition of the dissolution of personal existence, the extinction of individuals in death. This need to commemorate in the face of mortality is another of the topics in Sebald's seminal chapter on Rousseau in *Logis*. Some of the memorials Sebald displays and discusses in this essay are monuments once visited by Rousseau himself. The most poignant are the more modest ones, such as the carved initials of visitors to the rustic island house where Rousseau lived for a few happy months in 1765. "Running one's finger along the notches in the wood," Sebald writes, "one would like to know who they were and where they went from here."[17] Addressing the theme of commemoration in Rousseau's own life, Sebald produces at the end of the essay one of those startling historical connections for which he is known—Rousseau's funeral procession through Paris is led by none other than a captain of the United States Navy, carrying high the Stars and Stripes. Such details, the result of Sebald's documentary sleuthing, point to the origin and function of writing for a novelist like Sebald, whose interests are antiquarian and philological. And truly effective commemoration is made possible by filling in the gaps with newly unearthed historical evidence. "The point of origin of Sebald's oeuvre and the fixed centre around which it circles," writes the British scholar Arthur Williams, "is his awareness of the gaps in his knowledge and his need to find an appropriate form for the literary processing of them."[18] The genuineness of Sebald's search for historical answers, coupled with the often startling strangeness of the clues he discovers, gives the reader the sense that his prose is constantly breaking new ground, and accounts for the novelty of each succeeding book. And there are always more gaps to fill in; for the title character of *Austerlitz*, for instance, individual identity itself is the gap, forming an aching hollowness at the heart of the novel. To fill in the gap is also to teach, and Sebald, as a committed teacher, has simply found another outlet for his pedagogy. As Williams insists, learning and literature are for Sebald part of the same continuum.[19] This pedagogical aspect is a feature Sebald values in much Austrian literature, which for him possesses a clearer sense than the German that, "There is something worth passing on."[20] And the content of what is passed on is of the utmost importance—here the ethical dimension of Sebald's aesthetics becomes obvious, because it matters whether one "gets history right," and it matters both for the individual and for the collective. Despite the many literary allusions and the critical preoccupations traceable to his vocational and avocational study of European literature, Sebald's concept of literature is not "merely" aesthetic, but intimately concerned with questions of morality. Sebald's art is not art for its own sake. For him, literature must confront life honestly in order to maintain its integrity before society. This is the premise that led Sebald to criticize postwar German literature for failing to come to terms with the massive aerial bombardments that leveled most German and many Austrian cities during the Second World War. With the Zurich lectures that formed the basis for the book *Luftkrieg und Literatur,* Sebald caused considerable consternation among scholars and critics for his claim that postwar literature had refused, on the whole, to examine the apocalyptic destruction of German cities. It had failed to make succeeding generations understand the horror. It had not done justice to a subject of vital concern, and had mostly ignored a collective trauma. Sebald acknowledges only a handful of authors—Hans Erich Nossack, Heinrich Böll, and Alexander Kluge among them—as having confronted the bitter reality of the ruined cities and the human cost of the bombing. Negative response to Sebald consisted chiefly in naming authors and books Sebald had allegedly left out in order to prove his thesis. However, as Sebald himself points out in the text, the exceptions do not disprove the rule—the rarity of literary depictions of the bombings and their aftermath is the point of his argument, after all. Sebald also notes that it is a "quasi-natural reflex" to turn away and refuse to look, especially when one has brought the disaster on oneself. Such a response is based in "feelings of shame and defiance towards the victors" (40).

But what form would a literature of bombardment actually take? Writers whose intention is to create "aesthetic or pseudo-aesthetic effects from the ruins of a destroyed world" abrogate responsibility to both those who witnessed the events as well as their descendants (64). "The ideal of truthfulness requires an unaffected matter-of-factness as the only legitimate basis for continued literary work," Sebald concludes (64). Elsewhere in the book he calls for a "natural history of destruction," borrowing a term first used by the editor of *Horizon* magazine, Cyril Connolly, in 1946 (41). Sebald's own descriptions of the aftermath of air raids in *Luftkrieg und Literatur* are drawn to a large extent from reports by foreign observers—more proof that Sebald's thesis is accurate. One recalls the gardener at Somerlyton Hall in *The Rings of Saturn.* He watched wave after wave of bomber squadrons departing for Germany day after day in 1944 and 1945, but when he later learned German and went there he could find nothing to read on the subject. The postwar silence about what had happened is one of the reasons Sebald's generation, while coming of age in the 1960s, began to ask questions. There were also major trials of Holocaust perpetrators in Germany and Israel during the period. Not everyone in Germany had been silent, of course; some Germans took the position that they had disapproved of the Nazi regime all along. But postwar writers who offered the explanation that they had emigrated in spirit if not in body (*innere Emigration*) gave themselves away, according to Sebald in *Luftkrieg und Literatur,* by using a stilted vocabulary that is virtually identical with the code of fascist ideology (61). This brings us to the literary equivalent of the Hippocratic exhortation to "do no harm"—it is anathema to Sebald to revise historical events in literature to suit one's own ends. Not a few collaborators went to great lengths to rescript their pasts. Sebald has been criticized for "tacking on" an essay on the writer Alfred Andersch at the end of *Luftkrieg und Literatur,* but the Andersch essay is in fact thematically of a piece with the body of the book. Andersch, who participated in the war as a soldier, was a man who was blatantly dishonest in his life and literary career, especially—and most pointedly—during the postwar years, when he claimed to have been an opponent of the Nazi regime. He wrote to the Allied authorities, for instance, that his wife was Jewish, when in reality he had divorced her in order to advance his career, distancing himself from her and their daughter in February of 1942. Sebald demonstrates Andersch's galling mendacity by means of irrefutable documentation, but also notes autobiographical omissions and not-so-subtle falsehoods in Andersch's fiction. Andersch is for Sebald a parade example of the artist as charlatan. Andersch practiced his craft as an opportunist with no regard for the truth.

A further reason for focusing on, rather than turning away from, catastrophes like the destruction of Germany is the aesthetic principle operative throughout *The Rings of Saturn*—Walter Benjamin's insistence that history is a record of grinding destruction, that it is comprised of one calamity after another.[21] Though the idea seems at first glance a far too negative, pessimistic principle to foster creativity, its aesthetic manifestation offers a cathartic sense of resolution not unlike the effects of a ghost story or a horror film. The first mature expression of this "aesthetics of destruction" à la Benjamin is found in Sebald's 1980 study on Alfred Döblin. In it Sebald explores the author's preoccupation with the ultimate calamity: the Apocalypse. In this study the writer emerges as a literary prophet of destruction, helping the future to take shape, even if it is a disastrous future. Paradoxically, the fictional knowledge the writer expresses in the form of a disastrous teleology can provide redemption and release. By facing the truth of inevitable destructive power, one in effect transcends the dread associated with it. In this respect, Benjamin's is a new historical vision, which Sebald uses to describe the role of a highly experimental writer such as Döblin. He is the observer who has seen the terrible future—more terrible, even, than the terrible past—and lived to tell about it. For Sebald, Döblin's apocalyptic scenes represent "an exact illustration of the new concept of history, which is not based on the idea of progress, as the old, bourgeois concept was, but on the notion of self-perpetuating catastrophe."[22] To face that catastrophe is not to concede defeat, however. When viewed from the individual standpoint, the teleology of destruction is personal as well; every life is an apocalypse. The aesthetic response to mortality, however, is to write *in spite of* the power of destruction—to salvage and preserve in spite of the steady lapsing of all lives into oblivion. As the novel *Austerlitz* makes abundantly clear by means of—ironically—its painstaking effort at reconstruction and recollection, the history of most families, individuals, and things will never be told. Nonetheless, the fatalism one would expect from a proponent of such ideas about the inevitability of destruction does not, however, follow from Sebald's thought. Sebald never permits the world of his books to be as simple as reason would have it, and insists on calling into question the very scientific categories that underlie the entropy of his lapsing world. In *The Emigrants* and *Austerlitz,* especially, the dead return, one way or another—as a pile of bones beside a melting glacier or as the reproducible image on an obscure newsreel. The character Austerlitz even asserts that the realm of the dead intersects with ours, and is part of the same structure of "stereometrically interlocking spatial dimensions" (185). Like the fictional worlds in the Borges stories "Tlön, Uqbar, Orbis Tertium" and "The Library of Babel," Sebald's monistic universe contains everything simultaneously—the past, the future, the here-and-now. It is a dream universe, where anything can happen, where the past waits to occur again.

Aesthetic Continuity

The most comprehensive study of Sebald's aesthetics to date is Arthur Williams's "W. G. Sebald: A Holistic Approach to Borders, Texts, and Perspectives," which appeared in 2000. What Williams calls "holism" I have called "monism," preferring Borges's term, but in either case the emphasis in both concepts is on unity, continuity, and interconnectedness.[23] Sebald's writing is a consciously combinatory exercise, linking authors and texts of various languages as well as disparate media—prose, music, drama, film, photography—with a unifying vision of "historical metaphysics" in which destruction is a constant and time is non-linear. Moreover, the notion that everything fits into a continuum can be applied to the whole of the Sebaldian oeuvre, according to Williams, who sees in Sebald's work an uninterrupted continuity stretching from the first volume of poetry, through the three novels published prior to 2000, to the final essay of *Logis in einem Landhaus.* Sebald's "itinerary" begins with an exploration of a German artist and his art (Matthias Grünewald and his *Lindenhardt Altarpiece* in *Nach der Natur*) and "reaches its interim conclusion" with the essay on Jan Peter Tripp, a German painter and childhood friend born in the most recent period of major upheaval in Central Europe.[24] Sebald's novels, according to

149

Williams, begin with "a curiously encrypted literary and cultural past" (*Vertigo*), explore the effects of the persistent irrationality of European anti-semitism (*The Emigrants*), then move on to the history of European colonialism with its suppressed record of exploitation and extermination (*The Rings of Saturn*).[25] It is in a work of non-fiction, however, *Luftkrieg und Literatur,* that he first addresses the absence in his own life of "an adequate representation of the sufferings of the German civilian population in the Second World War."[26] But as Williams acknowledges, the context in which Sebald investigates German suffering—as well as German atrocities—is always a broadly European context. This fact is demonstrated once more, we might add, by the novel *Austerlitz,* in which the protagonist traverses the continent, from Prague to London. The character flaws in German politics, civilization, and culture that nurtured the missionary aggression and the absolutist racism of the Third Reich exist for Sebald in a wider context of European imperfections and wickedness. This is not to relativize German history but to give the many dastardly acts of European history their due; at the same time Sebald's approach opens up new perspectives for the future:

> He achieves this as a result of a combination of his physical distance from Germany, his journey through time and also, crucially, his engagement with aesthetic theories of the post-modern, which are essentially theories about perception and identity, both of which have implications for our reading of history and historiography.[27]

The theoretical aspect of Sebald's historical approach never displaces or overshadows the human experience of history, however. In Sebald's world, all history is personal, concrete, and, in the greater scheme of things, nothing if not disastrous.

Because Sebald's world is one of unity—where all things seem to be interconnected, where everything seems contingent and nothing merely coincidental—borders are constantly being crossed, perspectives reversed or merged, and time is repeatedly folded in upon itself. His prose celebrates borderlessness, but at the same time laments the uprootedness of lives in exile. The tentative, "guest status" of the resident alien is one Sebald knows personally, of course, and it is that experience that has elicited his interest in and sympathy for the various exiles and other marginalized victims described in his books. There is a strong first-person presence in his narratives at the same time as the distinction between subject and object is deemphasized. Sebald's concept of literature is in this sense eminently personal—the concerns expressed are real and his own, and even when quoting from others, Sebald expresses sentiments that seem keenly felt.

The personal nature of Sebald's writing is seen not only in his exchange with the living, but in his dynamic engagement with the dead. The intimate relationship he formed with the historical subjects he studied over the years is reflected in the familiar, yet distanced, objectifying voice of the narrator. It is the voice of a respectful, studious, contemplative person, the voice of an avid collector. Sebald's narrator is himself a character, but more importantly, he is a third party—a facilitator for the storytelling of others. Sebald explains the origins of his narrator's voice:

> I've always felt that the traditional novel doesn't give you enough infor- ✓
> mation about the narrator, and I think it's important to know the point of
> view from which these tales are told, the moral makeup of the teller. That's
> why my narrator has such a presence. I intimate that the narrator doesn't
> know more about the lives of other characters than they've told him. So
> you have [a] periscopic point of view through the layers of hearsay.[28]

Sebald has used the term periscopic before, in referring to the narrative perspective of Bernhard, and it is this perspective that is particularly marked in the case of *The Emigrants* and *Austerlitz,* and, to a lesser extent, *Vertigo* and *The Rings of Saturn.* (In the latter novels the narrator intrudes more often, and we experience with him his own moments of depression and destabilization.) It is important in this regard to observe that Sebald's narrative perspective evolved not only in the context of a career devoted to literature, but in the context of personal circumstances of middle age. In contemplating Sebald's late entry onto the literary scene, the originality of his style, and the paradoxical combination of strangeness and familiarity of his subjects, one is drawn once again to a comparison with the autobiography of Gregor von Rezzori. In an incident in "Löwinger's Rooming House" the narrator, having speculated at some length on the lives and personalities of a deceased couple on the basis of nothing more than the contents—clothing, jewelry, photographs—of their rather meager estate, is told by the fellow tenant Olschansky that he should put his narrative talents to work as a writer. "Jesus Christ! . . . That's it!" he cries, "I told you you should write, and you stupidly asked me what. This is it. Exactly as you just told it, word for word!"[29]

It was not until he was in his middle forties that Sebald realized he could write his own brand of literature, drawing from the reading, archival researches, and travels in which he was already engaged. The result was four remarkable novels, beginning with the publication of *Vertigo* in German in 1990 and ending with Sebald's tragic death shortly after *Austerlitz* appeared in English in 2001.

Notes

Introduction

1. This description of the circumstances of Sebald's childhood and youth, and those that follow are taken from an interview conducted by Claire Devarrieux, and published online in her review of Patrick Charbonneau's translation of *The Emigrants* into French, "Sebald, objectif hier. L'Europe de l'Allemand W. G. Sebald n'est pas celle de l'euro, mais de la ruine. Traduction des 'Emigrants,' quatre histoires d'exil passées au révélateur et submergées par le souvenir," available online at http://www.liberation.fr/livres/99janvier/0107sebald.html. Specific biographical information (dates, etc.) can be found in Markus Weber's entry on Sebald in the *Kritisches Lexikon zur deutschsprachigen Gegenwartsliteratur,* vol. 9. This lexicon of contemporary German-speaking authors is published in a binder format, which allows for individual articles, which are arranged alphabetically, to be updated occasionally, as deemed necessary by the editors. The article on Sebald was last updated on 1 April 2000 for the 65th edition of the *KLG*. I am indebted to Professor Sebald for furnishing the names of his parents and his two grandfathers.

2. *Nach der Natur: Ein Elementargedicht* (Frankfurt am Main: Eichborn, 1989). The source of the title is found in the first of the three sections of poems: "nach der Natur gemalt," i.e., "painted from nature." Michael Hamburger's translation *After Nature* was published in 2002 by Hamish Hamilton.

3. Thus argues a prominent Sebald scholar, Markus R. Weber. See his article "Phantomschmerz Heimweh: Denkfiguren der Erinnerung im literarischen Werk W. G. Sebalds," in *Neue Generation—Neues Erzählen: Deutsche Prosa-Literatur der achtziger Jahre* (Opladen: Westdeutscher Verlag, 1993), ed. Walter Delabar, Werner Jung, and Ingrid Pergande, 57–68. Weber also mentions several more compelling depictions of the Bering expedition that were published in the 1980s in Germany, overshadowing Sebald's.

4. Ransmayr was an early proponent of Sebald's poetry, and Enzensberger published Sebald's first novel in his series *Andere Literatur* (Other, i.e. different, literature). See Sven Boedecker's interview, "Mit der Schnauze am Boden," in the *Berliner Zeitung* of 13 Jan. 1996, available online at http://www.berlinonline.de/wissen/berliner-zeitung/archiv/1996/0113/kultur/0009/index.html

5. Ulrich Baron, "Dem Mäusevolk gilt heute meine Hoffnung," *Rheinischer Merkur,* 15 Jan. 1993: 20.

6. Irving Malin, "W. G. Sebald. *The Emigrants,*" *Review of Contemporary Fiction* (spring 1997): 173.

7. Cynthia Ozick, "The Posthumous Sublime," *New Republic,* 16 Dec. 1996: 33–38.

8. Susan Sontag, "A Mind in Mourning: W. G. Sebald's Travels in Search of Some Remnant of the Past," *Times Literary Supplement,* 25 Feb. 2000: 3.

9. James Wood, "The Right Thread," *New Republic,* 6 July 1998: 38.

10. A number of interviews have been published, so Sebald's autobiographical comments are generally accessible, but I have relied for these details of his life, work, and personality on an interview by James Atlas, "W. G. Sebald: A Profile," *Paris Review* 41 (1999): 278–95.

11. Anthony Lane, "Higher Ground: Adventures in Fact and Fiction from W. G. Sebald," *New Yorker,* 29 May 2000: 130.

12. The original German reads: "Die bewundernswerte innere Sicherheit Hebels kommt allerdings weniger aus dem, was er weiß von der Natur der Dinge, als aus der Anschauung dessen, was über den Verstand geht" W. G. Sebald, *Logis in einem Landhaus: Über Gottfried Keller, Johann Peter Hebel, Robert Walser und andere* (Frankfurt: Fisher, 2000), 17. *Logis in einem Landhaus* was first published by Hanser in 1998.

13. Atlas, "Profile," 295.

14. Joyce Hackett, "*The Rings of Saturn* by W. G. Sebald," "Salon Magazine," 30 Dec. 1998, available online at http://www.com/books/reviews/981230/rings.saturn/salon/

15. Or, as Tess Lewis puts it, "He has effecticely created a new genre by combining travelogue, biography, memoir, speculation, literary criticism, and erudite detail into an elaborate structure founded on the restless sensibility of a melancholic aesthete." See "W. G. Sebald: The Past is Another Country," *New Criterion,* Dec. 2001: 86.

16. This "unpromising name" comes from Wyatt Mason, "Mapping a Life: A Review of W. G. Sebald," *The American Book Review,* May/June 1999: 20.

17. See "Surveying the Scene—Some Introductory Remarks" in W. G. Sebald, ed. *A Radical State. Theatre in Germany in the 1970s and 1980s* (Oxford: Berg, 1987), 1.

18. James Wood, "W. G. Sebald's Uncertainty," in *The Broken Estate. Essays on Literature and Belief* (New York: Random House, 1999), 232.

Chapter 1: Blending Fact, Fiction, Allusion, and Recall

1. *The Emigrants,* trans. Michael Hulse (New York: New Directions Books, 1996), 225. The original German reads: "[Ich] spürte . . . die rings um mich umgebende Geistesverarmung und Erinnerungslosigkeit der Deutschen, das Geschick, mit dem man alles bereinigt hatte" *Die Ausgewanderten* (Frankfurt: Fischer, 1998), 338. Original quotations of any length will be given in endnotes throughout, whereas short passages will include only the page numbers for the English-language edition. Self-explanatory and/or single-word quotations will not include either page numbers or endnotes.

2. James Wood, "An Interview with W. G. Sebald," *Brick* 59 (spring 1998): 27.

3. The phrase "zugewinkt . . . von der anderen Seite" appears in Sebald's essay on the writer Robert Walser. See *Logis in einem Landhaus,* 139.

4. Wood, "An Interview," 27.

5. Thomas Bernhard, *Verstörung* (Frankfurt am Main: Suhrkamp, 1970), 16. Richard and Clara Winston translate the line as "everything is *fundamentally sick and sad,*" see Thomas Bernhard, *Gargoyles* (Chicago: University of Chicago Press, 1970), 11.

6. Wood, "The Right Thread," 42.

7. See Eva Juhl's remarks in "Die Wahrheit über das Unglück. Zu W. G. Sebald *Die Ausgewanderten,*" in *Reisen im Diskurs. Modelle der literarischen Fremderfahrung von den Pilgerberichten bis zur Postmoderne. Tagungsakten des internationalen Symposiums zur Reiseliteratur University College Dublin vom 10.–12. März 1994,* ed. Anne Fuchs and Theo Harden (Heidelberg: Carl Winter, 1995), 642.

8. Sigmund Freud, "The Uncanny," in *The Standard Edition of the Complete Psychological Works of Sigmund Freud,* vol. 17, ed. James Strachey (London: The Hogarth Press, 1955), 220.

9. Ibid., 221.

10. Ibid., 237–38.

11. *Die Beschreibung des Unglücks. Zur österreichischen Literatur von Stifter bis Handke* (Frankfurt am Main: Fischer, 1994), 132. Here Sebald quotes from Benjamin's essay on surrealism, "Angelus Novum," in *Walter Benjamin: Gesammelte Schriften,* vol. 2, ed. Rolf Tiedemann and Hermann Scheppenhäuser (Frankfurt: Suhrkamp, 1980), 307: "Es bringt uns nämlich nicht weiter, wenn wir die rätselhafte Seite am Rätselhaften pathetisch oder fanatisch unterstreichen; vielmehr durchdringen wir das Geheimnis nur in dem Grade, als wir es im Alltäglichen wiederfinden."

12. Benjamin Kunkel, "Germanic Depressive," *Village Voice,* 6 June 2000: 125.

13. Ibid.

14. Sontag, "A Mind in Mourning," 3.

15. Wood, "An Interview," 25.

16. Roland Barthes, *Camera Lucida. Reflections on Photography,* trans. Richard Howard (New York: Noonday Press, 1981), 83.

17. *Austerlitz,* trans. Anthea Bell (New York: Random House, 2001), 262. "Man habe den Eindruck, sagte sie, es rühre sich etwas in ihnen, als vernehme man kleine Verzweiflungsseufzer, gémissements de désespoir, so sagte sie, sagte Austerlitz, als hätten die Bilder selbst ein Gedächtnis und erinnerten sich an uns, daran, wie wir, die Überlebenden, und diejenigen, die nicht mehr unter uns weilen, vordem gewesen sind" *Austerlitz* (Munich and Vienna: Hanser, 2001), 262.

18. John Tagg, "The Violence of Meaning," *Crossings* 3 (1999): 189.

19. See *Schwindel. Gefühle* (Frankfurt, Fischer, 1994), 22–23. One might also note the similarity with the title of Thomas Bernhard's 1983 novel *Der Untergeher* (Going under). *Schwindel. Gefühle* was first published by Eichborn in 1990.

20. Ernestine Schlant, *The Language of Silence. West German Literature and the Holocaust* (New York and London: Routledge, 1999) 225.

21. *Vertigo,* trans. Michael Hulse (New York: New Directions Books, 2000), 95. "Ich [sagte], daß ich . . . in zunehmendem Maße das Gefühl habe, es handle sich um einen Kriminalroman" *Schwindel. Gefühle,* 113.

✓ 22. Sebald himself always insisted that his medium was "prose, not the novel." See Sigrid Löffler's interview "Wildes Denken" (Thinking wildly) as cited in *W. G. Sebald,* ed. Franz Loquai (Eggingen: Isele, 1997), 135–37.

23. Schlant, *Language of Silence,* 225.

24. Hackett, *"Rings,"* ibid.

25. *The Emigrants,* 41–42. "Aber nicht nur die Musik löste in Paul solche Anwandlungen aus; vielmehr konnte es jederzeit, mitten im Unterricht, während der Pause oder wenn wir unterwegs waren, geschehen, daß er abwesend und abseits irgendwo saß oder stehenblieb, als wäre er, der immer gut gelaunt und frohsinnig zu sein schien, in Wahrheit die Untröstlichkeit selbst" *Die Ausgewanderten* (Frankfurt: Fischer, 1994), 62. *Die Ausgewanderten* was first published by Eichborn in 1992.

26. A phrase from Virgil's *Aeneid,* meaning literally "there are tears for things," quoted in Stendhal's autobiography, *The Life of Henry Brulard,* trans. John Sturrock (New York: Penguin Books, 1995), 155.

27. *The Rings of Saturn,* trans. Michael Hulse (New York: New Directions Books, 1996), 36. "Jedesmal, bevor sie kehrtmachte, . . . schüttelte [die Wachtel] den Kopf . . . als begreife sie nicht, wie sie in diese aussichtslose Lage geraten sei" *Die Ringe des Saturn: Eine englische Wallfahrt* (Frankfurt: Fischer, 1997), 50. *Die Ringe des Saturn* was first published by Eichborn in 1995.

28. Sebald responds to Alexander and Margarete Mitscherlich's now famous assertion that West German society has been "incapable of grieving" since the Second World War in "Konstruktion der Trauer. Zu Günter Grass 'Tagebuch einer Schnecke' und Wolfgang Hildesheimer, 'Tynset,'" *Der Deutschunterricht* 35 (1983): 32–47.

29. *Vertigo,* 187. "In fast jeder Wochenschau sah man auch die Ruinenhaufen von Städten wie Berlin oder Hamburg, die ich . . . für eine sozusagen natürliche Gegebenheit aller größeren Städte gehalten habe" *Schwindel. Gefühle,* 213.

30. Ibid., 66–67. "Als eine Art feste Insel ragte [das Stehbuffet] heraus aus der wie ein Ährenfeld im Wind schwankenden Menge der Menschen, die teils zu den Eingängen herein-, teils aus ihnen hinaus-, teils um das Buffet herum- und teils um das zu den ein Stück weit entfernt auf erhobenem Posten sitzenden Kassiererinnen hinüberwogte" Ibid., 80.

31. Ibid., 67. "Diese kaum sich rührende Kellnerschaft [glich] nicht anders als die ihr verwandten Schwestern, Mütter und Töchter hinter den Registrierkassen einer eigenartigen Versammlung höherer Wesen, die hier nach einem dunklen System über ein von endemischer Gier korrumpiertes Geschlecht Gerichtstag hielten" Ibid., 81.

32. On the subject of the travel genre in German literature, see Peter J. Brenner, *Der Reisebericht in der deutschen Literatur. Ein Forschungsüberblick als Vorstudie zu einer Gattungsgeschichte* (Tübingen: Niemeyer, 1990). For recent examples of travel literature in German, see Gerhard Sauder, "Formen gegenwärtiger Reiseliteratur," in Fuchs and Harden, *Reisen im Diskurs,* 552–73.

33. Joseph Roth, *The Radetzky March,* trans. Joachim Neugroschel (Woodstock, N.Y.: Overlook Press, 1995), 61.

34. Fin Keegan's online review of *The Rings of Saturn,* revised to account for Sebald's death, is available online at http://www.thesecondcircle.com/fjk/seba.html.

35. Pico Iyer, "The Strange, Haunted World of W. G. Sebald," *Harper's Magazine,* (October 2000): 87.

36. David Auerbach, "W. G. Sebald: History as Memoir," *Rain Taxi* 5 (summer 2000): 23.

37. *Vertigo,* 176. "Ich verwunderte mich über die Geröllhalden, die von den Bergen herunter in die Wälder hineingriffen so wie Finger ins Haar, und es erstaunte mich wieder die schleierhafte Zeitlupenhaftigkeit der, wenigstens solange ich denken konnte, unverändert über die Felswände herabstürzenden Bäche. An einer Wegkehre sah ich aus dem sich drehenden Autobus in die Tiefe hinunter und erblickte die dunkeltürkisgrünen Flächen des Fernstein-Sees und des Samaranger Sees, die mir schon in der Kindheit, als wir . . . den ersten Ausflug ins Tirol machten, wie der Inbegriff aller nur erdenklichen Schönheit vorgekommen waren" *Schwindel. Gefühle,* 200–201.

38. The phrase comes from Martin Chalmers's review of *The Emigrants,* "Angels of History," *New Statesman,* 12 July 1996: 45. Anthony Lane used the title "Higher Ground: Adventures in Fact and Fiction from W. G. Sebald" for his review of *Vertigo.*

39. *The Rings of Saturn,* 266. ". . . wo die Kronen der großen Bäume des benachbarten bischöflichen Parks gebogen und durchfurcht wurden wie Wasserpflanzen in einer dunklen Strömung" *Die Ringe des Saturn,* 316.

40. Both writers are discussed in Sebald's monograph on "unhappiness" in Austrian Literature, *Die Beschreibung des Unglücks.* Gabriele Annan mentions the affinity with Stifter in her review of *The Emigrants* titled "Ghosts," *New York Review of Books,* 25 Sept. 1997: 29.

41. Wood, "Thread," 40.

42. Ibid., "An Interview," 28.

43. The German critic Martin Lüdke was perhaps the first to suggest this line of succession, in his February 2001 review for "Rheinland-Pfalz Aktuell," a website of the broadcast network Südwest Fernsehen, available online at http://www.swrl.de/rp/aktuell/lesetipp/10201.html

44. Wood, "Thread," 40.

45. Ibid.

46. Tim Parks, "The Hunter," *New York Review of Books,* 15 June 2000: 52.

47. Hackett, *"Rings,"* ibid.

48. See Sebald's remarks on narrative in Wood, "An Interview," 28–29.

49. According to Sebald, a writer of fiction must "atone" for his or her exaggerations by being as meticulous as possible, particularly about objects, interiors, landscapes. See Wood, "An Interview," 28.

50. Randolph Stow, "The Plangency of Ruins," *Times Literary Supplement,* 31 July 1998: 11.

51. Blake Morrison, "Suffolk Through Death-tinted Specs," *New Statesman*, 5 June 1998: 45.

52. In fact, the ending of chapter 3 of *The Rings of Saturn* seems nearly to merge with the ending of "Tlön, Uqbar, Orbis Tertius." See Jorge Luis Borges, *Ficciones*, ed. Anthony Kerrigan (New York: Grove Press, 1962), 34–35.

53. Borges, *Ficciones*, 25.

54. Ibid.

55. Ibid., 26.

56. *Austerlitz*, 265. "Doch ist es mir immer mehr, als gäbe es keine Zeit, sondern nur verschiedene, nach einer höheren Stereometrie ineinander verschachtelte Räume, zwischen denen die Lebendigen und die Toten . . . hin und her gehen können" *Austerlitz*, 269.

57. Ibid., 100. "Wenn Newton gemeint hat, . . . die Zeit sei ein Strom wie die Themse; wo ist dann der Ursprung der Zeit und in welches Meer mündet sie endlich ein? Jeder Strom ist, wie wir wissen, notwendig zu beiden Seiten begrenzt. Was aber wären, so gesehen, die Ufer der Zeit?" Ibid., 146.

58. Ibid., 101. ". . . in der Hoffnung, . . . daß die Zeit nicht verginge, nicht vergangen sei, daß ich hinter sie zurücklaufen könne, daß dort alles so wäre wie vordem oder, genauer gesagt, daß sämtliche Zeitmomente gleichzeitig nebeneinaner existieren" Ibid., 148.

59. See Arthur Williams, "W. G. Sebald: A Holistic Approach to Borders, Texts and Perspectives" in *German-Language Literature Today: International and Popular?* ed. Arthur Williams et al. (Bern: Peter Lang, 2000), 106. Williams prefers the term "holism" to describe Sebald's unifying approach.

60. Anastomosis is the connecting of branches or lines in the form of a network, as in the veins of a leaf, or the blood vessels of the human body. The quotation comes from Nabokov's ironic review of his own memoir, published as the sixteenth chapter of *Speak, Memory* (New York and Toronto: Alfred A. Knopf, 1999), 247–62. The original version, published by Putnam in 1951, did not include the final chapter, nor did the 1966 revised version.

61. Lane, "Higher Ground," 133.

62. Ibid., 134.

63. This observation about the "indescribability" of Sebald's books is made, for instance, in Wood, "Thread," 42.

64. Margo Jefferson, "Writing in the Shadows," *New York Times Book Review*, 18 March 2001: 27.

65. Andre Aciman, "Out of Novemberland," *New York Review of Books*, 3 Dec. 1998: 47.

66. The influence of twentieth-century physics on art can be traced to Einstein, whose concept of relativity—or more precisely, a popular understanding of his concept of relativity—influenced literature and the visual arts from 1905 onward. For more on the scientific origins of the notion of the "indeterminacy of the text," see Christine Froula, "Quantum Physics/Post-modern Metaphysics: The Nature of Jacques Derrida," *Western Humanities Review* 39 (1985): 287–313.

67. For Hofmannsthal's best-known expression of the need for a "new language," see "The Letter of Lord Chandos," *Hugo von Hofmannsthal: Selected Prose*, trans. Mary Hottinger and Tania & James Stern (New York: Pantheon Books, 1952), 129–41.

68. Aciman, "Novemberland," 47.

69. Iyer, "Strange, Haunted World," 88.

70. Wood, "Thread," 39.

Chapter 2: *The Emigrants*

1. See Annan, "Ghosts," 29.

2. *The Emigrants*, 4. ". . . eine ganz und gar zwecklose, aus der Entfernung allerdings sehr eindrucksvolle Kulisse" *Die Ausgewanderten*, 9.

3. Ibid., 5. "Obzwar groß gewachsen und breit in den Schultern, wirkte er untersetzt, ja, man hätte sagen können, wie ein ganz kleiner Mensch" Ibid., 10

4. A good critical discussion of the film is Jonathan Romney's "The Man who Fell to Earth," *Sight and Sound* 10 (October 2000): 24–26.

5. *The Emigrants*, 18–19. "Die Kamera bewegt sich dann von rechts nach links in einem weiten Bogen und zeigt uns das Panorama einer von Bergzügen umgebenen, sehr indisch aussehenden Hochebene, auf der zwischen grünem Gebüsch und Waldungen pagodenartige Turm- oder Tempelbauten mit seltsamen dreieckigen Fassaden aufragen, Follies, die in dem pulsierend das Bild überblendenden Licht mich stets von neuem erinnern an die Segel der Windpumpen von Lasithi, die ich in Wirklichkeit noch gar nicht gesehen habe" *Die Ausgewanderten*, 29.

6. Lane, "Higher Ground," 126.

7. Romney, "The Man Who Fell to Earth," 24–25.

8. *The Emigrants*, 23. "So also kehren sie wieder, die Toten. Manchmal nach mehr als sieben Jahrzehnten kommen sie heraus aus dem Eis und liegen am Rand der Moräne, ein Häufchen geschliffener Knochen und ein Paar genagelte Schuhe" *Die Ausgewanderten*, 37.

9. Hebel (1760–1826) wrote unpretentious, gentle, often whimsical tales that Sebald admired (see his essay on Hebel in *Logis in einem Landhaus*.) Hebel's story "Kannitverstan" is mentioned in *The Rings of Saturn*.

10. *The Emigrants*, 28. "Wir in der Schule . . . hatten . . . ausschließlich vom Paul gesprochen, wenn auch nicht geringschätzig, sondern vielmehr wie von einem vorbildlichen älteren Bruder und so, als gehöre er zu uns und wir zu ihm" *Die Ausgewanderten*, 43.

11. Ibid., 25. "Manche Nebelflecken löset kein Auge auf" Ibid., 39.

12. Ibid., 45. ". . . die in der Ferne fast verschimmernden Glaciers de la Vanoise und das den halben Horizont einnehmende Alpenpanorama hätten ihr zum erstenmal in ihrem Leben ein Gefühl vermittelt für die widersprüchlichen Dimensionen unserer Sehnsucht" Ibid., 68.

13. Ibid., 61. ". . . das Sinn- und Abbild von Pauls deutschem Unglück" Ibid., 91.

14. Ibid, 88. "Es . . . war . . .als werde er bloß noch von seinen Kleidern zusammengehalten" Ibid., 129.

15. Sebald's phrase is "der Rand der Finsternis" Ibid., 88.

16. *The Emigrants,* 109. ". . . jene Zirbelhütten, wie sie die österreichischen Erzherzöge und Landesfürsten zu Ende des letzten Jahrhunderts überall in ihren steirischen und Tiroler Revieren . . . hatten errichten lassen" *Die Ausgewanderten,* 159.

17. Ibid., 110. "[Die] Preisgabe [des Hauses Samaria] war die Voraussetzung für meine Auslösung aus dem Leben" Ibid., 161.

18. Ibid., 112. "Dem Mäusevolk gilt heute meine Hoffnung" is the first expression (165), while final state of the sanatorium in Dr. Abramsky's dream is as "ein Häufchen puderfeines, blütenstaubähnliches Holzmehl" Ibid., 166.

19. Ibid., 130. "Niemand . . . würde eine solche Stadt vorstellen können. So viel verschiedenes Grün. Pinienkronen hoch in der Luft. Akazien, Korkeichen, Sykomoren, Eukalyptus, Wacholder, Lorbeer, wahre Baumparadies und Schattenhalden und Haine mit rauschenden Brunnen" Ibid., 192.

20. Ibid., 144. ". . . als befinde sie sich an dem eigens ihr gehörigen Platz" Ibid., 214.

21. The Aurach/Ferber character is also based on Sebald's landlord when he first lived in England. See Annan, "Ghosts," 30. The name Max Aurach, which contains Sebald's own nickname as well as a surname resembling the English painter's, was changed in the English version out of respect for Auerbach's privacy. See Carole Angier, "Who is W. G. Sebald?" *Jewish Quarterly* 43 (winter 1996/97): 14.

22. *The Emigrants,* 150. ". . . die seltsam gerippte Flanke eines kahlen und langestreckten Berges . . . der, wie mir vorkam, gleich einem ungeheuren liegenden Körper atmend manchmal ein wenig sich hob und senkte" *Die Ausgewanderten,* 220. "Eine Nebeldecke . . . hatte sich ausgebreitet über die ein Gebiet von tausend Quadratkilometern überziehende, aus unzähligen Ziegeln erbaute und von Millionen von toten und lebendigen Seelen bewohnte Stadt" Ibid., 221.

23. Ibid., 160. "In einem dieser Gebäude war das Atelier untergebracht, das ich in den kommenden Monaten . . . aufsuchte, um Gespräche zu führen mit dem Maler, der dort seit Ende der vierziger Jahre arbeitete, Tag für Tag, den siebten Tag nicht ausgenommen" Ibid., 236.

24. Vladimir Nabokov, *Speak, Memory: An Autobigraphy Revisited.* (New York and Toronto: Alfred A. Knopf, 1999) 88.

25. *The Emigrants,* 161. "Nirgends befinde er sich wohler als dort, wo die Dinge ungestört und gedämpft daliegen dürfen unter dem grausamtenen Sinter, der entsteht, wenn die Materie, Hauch um Hauch, sich auflöst in nichts" *Die Ausgewanderten,* 238.

26. Frank Auerbach refused to allow the drawing to be used in the English version, according to Maya Jaggi's interview with Sebald in the *Guardian* on 22 Sept., 2001. Her "Recovered Memories" is available online at http://books.guardian.co.uk/ departments/politicsphilosophyandsociety/story/0,6000,555839,00

27. *The Emigrants,* 170. "Die extremistische, eine jede Einzelheit durchdringende, sämtliche Glieder verrenkende und in den Farben wie eine Krankheit sich ausbreitende Weltsicht dieses seltsamen Mannes war mir, wie ich immer gewußt hatte und nun durch den Augenschein bestätigt fand, von Grund auf gemäß" *Die Ausgewanderten,* 253.

28. Sebald's phrase is "Lagune der Erinnerungslosigkeit" Ibid., 269.

29. Arthur Williams comments at length on the "complex interplay" of motifs, contemporary aesthetic insights, and images within the highly musical structure of *The Emigrants*. See his article "The Elusive First Person Plural: Real Absences in Reiner Kunze, Bernd-Dieter Hüge, and W. G. Sebald," in *"Whose Story?"—Continuities in Contemporary German-language Literature,* ed. Arthur Williams, Stuart Parkes, and Julian Preece (Bern: Peter Lang, 1998), 85–115.

30. *The Emigrants,* 181. "Die Zeit . . . ist nichts als das Rumoren der Seele" *Die Ausgewanderten,* 270.

31. Ibid., 191. ". . . um mich zu immunisieren gegen das von den Eltern erlittene Leid und gegen mein eigenes" Ibid., 285. Michael Hulse's translation is less literal than mine, "to keep at bay thoughts of my parents' sufferings and of my own misfortune" *The Emigrants,* 191.

32. Ibid., 191. "Das Unglück meines jugendlichen Noviziats hatte so tief Wurzel gefaßt in mir, daß es später wieder aufschießen, böse Blüten treiben und das giftige Blätterdach über mir aufwölben konnte, das meine letzten Jahre so sehr überschattet und verdunkelt hat" Ibid., 185–86.

33. Ibid., 193. ". . . wie eines jener bösen deutschen Märchen, in denen man, einmal in den Bann geschlagen, mit einer angefangenen Arbeit, in diesem Fall also mit dem Erinnern, dem Schreiben und dem Lesen, fortfahren muß, bis einem das Herz bricht" Ibid., 289.

34. Ibid., 195. ". . . das schönste Mädchen weit und breit . . . eine wahre Germania" Ibid., 291.

35. Ibid., 207. "Die Zeit. In welcher Zeit ist das alles gewesen? Und wie langsam neigten sich nicht damals die Tage? Und wer war dieses fremde Kind auf dem Heimweg, müde, mit einer winzigen weißblauen Häherfeder in der Hand?" Ibid., 310.

36. Ibid., 214. "Obgleich alles um mich herum verschwamm, [sah ich] mit größter Deutlichkeit den russischen Knaben, den ich längst vergessen gehabt hatte, mit seinem Schmetterlingsnetz durch die Wiesen springen als den wiederkehrenden Glücksboten jenes Sommertags, der nun aus seiner Botanisiertrommel sogleich die schönsten Admirale, Pfauenaugen, Zitronenfalter und Ligusterschwärmer entlassen würde zum Zeichen meiner endlichen Befreiung" Ibid., 321.

37. Ibid., 220. "Unsere Welt ist eine Glocke, die einen Riß hat und nicht mehr klingt" Ibid., 330.

38. Ibid., 224. "Das gab mir den Gedanken ein, daß die Deutschen den Juden vielleicht nichts so mißgönnt haben als ihre schönen, mit dem Land und der Sprache, in der sie lebten, so sehr verbundenen Namen" Ibid., 335.

39. The German version spells Mr. Stern's first name Meier, though the gravestone in the picture clearly shows "Maier." This discorrespondence suggests the arbitrariness of names, and highlights the delusion that they are somehow essential to identity. In "Paul Bereyter," Sebald pokes fun at the two clergymen, the catechist whose name is spelled Meier and the beneficiary whose name is spelled Mayer. (35) In a famously regrettable error, Jean Améry's original name, Hans Mayer, was given as Hans Meyer

when, in 1980, his 1966 volume of essays *At the Mind's Limits* was reissued with a new afterward.

40. Ibid., 225. "Ich spürte' daß die rings um mich umgebende Geistesverarmung und Erinnerungslosigkeit der Deutschen, das Geschick, mit dem man alles bereinigt hatte, mir Kopf und Nerven anzugreifen begann" Ibid., 338.

41. Ibid., 237 ". . . die Töchter der Nacht, mit Spindel und Faden und Schere" Ibid., 335.

42. Writing for the *Frankfurter Allgemeine Zeitung* on 17 Nov., 1992, Heinrich Detering was the first to use the term. His review, "Große Literatur für kleine Zeiten" (Great literature for minor times) can be found in Loquai, ed., *W. G. Sebald*, 82–87, along with several other German reviews from major newspapers and journals.

43. Philip Brady, "Ghosts of the Present," *Times Literary Supplement,* 12 July 1996: 22.

44. Larry Wolff, "When Memory Speaks," *New York Times Book Review,* 30 March 1997: 19.

45. Ozick, "Sublime," 34.

46. Ibid., 38.

47. Angier, "Who is W. G. Sebald," 14. The biographer Angier goes on to say: "Curiously, the final proof [of the greatness of *The Emigrants*] is not a photograph, but the absence of one. . . . I am convinced that I have seen [the picture of the three Jewish women sitting at the carpet loom] on the last page; I remember the loom, their hands, their faces. But it isn't there."

48. Chalmers, "Angels of History," 45. The original German is found in Walter Benjamin, *Gesammelte Schriften,* 6 vols., ed. Rolf Tiedemann and Hermann Schweppenhäuser in collaboration with Theodor W. Adorno and Gershom Scholem (Frankfurt: Suhrkamp, 1990) 2: 697. An English version, "Theses on the Philosophy of History," can be found in Hannah Arendt's book of selections from Benjamin's essays, *Illuminations,* trans. Harry Zohn (New York: Harcourt, Brace & World, 1968), 255–69.

49. Ann Parry, "Idioms for the Unrepresentable," in *The Holocaust and the Text: Speaking the Unspeakable,* ed. Andrew Leak and George Paizis (New York: St. Martin's, 2000), 109–24.

50. Ibid., 117.

51. Williams, "First Person Plural," 107.

52. Ibid.

53. Ibid., 112n. 30.

Chapter 3: *The Rings of Saturn*

1. Freud, "The Uncanny," 237.

2. Ibid.

3. Ibid.

4. See Friedrich Nietzsche, section 341 of *The Gay Science with a Prelude in Rhymes and an Appendix of Songs,* trans. Walter Kaufmann (New York: Random

House, 1974), 273–74. "What if some day or night a demon were to steal after you into your loneliest loneliness and say to you: 'This life as you now live it and have lived it, you will have to live once more and innumerable times more. . . .' Would you not throw yourself down and gnash your teeth and curse the demon who spoke thus?" The passage in its entirety was considered by Nietzsche to be the first expression of the basic idea of *Thus Spake Zarathustra*. While I argue Sebald's "patterns of repetition" and coincidence have more to do with Freud's ideas than Nietzsche's, there is undoubtedly some overlapping, given the highly referential nature of Sebald's writing. In this same passage, for instance, Nietzsche quotes the demon as saying "even this spider and this moonlight between the trees, and even this moment and I myself [would recur eternally]." Could this striking scene be related to the "shudder" the narrator of *The Rings of Saturn* feels as he perceives the water beetle crossing the well in the moonlight? (see p. 190)

5. Auerbach, "History as Memoir," 22.

6. Merle Rubin, "Random Sights, Curious Patterns," *Wall Street Journal*, Oct. 28, 1998

7. *The Rings of Saturn*, 3. ". . . das lähmende Grauen, das mir verschiedentlich überfallen hatte" *Die Ringe des Saturn*, 11.

8. Ibid., 23. "Ähnlich wie in diesem fortwährenden Prozeß des Fressens und des Gefressenwerdens hat auch für Thomas Browne nichts Bestand" Ibid., 35.

9. Ibid., 48. "Die bessere Gesellschaft . . . drehte . . . sich . . . zu den Klängen des Orchesters im Kreise . . . und . . . schwebte . . . gleichsam . . . in einer Lichterwoge" Ibid., 64.

10. Both stories can be found in Borges, *Ficciones*, ed. Anthony Kerrigan (New York: Grove Press, 1962). The quotation from "Pierre Menard" is found on p. 49.

11. *The Rings of Saturn*, 77. "Selbst gefeierte Seeschlachtenmaler wie Storck, van der Velde oder de Loutherbourg . . . vermögen . . . keinen wahren Eindruck davon zu vermitteln, wie es auf einem der mit Gerät und Mannschaften bis zum äußersten überladenenen Schiffe zugegangen sein muß, wenn brennende Masten und Segel niederstürzten oder Kanonenkugeln die von einem unglaublichen Leibergewimmel erfüllten Zwischendecks durchschlugen" *Die Ringe des Saturn*, 95–96.

12. *Logis in einem Landhaus*, 32.

13. *The Rings of Saturn*, 79. "Gleich einer Schleppe wird der Nachtschatten über die Erde gezogen, und da nach Sonnenuntergang fast alles von einem Weltgürtel zum nächsten sich niederlegt, . . . könnte man . . . die von uns bewohnte Kurgel andauernd voller hingestreckter, wie von der Sense Saturns umgelegter und geernteter Leiber erblicken" *Die Ringe des Saturn*, 97.

14. Gareth Howell-Jones, "A Doubting Pilgrim's Happy Progress," *The Spectator*, 30 May 1998: 35.

15. *The Rings of Saturn*, 78. "Eine Weile bloß glitten diese seltsamen, auf Namen wie *Stavoren, Resolution, Victory, Groot Hollandia* und *Olyfan* getauften Wesen, vom Weltatem getrieben, über das Meer, und schon waren sie wieder verschwunden" *Die Ringe des Saturn*, 96.

16. Ibid., 96. "Ich fühlte mich eine Weile schon wie im ewigen Frieden" Ibid., 119.

17. Ibid., 99. "In seiner Eigenschaft [als Generalsekretär der Vereinten Nationen] ist es angeblich gewesen, daß [Kurt Waldheim], für allfällige außerirdische Bewohner des Universums, eine Grußbotschaft auf Band gesprochen hat, die jetzt, zusammen mit anderen Memorabilien der Menscheit, an Bord der Raumsonde *Voyager II* die Außenbezirke unseres Sonnensystems ansteuert" Ibid., 122–23.

18. "It so happens," as Sebald told more than one interviewer, "that a friend of mine was in the process of translating into German—which is a quite impossible task— Aubrey's *Brief Lives,* and he did it in the most brilliant way by inventing an artificial seventeenth-century German, and so I got more and more into reading seventeenth and early eighteenth-century English authors, and the density of the miraculous achievements there is staggering." See Robert McCrum, "'Characters, Plot, Dialogue? That's Not Really My Style . . .': The Books Interview," *Observer,* 7 June 1998: 17.

19. *The Rings of Saturn,* 134. "Es . . . war . . . möglicherweise gerade die Homosexualität Casements. . . , die ihn befähigte, über die Grenzen der gesellschaftlichen Klassen und der Rassen hinweg die andauernde Unterdrückung, Ausbeutung, Versklavung und Verschrottung derjenigen zu erkennen, die am weitesten entfernt waren von den Zentren der Macht" *Die Ringe des Saturn,* 162.

20. Ibid., 123. "Jedenfalls entsinne ich mich genau, daß mir bei meinem ersten Besuch in Brüssel im Dezember 1964 mehr Bucklige und Irre über den Weg gelaufen sind als sonst in einem ganzen Jahr" Ibid., 149.

21. Ibid., 159. The word "power" is not as descriptive as the German "Sog," which suggests being swallowed up, as the wake of a large ship, or being pulled away, as by an undertow. "Wenn man . . . in die Richtung hinausblickt, wo die Stadt einst gewesen sein muß, dann spürt man den gewaltigen Sog der Leere." Ibid., 192.

22. Ibid., 159. "In Brasilien erlöschen bis heute halbe Provinzen wie Feuerbrünste, wenn das Land durch Raubbau erschöpft ist und weiter im Westen neuer Raum aufgetan wird" Ibid., 191.

23. Ibid., 170. "Die ganze Menschheitszivilisation war von Anfang an nichts als ein von Stunde zu Stunde intensiver werdendes Glossen, von dem niemand weiß, bis auf welchen Grad es zunehmen und wann es allmählich ersterben wird" Ibid., 203.

24. Ibid., 177. "[Das Ereignis] führte uns vor Augen. . . , mit welchen Ungeheuerlichkeiten das Überwechseln in ein neues Land unter den gegebenen Umständen verbunden war" Ibid., 210.

25. Ibid., "Schaue ich heute . . . zurück auf Berlin, dann sehe ich bloß einen schwarz-blauen Hintergrund und darauf einen grauen Fleck, eine Griffelzeichnung, undeutliche Ziffern und Buchstaben, ein scharfes Eß, ein Zet, ein Vogelvau, mit dem Tagellappen verschmiert und ausgelöst" Ibid., 212. Note that Germans use a damp rag, not a dry chalk eraser, to wipe off school blackboards.

26. Ibid., 182. ". . . die Unwägbarkeiten, die in Wahrheit unsere Laufbahn bestimmen" Ibid., 217.

27. Ibid., 187. "Sooft ich mir sage, daß dergleichen Zufälle sich weitaus häufiger ereignen, als wir ahnen, weil wir uns alle, einer hinter dem anderen, entlang derselben, von unserem Herkommen und unseren Hoffnungen vorgezeichneten Straßen bewegen,

sowenig vermag ich mit meiner Vernunft gegen die mich immer öfter durchgeisternden Phantome der Wiederholung" Ibid., 223.

28. Ibid., 188. "Möglicherweise handelt es sich bei diesem Phänomen, für das es bis heute keine rechte Erklärung gibt, um so etwas wie ein Vorwegnehmen des Endes, um ein Ins-Leer-Treten oder um eine Art Ausrasten, das ähnlich wie bei einem immer wieder durch die gleiche Tonfolge laufenden Grammophon, weniger etwas mit einem Schaden der Machine zu tun hat als mit einem irreparablen Defekt des der Maschine eingegebenen Programms" Ibid., 224.

29. Ibid., 210. "Unter ihrem eigenen Dach lebten [die Ashburys] wie Flüchtlinge, die Furchtbares mitgemacht haben und die es nicht wagen, an dem Platz, an dem sie gestrandet sind, sich niederzulassen" Ibid., 250.

30. Ibid, 226. "Der Verlauf der Geschichte ist dann natürlich ein ganz anderer gewesen, weil es ja immer, wenn man gerade die schönste Zukunft sich ausmalt, bereits auf die nächste Katastrophe zugeht" Ibid., 270.

31. Ibid., 234. ". . . zugleich vollkommen befreit und maßlos bedrückt" Ibid., 279.

32. Ibid., 248. "Der Tempel, sagte Alec Garrard, indem wir seine Werkstatt verließen, hat ja nur hundert Jahre überdauert. *Perhaps this one will last a little longer*" Ibid., 294.

33. Ibid., 253. "Wird überhaupt irgend jemand es noch begreifen können in einer von Grund auf veränderten Welt?" Ibid., 300.

34. Ibid., 266. ". . . eine schauderhafte Leere . . . eine gestaltlose, in die Unterwelt übergehende Szene" Ibid., 316.

35. Ibid., 294. ". . . bis das ganze Tötungsgeschäft vollendet ist" Ibid., 348.

36. Morrison, "Death-tinted Specs," 45.

37. See for example Morrison, "Death-tinted Specs," 46. The novelist Andre Aciman finds many of Sebald's connections not only tenuous, but "forced" in his review of *The Emigrants* and *The Rings of Saturn*, "Novemberland," 46.

38. Auerbach, "History as Memoir," 22.

39. Aciman, "Novemberland," 46.

40. Morrison sees a good deal of *Tristram Shandy* in the techniques of Sebald's prose. See "Death-tinted Specs," 46.

41. Richard Eder, "Excavating a Life," *New York Times Review of Books,* 28 Oct. 2001: 10.

42. Ibid.

43. Melville is not an acknowledged influence, though the parallel is apt in terms of the mood of uncanniness in *Moby Dick* as well as its theme of travel. (Melville was also a literary disciple of Sir Thomas Browne.) See Mason, "Mapping a Life," 19.

44. James Wood, "The Right Thread," *New Republic,* 6 June 1998: 38.

Chapter 4: *Vertigo*

1. From the essay, "William Faulkner: Three Reviews," as cited in *Borges: A Reader. A Selection from the Writings of Jorge Luis Borges,* ed. Emir Rodriguez Monegal and Alastair Reid (New York: E. P. Dutton, 1981), 92.

2. Stendhal, *The Life of Henry Brulard,* trans. John Sturrock (New York: Penguin, 1995) 49–52.

3. *Vertigo,* 5. "[Immer] wieder stößt er auf Bilder von solch ungewöhnlicher Deutlichkeit, daß er ihnen nicht glaubt trauen zu dürfen, beispielsweise auf dasjenige des Generals Marmont, den er in Martigny zur Linken des Weges, auf welchem sich der Troß voranbewegte, in dem himmel- und königsblauen Kleid eines Staatsrats gesehen zu haben meint, . . . obschon Marmont ja damals, wie Beyle sehr wohl weiß, seine Generaluniform und nicht das blaue Staatskleid getragen haben muß" *Schwindel. Gefühle,* 9.

4. Ibid., 17. "Die Entscheidende Wendung . . . war ihm aus zahllosen Erzählvarianten vertraut, und auch er selbst hatte sie sich verschiedentlich und in vielerlei Farben ausgemalt" Ibid., 21.

5. Ibid., 17. "Die Differenz zwischen den Bildern der Schlacht, die er in seinem Kopf trug, und dem, was er als Beweis dessen, daß die Schlacht sich wahrhaftig ereignet hatte, nun vor sich ausgebreitet sah, diese Differenz verursachte ihm ein noch niemals zuvor gespürtes, schwindelartiges Gefühl der Irritation" Ibid., 22. Sebald is indulging in an Anglicism when he uses of the word "Differenz," usually restricted to mathematics, instead of "Unterschied" or "Kontrast."

6. Ibid., 15. "Der Applaus, der das Opernhaus am Ende der Aufführung durchtoste, kam ihm vor wie der Schlußakt von einer Zerstörung, wie das von einem riesigen Brand verursachte Prasseln, und lange Zeit blieb er noch sitzen wie betäubt von der Hoffnung, daß das Feuer ihn aufzehren möge" Ibid., 19.

7. Ibid., 30. "Am Abend des 22. März 1842, der Vorfrühling lag bereits in der Luft, wirft ihn ein apoplektischer Anfall auf das Trottoir der Rue Neuve-des-Capucines" Ibid., 37.

8. Ibid., 33. "Ich war damals, im Oktober 1980 ist es gewesen, von England aus, wo ich nun seit nahezu fünfundzwanzig Jahren in einer meist grau überwölkt Grafschaft lebe, nach Wien gefahren in der Hoffnung, durch eine Ortsveränderung über eine besonders ungute Zeit hinwegzukommen" Ibid., 41.

9. Ibid., 35. ". . . des Übelkeit und des Schwindels" Ibid., 44.

10. Ibid., 42. "Der Lauf des Stroms wurde dadurch begradigt und bietet jetzt einen Anblick, dem die Erinnerungskraft nicht mehr lange gewachsen sein wird" Ibid., 51–52.

11. Ibid., 48. "England ist bekanntlich eine Insel für sich. Wenn man nach England reisen will, braucht man einen ganzen Tag" Ibid., 59.

12. The similarity ends there, since there is none of the fawning flattery of Mann's Venetian barber, who persuades the elderly Aschenbach, hopelessly infatuated with a teenage boy, to wear makeup in order to make himself more attractive.

13. Ibid., 52. "Wer hineingeht in das Innere dieser Stadt, weiß nie, was er als nächstes sieht oder von wem er im nächsten Augenblick gesehen wird. Kaum tritt einer auf, hat er die Bühne durch einen anderen Ausgang schon wieder verlassen. Diese kurzen Expositionen sind von einer geradezu theatralischen Obszönität und haben

zugleich etwas von einer Verschwörung an sich, in die man ungefragt und unwillentlich einbezogen wird" Ibid., 63.

14. Ibid., 54. Sebald uses the term "das unsichtbare Prinzip" Ibid., 65.

15. On the night between October and November Orlando begins his amorous quest, according to the first line of the seventh stanza of canto IX. A generally available English translation is by Guido Waldman, *Orlando Furioso* (Oxford University Press, 1998), 82.

16. *"Ci vediamo a Gerusalemme."* Ibid., 62, also in the German edition, Ibid., 75.

17. Ibid., 65. "[Ich kam mir vor] . . . wie ein Aufgebahrter" Ibid., 78.

18. Ibid., 73. ". . . allem . . . wird . . . durch nichts geschmälerte Daseinsberechtigung zugesprochen" Ibid., 88.

19. Ibid., 81. ". . . um meine schemenhaften Erinnerungen an die damalige gefahrvolle Zeit genauer überprüfen und vielleicht einiges davon aufschreiben zu können" Ibid., 97.

20. The phrases appear in Italian in both the English and the German versions of the book, pp. 86–87 and 103 respectively.

21. Ibid., 93. "Schwaben, Franken und Bayern hörte ich die unsäglichsten Dinge untereinander reden" Ibid., 111.

22. Sebald quotes Fitzgerald's line from *The Rubaiyat* ("'Tis nothing but a Magic Shadow-Show, / Play'd in a Box whose Candle is the Sun, / Round which the Phantom Figures come and go") in *The Rings of Saturn* (p. 201). Sebald uses the word *Offenbarungen* for "revelations." Ibid., 141.

23. Ibid., 112. My translation. Michael Hulse leaves out the line "Aus dem Schnürboden senkte der Schlaf sich hernieder." Ibid., 132. Literally, the sentence means, "Sleep sank down from above the stage."

24. Ibid., 129. "Eigenartig, sagte Salvatore noch, wie in diesem Jahr alles auf einen einzigen Punkt zustrebte, an dem sich, ganz gleich, was es kostete, irgend etwas ereignen mußte" Ibid., 152.

25. Apparently part of a draft of a story, the angel's descent from the opened ceiling, was recorded on 25 June 1914. See Franz Kafka, *The Diaries: 1910–1923*, ed. Max Brod, trans. Joseph Kresch and Martin Greenberg (New York: Schocken, 1948–49), 291–92. The murderous "iron angel" mentioned by Sebald does not, however, stem from Kafka's writings, and is not mentioned in Robert Alter's book *Necessary Angels: Tradition and Modernity in Kafka, Benjamin, and Scholem* (Cambridge: Harvard University Press, 1991).

26. The name Sandwirth represents a subtle link with the first chapter, in which ✓ Mme. Ghrerardi purchases a hat in the style of Andreas Hofer, whom Sebald describes only as the leader of a rebellion. In fact, Hofer was called, like his father, Sandwirth (innkeeper of the public house on a sandy split of land formed by the Passeyr River), and his rebellion was an uprising against the Bavarian occupiers of the Tyrol in 1808. He also led several campaigns against Napoleon's forces in the Tyrol as well as Northern Italy, and was executed in Mantua in February of 1810.

27. Kafka's letters and notes from the period of his trip to Vienna, Venice, and Verona (autumn 1913) can be found in Erich Heller and Jürgen Born, eds., *Franz Kafka: Letters to Felice* (New York: Schocken Books, 1973), 317–22.

28. *Vertigo,* 158. "Die Felswande erheben sich aus dem Wasser in das schone Herbstilcht, so halb un halb grun, als ware die ganze Gegend ein Album und die Berge waren von einem feinsinnigen Dilettanten der Besitzerin des Albums aufs leere Blatt hingezeichnet worden, zur Erinnerung" *Schwindel. Gefühle,* 180. Walser's story concerns a visit by the Romantic-era writer Heinrich von Kleist to Thun in Switzerland, and includes the words: "The mountains are like the illusion created by a skilled set designer, or they look as if the whole location were an album and the mountains had been drawn on an empty page by a sensitive dilettante, as a souvenir. The album has a pale green binding" (translation mine). See Robert Walser, *Dichtungen in Prosa,* vol. 5 (Geneva: Kossodo, 1961), 197–98.

29. Ibid., 163. "Im Verlauf der nachfolgenden Jahre legten sich lange Schatten über die, wie Dr. K. sich gelegentlich sagte, ebenso schönen wie entsetzlichen Herbsttage in Riva, und aus den Schatten tauchten allmählich die Umrisse einer Barke auf mit unverständlich hohen Masten und finsteren faltigen Segeln" Ibid., 185–86.

30. Ibid., 165. The entire passage in the original German reads as follows: "Da es aber Dr. K. gewesen ist, der die Geschichte ersonnen hat, kommt es mir vor, als bestünde der Sinn der unablässigen Fahrten des Jägers Gracchus in der Abbuße einer Sehnsucht nach Liebe, die Dr. K., wie er in einem seiner zahllosen Fledermausbriefe an Felice schreibt, immer genau dort ergreift, wo scheinbar und gesetzmäßig nichts zu genießen ist" Ibid., 188–89.

31. See Kafka's letter of 23 February 1913, *Letters to Felice,* 203.

32. *Vertigo,* 167. "Dieser ängstliche Blick," Sebald writes, makes one want to spare Muzzi "die Schrecknisse der Liebe" *Schwindel. Gefühle,* 190.

33. Ibid., 223. The original German phrase is terser: "Zeichen einer langsamen Auflösung" Ibid., 254.

34. See, for instance, Marcel Atze's article "Koinzidenz und Intertextualität" in Loquai, ed., *W. G. Sebald,* 151–75. Peter Weiss's novel, *Der Schatten des Körpers des Kutschers* appeared in 1952 and was first translated into English by E. B. Garside in 1969.

35. Hölty died of tuberculosis at the age of twenty-seven, before he could publish little more than a handful of poems. The most recent critical edition of his works is *Ludwig Christoph Heinrich Hölty: Gesammelte Werke und Briefe,* ed. Walter Hettche (Göttingen: Wallstein, 1999), 226–27.

36. *Vertigo,* 253. Sebald refers to "das mir von jeher unbegreifliche, bis in den letzten Winkel aufgeräumte und begradigte deutsche Land" *Schwindel. Gefühle,* 287.

37. Ibid., 254. "Tatsächlich schien es, als habe unsere Art bereits einer anderen Platz gemacht oder als lebten wir doch zumindest in einer Form der Gefangenschaft" Ibid., 288.

38. *Vertigo,* 254. "Es wiederholten sich beim Hinausschauen auf das restlos aufgeteilte und nutzbar gemachte Land . . . unausgesetzt nur die Worte 'der südwestdeutsche Raum'" *Schwindel. Gefühle,* 288–89.

39. Ibid., 263. "Westwärts, bis über Windsor Park hinaus" is the German phrase Ibid., 299.

40. Lane, "Higher Ground," 132.

41. Ibid., 128.

42. Reviews by these critics and others can be found in Loquai, ed., *W. G. Sebald.*

43. See Antonio Fian's article "Ein paar Vorurteile . . ." (A few prejudices . . .) in *Wespennest* 83 (1991): 76–78

44. Anita Brookner, "Pursued Across Europe by Ghosts and Unease," *Spectator,* 18 Dec. 1999: 65.

45. Sontag, "A Mind in Mourning," 4.

46. Ibid.

47. Ibid., 3.

48. Ibid., 4. The line from *The Rings of Saturn* can be found on p. 93.

49. Joyce Hackett, "*Vertigo* by W. G. Sebald," *Boston Review* 25 (summer 2000): 34.

50. Ibid., 35.

51. Parks, "The Hunter," 52.

52. Iyer, "Strange, Haunted World," 90.

53. Ibid., 87.

Chapter 5: *Austerlitz*

1. Gregor von Rezzori, *Memoirs of an Anti-Semite* (New York: Viking Press, 1981), 138. It is worth noting, too, that von Rezzori's autobiography *Snows of Yesteryear* (New York: Alfred & Knopf, 1989) displays photographs at the beginning of each chapter. In hindsight they appear distinctly "pre-Sebaldian." The introductory sentence in the German version of *Austerlitz* begins, "In der zweiten Hälfte der sechziger Jahre bin ich, teilweise zu Studienzwecken, teilweise aus anderen, mir selber nicht recht erfindlichen Gründen, von England aus wiederholt nach Belgien gefahren" *Austerlitz, 5.*

2. *Austerlitz, 5.* "Etliche von [den Tieren] . . . hatten . . . auffallend große Augen . . . und jenen unverwandt forschenden Blick, wie man ihn findet bei bestimmten Malern und Philosophen, die vermittels der reinen Anschauung und des reinen Denkens versuchen, das Dunkel zu durchdringen, das uns umgibt" Ibid., 7.

3. The French term *salle des pas perdus* means literally "the room of lost steps," referring to the pacing that goes on in a hall where people wait for their train to arrive. Prior to the introduction of train travel, the name referred to waiting room of a law court.

4. *Austerlitz, 77.* "Besonders in den Bann gezogen hat mich . . . stets der Augenblick, in dem man auf dem belichteten Papier die Schatten der Wirklichkeit sozusagen aus dem Nichts hervorkommen sieht, genau wie Erinnerungen, . . . die ja auch inmitten der Nacht in uns auftauchen und die sich dem, der sie festhalten will, so schnell wieder verdunkeln, nicht anders als ein photographischer Druck, den man zu lang im Entwicklungsbad liegenläßt" Ibid., 113.

5. Ibid., 40. Sebald refers to "den entsetzten Ausdruck, den sie beide trugen in ihrem Gesicht" Ibid., 58.

6. Ibid., 41. "Mehr und mehr dünkt es mich . . . jetzt, sobald ich irgendwo auf eine Photographie von Wittgenstein stoße, als blicke mir Austerlitz aus ihr entgegen, oder, wenn ich Austerlitz anschaue, als sehe ich in ihm den unglücklichen, in der Klarheit seiner logischen Überlegungen ebenso wie in der Verwirrung seiner Gefühle eingesperrten Denker" Ibid., 60.

7. Ibid., 283. "die Grenze zwischen dem Tod und dem Leben [ist] durchlässiger . . . als wir gemeinhin glauben" Ibid., 397.

8. As Sebald hints in the book, he was prompted to use the name by a radio program on the life of the dancer Fred Astaire, whose surname was originally Austerlitz. See Sebald's remarks in the *Der Spiegel* interview of 12 Mar. 2001, p. 230. The name "Jacques," rare in German-speaking Europe, is used for a Jewish Viennese in a theatrical parody in von Rezzori's *Memoirs of an Anti-Semite*, 236. Jacques is also the name of a manservant in Roth's *Radetsky March*.

9. Ibid., 8–9. "Während der beim Reden eintretenden Pausen merkten wir beide, wie unendlich lang es dauerte, bis wieder eine Minute verstrichen war, und wie schrecklich uns jedesmal, trotzdem wir es doch erwarteten, das Vorrücken dieses, einem Richtschwert gleichenden Zeigers schien, wenn er das nächste Sechzigstel einer Stunde von der Zukunft abtrennte mit einem derart bedrohlichen Nachzittern, daß einem beinahe das Herz aussetzte dabei" Ibid., 13.

10. Annan, "Ghost Story," 26.

11. *Austerlitz*, 112. "[Wir] schauten bis zu ihrem Erlöschen, die Bilder uns an, die von den waagerecht durch das bewegte Gezweig eines Weißdorns dringenden letzten Strahlen der Sonne an die Wand gegenüber dem hohen Spitzbogenfenster geworfen wurden. Die schütteren Muster, die dort in ständiger Folge auf der lichten Fläche erschienen, hatten etwas Huschendes, Verwehtes, das sozusagen nie über den Moment des Entstehens hinauskam, und doch waren hier, in diesem immer neu sich zusammensetzenden Sonnen- und Schattengeflecht, Berglandschaften mit Gletscherflüssen und Eisfeldern zu sehen, Hochebenen, Steppen, Wüsteneien, Blumensaaten, Seeinseln, Korallenriffe, Archipelagos und Atolle, vom Sturm gebeugte Wälder, Zittergras und treibender Rauch" Ibid., 162.

12. In an interview with Robert McCrum, Sebald said: "I think [beginning to write] had to do with the fact that my professional life as a teacher at a British university became much more stressed than it had been before. I mean, conditions in British universities were absolutely ideal in the Sixties and Seventies. Then the so-called reforms began and life became extremely unpleasant. I was looking around for a way of re-establishing myself in a different form simply as a counterweight to the daily bother in the institution," Robert McCrum, "McCrum on W. G. Sebald," *Observer*, 7 June 1998: 17.

13. Ibid., 137. "Eine furchtbare Müdigkeit überkam [mich] bei dem Gedanken, nie wirklich am Leben gewesen zu sein oder jetzt erst geboren zu werden, gewissermaßen am Vortag meines Todes" Ibid., 198.

14. The bewitching power of the blue shoe is described in Mary Hottinger's excellent translation of the story in *Hugo von Hofmannsthal: Selected Prose* (New York: Pantheon Books, 1952), 10. In his essay on Hofmannsthal's tale, Sebald interprets the√ shoe as a symbol of the forbidden pleasure of art. See "Venezianisches Kryptogramm: Hofmannsthals *Andreas*" (A Venetian cryptograph: Hofmannsthal's Andreas) in *Die Beschreibung des Unglücks*, 76–77.

15. *Austerlitz*, 184. The full quotation from the German original is: "Und immer fühlte ich mich dabei durchdrungen von dem forschenden Blick das Pagen, der gekommen war, sein Teil zurückzufordern und der nun im Morgengrauen auf dem leeren Feld darauf wartete, daß ich den Handschuh aufheben und das ihm bevorstehende Unglück abwenden würde" Ibid., 264.

16. For discussion of images of Hitler, including childhood photographs, see Ron Rosenbaum, "Explaining Hitler," *New Yorker*, 1 May 1995: 50–70.

17. *Austerlitz*, 23. "Das waren die Familienväter und die guten Söhne aus Vilsbiburg und aus Fuhlsbüttel, aus dem Schwarzwald und aus dem Münsterland" Ibid., 33.

18. Ibid., 182. "Man habe den Eindruck . . . als hätten die Bilder selbst ein Gedächtnis und erinnerten sich an uns, daran, wie wir, die Überlebenden, und diejenigen, die nicht mehr unter uns weilen, vordem gewesen sind" Ibid., 262.

19. Ibid., 185. "Doch ist es mir immer mehr, als gäbe es überhaupt keine Zeit, sondern nur verschiedene, nach einer höheren Stereometrie ineinander verschachtelte Räume, zwischen denen die Lebendigen und die Toten, je nachdem es ihnen zumute ist, hin und her gehen können" Ibid., 265.

20. Ibid., 190. "Am unheimlichsten aber schienen mir die Türen und Tore von Terezin, die sämtlich . . . den Zugang versperrten zu einem nie noch durchdrungenen Dunkel" Ibid., 272–76.

21. Writing in the Berlin newspaper *Die Tageszeitung* on 9 July 1993 ("Zartbitterstes. Ist es versuchte Nähe, ist es 'Abwehrzauber'? Warum nur lieben alle den Kitsch W. G. Sebalds?" 16), Sibylle Cramer even accuses *Die Ausgewanderten* of being in bad taste ("kitsch"). The title of the article in English reads Bittersweet in the extreme. Is it an attempt at intimacy or the "magic of repulsion"? Why does everybody love Sebald's kitsch? Iris Radisch roundly castigates Sebald for the tastelessness of the allegedly relativizing effects of his correspondences in her review of *Austerlitz*, "Der Waschbär der falschen Welt: W. G. Sebald sammelt Andenken und rettet die Vergangenheit vorm Vergehen" (Raccoon of the false world: W. G. Sebald collects mementos and saves the past from passing), *Die Zeit*, 5 April 2001: 55–56.

22. Ibid., 221. ". . . dass diese . . . gußeiserne Säule sich erinnerte an mich und, wenn man so sagen kann, . . . Zeugnis ablegte von dem, was ich selbst nicht mehr wußte" Ibid., 316.

23. The startling image of the dead child treated as luggage has its roots in real-√ ity. Sebald recounts the experience of a German woman who witnessed the arrival in Stralsund of a trainload of refugees from Hamburg, following its bombardment in the summer of 1943. More than one distraught mother on the train was carrying in her suitcase the corpse of her child. See *Luftkrieg und Literatur* (Munich: Hanser, 1999), 102–3.

24. *Austerlitz*, 275. ". . . als kannte sie ihr eigenes Los und auch das derjenigen, in deren Gesellschaft sie sich befand" Ibid., 386–87.

25. Though Sebald uses many of Jacobson's details about "Fort IX" from chapter 15, he does not mention the most unspeakable, i.e., that the dead were exhumed and their corpses burned in order to destroy the evidence of Nazi crimes. Thus the Jews were desecrated twice. As a crowning insult, the prisoners forced to execute the exhumations and incinerations were shot to death immediately upon completion of the task. See Dan Jacobson, *Heshel's Kingdom* (Evanston, Ill.: Northwestern University Press, 1998), 167.

26. See "Ich fürchte das Melodramatische" (I dread the melodramatic), *Der Spiegel*, 12 March 2001: 228–34. Sebald always obtains permission to use biographical details in creating his characters. In the case of Austerlitz, Sebald combined features from the lives of an elderly friend whose research into his origins lead to an identity crisis, and a woman (Susie Bechhofer) who as a child had been in the *Kindertransport* from Munich to England—the rest of her childhood was spent in Wales, where she was brought up by a fundamentalist pastor. In an interview with Kenneth Baker in the *San Francisco Chronicle* ("W. G. Sebald: Up against Historical Amnesia," *San Francisco Chronicle*, 7 Oct. 2001: R 2.), Sebald responded affirmatively to the suggestion that Ludwig Wittgenstein's personality influenced the creation of the character of Austerlitz, and to some extent, Paul Bereyter.

27. Gerald Heidegger, "Ein Mann namens Austerlitz" (A man called Austerlitz), available online at http://kultur.orf.at/orfon/kultur/010305–5102/5117txt_story.html

28. Radisch, "Waschbär," 55.

29. Ibid., 56.

30. Ibid.

31. Sebald cites the example of Alfred Andersch's novel *Ephraim*, which he says was a blatant attempt to capitalize on the Holocaust. See "Ich fürchte das Melodramatische," 231–32. Sebald devoted the final section of *Luftkrieg und Literatur* to a study of Andersch's literary opportunism.

32. Peter Craven, "W. G. Sebald: Anatomy of Faction," *Heat* 13 (1999): 218.

33. Daniel Mendelsohn, "Foreign Correspondents," *New York*, 8 Oct. 2001: 70.

34. Ibid.

35. Ibid.

36. Michael Dirda, "*Austerlitz* by W. G. Sebald," *Washington Post*, 14 Oct. 2001: BW 15.

37. Michiko Kakutani, "Life in a No Man's Land of Memory and Loss," *New York Times*, 27 Oct. 2001: E 40.

38. Eder, "Excavating a Life," E 40.

39. Ibid.

40. Benjamin Markovits, "What Was It That So Darkened Our World," *London Review of Books*, 18 Oct. 2001: 24.

41. Ibid., 23.

42. Annan, "Ghost Story," 27.

43. John Banville, "The Rubble Artist," *New Republic*, 26 Nov. 2001: 37.

44. Medicus's obituary "Leichtfüßiger Schwerarbeiter der Erinnerung" (Lightfooted heavy-lifter of memory) appeared on 17 Dec., 2001.

Chapter 6: The Plangent Parting

1. John Banville makes this observation "The Rubble Artist," 37.

2. In fact, one of the characteristics of Sebald's prose fiction is a posture of indifference as to whether his reader understands. One would have to be a Germanist of similar erudition, not to mention a comparatist conversant in French, German, Italian, and English literature, in order to appreciate completely Sebald's intertextuality. The term *Prätext* comes from the scholar Manfred Pfister and is defined in his article "Konzepte der Intertextualität" in *Intertextualität*, ed. Ulrich Broich (Tübingen: Niedermeyer, 1985), see especially p. 11.

3. *The Emigrants*, 230–31. "Es war ein äußerst mühevolles, oft stunden- und tagelang nicht vom Fleck kommendes und nicht selten sogar rückläufiges Unternehmen, bei dem ich fortwährend geplagt wurde von einem immer nachhaltiger sich bemerkbar machenden und mehr und mehr mich lähmenden Skrupulantismus. Dieser Skrupulantismus bezog sich sowohl auf den Gegenstand meiner Erzählung, dem ich, wie ich es auch anstellte, nicht gerecht zu werden glaubte, als auch auf die Fragwürdigkeit der Schriftstellerei überhaupt. Hunderte von Seiten hatte ich bedeckt mit meinem Bleistift- und Kugelschreibergekritzel. Weitaus das meiste davon war durchgestrichen, verworfen oder bis zur Unleserlichkeit mit Zusätzen überschmiert. Selbst das, was ich schließlich für die 'endgültige' Fassung retten konnte, erschien mir als ein mißratenes Stückwerk" Ibid., 344–45.

4. *Die Beschreibung des Unglücks*, 12.

5. Michael Butler, "The Human Cost of Exile," *Times Literary Supplement*, 2 Oct. 1998: 10.

6. Ibid.

7. Ibid.

8. Ibid.

9. *Logis in einem Landhaus*, 64.

10. "Der metaphysische Augen- und Überblick entspringt einer profunden Faszination, in welcher sich eine Zeitlang unser Verhältnis zur Welt verkehrt. Im Schauen spüren wir, wie die Dinge uns ansehen, verstehen, daß wir nicht da sind, um das Universum zu durchdringen, sondern um von ihm durchdrungen zu sein" *Unheimliche Heimat* (Frankfurt: Fischer, 1995), 158.

11. Arthur Williams draws the connection to Merleau-Ponty's *L'Œil et l'Esprit* (1964) in his article, "A Holistic Approach," 107. He also notes the influence of Susan Sontag's *On Photography* (1977), and the writings of Roland Barthes.

12. Kenneth Baker, "Historical Amnesia," R 2.

13. Sebald observes that Stifter's texts "tendieren . . . ins Hermetische," and contain little development or reflection. *Die Beschreibung des Unglücks*, 17.

14. "Die Beschreibung der Natur, auch die literarische, entwickelte sich erst mit der kommerziellen Erschließung der Welt." Ibid., 25.

15. "Vielleicht ist Stifters Bemühen um eine Verewigung der Schönheit am ehesten faßbar in seinen Beschreibungen der Natur." Ibid., 24.

16. "Photographien sind die Mementos einer im Zerstörungsprozeß und im Verschwinden begriffenen Welt." Ibid., 178.

17. *Logis in einem Landhaus*, 49. "Wenn man mit dem Finger die Kerben im Holz nachfährt . . . möchte man . . . wissen, wer sie gewesen und wohin sie gegangen sind."

18. Williams, "A Holistic Approach," 102.

19. Ibid., 99.

20. Many Austrian writers possess "eine Haltung, die dafur einstehen hann, dab es einen sinn hat, etwas weiterzugeben," *Die Beschreibung des Unglücks*, 13.

21. Useful in understanding Sebald's reliance on Benjamin is the influential study by Susan Sontag, "Under the Sign of Saturn," in *Under the Sign of Saturn* (New York: Farrar, Strauss and Giroux, 1980), 109–36. It was the melancholy Benjamin's bon mot that he had been "born under the sign of Saturn" (115).

22. *Der Mythus der Zerstörung im Werk Döblins* (Stuttgart: Klett, 1980), 58.

23. The roots of Sebald's monism can be found not just in Borges, but also in his reading of Hugo von Hofmannsthal, whose "Letter of Lord Chandos" includes the following lines: "To sum up: In those days I, in a state of continuous intoxication, conceived the whole of existence as one great unit: the spiritual and physical worlds seemed to form no contrast, as little as did courtly and bestial conduct, art and barbarism, solitude and society; in everything I felt the presence of Nature, in the aberrations of insanity as much as in the utmost refinement of the Spanish ceremonial; in the boorishness of young peasants no less than in the most delicate of allegories; and in all expressions of Nature I felt myself." See *Hugo von Hofmannsthal: Selected Prose*, trans. Mary Hottinger and Tania & James Stern (New York: Pantheon, 1952), 132.

24. Williams, "A Holistic Approach," 104.

25. Ibid.

26. Ibid.

27. Ibid.

28. Baker, "Historical Amnesia," R 2.

29. von Rezzori, *Memoirs of an Anti-Semite*, 180. First published by Viking Press in 1981.

Bibliography

Works by W. G. Sebald

Poetry and Fiction

Nach der Natur. Ein Elementargedicht. Nördlingen: Greno, 1988. This, Sebald's first non-scholarly book, did not appear in English until 2002. The publisher, Random House, used the literal translation *After Nature*, but my rendering of the title is "Painted from Nature," based on a key line in the text. The central themes are the relationship of art and nature, transience, and mortality. After the success of his first two novels in Germany, the book was reissued by Fischer in paperback, beginning in 1995. The English translation was done by Sebald's friend Michael Hamburger.

Schwindel. Gefühle. Frankfurt: Eichborn, 1990. Michael Hulse's translation, *Vertigo*, was published in the United States by New Directions Books in 2000. Sebald's first novel.

Die Ausgewanderten. Frankfurt: Eichborn, 1993. Translated by Michael Hulse and published as *The Emigrants* by New Directions Books in 1996. Sebald's second novel, but the first to appear in English.

Die Ringe des Saturn: Eine englische Wallfahrt. Frankfurt: Eichborn, 1995. *The Rings of Saturn*, also translated by Michael Hulse, appeared in 1998, published by New Directions Books. Sebald's third novel.

"In Bamberg," "Am 9. Juni 1904" (On the ninth of June, 1904), "Neunzig Jahre später" (Ninety years later), and "Ein Walzertraum" (A waltz dream) are poems that appeared in Franz Loquai, ed. *W. G. Sebald.* Eggingen: Isele, 1997, 13–20. Other pre-1997 poems can be found in the bibliography to this edition, on p. 271.

— "I remember," and "October Heat Wave," *Pretext* 2 (2000): 22–25. These poems mark Sebald's poetic debut in English and are, like most of his work, reconstructions of scenes from his travels.

"Gedichte" (Poems), *Akzente.* April 2001: 112–21. The journal *Akzente* publishes works of poetry and short fiction by contemporary authors. The six poems in this issue are, again, products of Sebald's travels, representing scenes from hotels, trains, and poetry readings.

Austerlitz. Munich and Vienna: Hanser, 2001. Sebald's fourth and last novel, translated by Anthea Bell and published in the U.S. by Random House.

— *For Years Now.* London: Hamish Hamilton, Short Books, 2001. Consists of twenty-three poems in English. Illustrated by the painter Tess Jaray.

Radio Plays

"Max Aurach." Bayerischer Rundfunk. 20 May 1994. This radio play is based on the chapter of *The Emigrants* titled "Max Ferber" in the English version. The subject is a German-born painter living in Manchester, England. Ulrich Gerhardt produced this broadcast, with the actors Bruno Ganz and Michael König reading.
"Aurachs Mutter." Bayerischer Rundfunk. 10 Feb. 1995. Sebald reads from his summary of the remembrances of Aurach's (Ferber's) mother, who described her life as a Jew in Bad Kissingen and its environs before the Nazi persecutions began. Also produced by Ulrich Gerhardt. Corinna Kirchhoff and Michael König read.

Literary Criticism

Carl Sternheim: Kritiker und Opfer der Wilhelminischen Ära (Carl Sternheim: critic and victim of the Wilhelminian era). Stuttgart: Kohlhammer, 1969. One of the early products of Sebald's fascination with "problematic" writers and their flaws. Sternheim is a lesser-known Jewish writer whose works Sebald associates with fascist ideology, a charge that proved controversial in critical circles.
Der Mythus der Zerstörung im Werk Alfred Döblins (The Myth of destruction in the work of Alfred Döblin). Stuttgart: Klett, 1980. An examination of the prolific and unconventional writings of the Jewish physician best known for his authorship of the novel *Berlin Alexanderplatz.*
Die Beschreibung des Unglücks: Zur österreichischen Literatur von Stifter bis Handke (Describing unhappiness: Austrian literature from Stifter to Handke). Salzburg and Vienna: Residenz, 1985. In this collection of ten articles, Sebald elaborates on his thesis that "depressive" or melancholy writing represents an attempt to resist the power of depression, rather than acquiescence to it. A paperback edition was published by Fischer Taschenbuch Verlag in 1994.
A Radical Stage: Theatre in Germany in the 1970s and 1980s. Edited by W. G. Sebald. Oxford, New York, Hamburg: Berg, 1988. Here Sebald has gathered together critical articles on the major figures of "radical theater" in Germany, Switzerland, and Austria, which he argues is the only original development in German drama since before the Second World War. The writers treated include Herbert Achternbusch, Volker Braun, Heiner Müller, and Botho Strauss.
Unheimliche Heimat: Essays zur österreichischen Literatur. (Alien homeland: essays on Austrian literature). Salzburg and Vienna: Residenz, 1991. In this book, Sebald turns away from the earlier, psychological determinants that affected Austrian writers, and explores the sociological factors that have influenced and shaped the works of Karl Postl (better known as Charles Sealsfield), Franz Kafka, Joseph Roth, Hermann Broch, and Peter Handke. There are also thematic essays on the literature of the Jewish ghetto and on Austria's literary relations with France. A paperback edition of *Unheimliche Heimat* was published by Fischer Taschenbuch Verlag in 1995.
Logis in einem Landhaus (Lodgings in a country house). Munich: Hanser, 1998. This book consists of five essays on literary figures, and one on the visual artist Jan Peter Tripp. Of the writers discussed, Rousseau is the best known in the English-speaking

world. The others—Gottfried Keller, Johann Peter Hebel, Robert Walser, and Eduard Mörike—are nonetheless interesting in Sebald's sympathetic and painstakingly researched treatments. The common subject of all six essays is the relationship of life and art. Fischer published a paperback edition in 2000.

Luftkrieg und Literatur. Munich: Hanser, 1999. This volume grew out of lectures held at the University of Zurich in the autumn of 1997. Sebald contrasts the extent and duration of the effort to destroy Germany's cities from the air with the paucity of references to the horror of aerial bombardment in the literature of the postwar period. He also cites numerous responses to the content of his lectures as yet further proof that Germany still has found no commonly accepted means of coming to terms with the disaster of the Allied air raids. A final chapter on the author Alfred Andersch illustrates the lengths to which some Germans were willing to go in order to deny their own participation in the aggression that—in the final analysis—brought on the destruction of Germany's cities. The English translation, *On the Natural History of Destruction,* was done by Anthea Bell and published in London by Hamish Hamilton in 2002.

Critical Works on W. G. Sebald

Bibliographies

Smith, Duncan. "W. G. Sebald" In *Encyclopedia of German Literature*, vol. 2, edited by Matthias Konzett, 890–91. Chicago and London: Fitzroy Dearborn, 2000. Smith lists Sebald's major works prior to *Austerlitz*, both critical and belletristic, and fourteen important reviews.

Weber, Markus R. "W. G. Sebald." *Kritisches Lexikon zur deutschsprachigen Gegenwartsliteratur* 65 (2000). This reference work is published in binder format, and is updated regularly, since its subject is contemporary German writers. Hence, the articles are in alphabetical order without continuous pagination. I have indicated the most recent version of the article on Sebald at the time of this writing. The bibliography, including mostly German works, was current on 1 April 2000.

Articles

Craven, Peter. "W. G. Sebald: Anatomy of Faction." *Heat* 12 (1999): 212–24. An ebullient discussion of Sebald's "unclassifiable" prose and its relation to documentation. In Sebald, fiction blends with fact to yield "faction."

Lewis, Tess. "W. G. Sebald: The Past is Another Country." *New Criterion* (December 2001): 85–90. Lewis summarizes Sebald's novels thus far and proclaims *Austerlitz* the most emotionally powerful and "the most unobtrusively constructed" of them all. Lewis also delves into *Luftkrieg und Literatur* and notes that the furor raised by Sebald's claims about willful amnesia among the Germans has led to the rediscovery of Gert Ledig's novel *Retribution*.

Parry, Ann. "Idioms for the Unrepresentable: Postwar Fiction and the Shoah." In *The Holocaust and the Text: Speaking the Unspeakable*, edited by Andrew Leak and

George Paizis, 109–24. New York: St. Martin's Press, 2000. Parry discusses the difficulties inherent in attempting fictional representations of the holocaust by comparing Emmanuel Litvinoff's *The Lost Europeans*, Robert Harris's *Fatherland*, and W. G. Sebald's *The Emigrants*.

Sill, Oliver. "Migration als Gegenstand der Literatur: W. G. Sebalds *Die Ausgewanderten*" (Migration as a subject of literature: W. G. Sebald's *The Emigrants*). In *Nation, Ethnie, Minderheit: Beiträge zur Aktualität ethnischer Konflikte* (Nation, ethnicity, minority: contributions on the topicality of ethnic conflict), edited by Armin Nassehi, 309–30. Cologne, Weimar, Vienna: Böhlau, 1997. Sill's is a careful analysis of Sebald's prose, with special emphasis on its complex intertextuality as the source of an idiosyncratic aesthetic (rather than documentary) truth.

Steinfeld, Thomas. "Der Eingewanderte. Literarische Größe: W. G. Sebald und Angelsachsen" (The immigrant. Literary greatness: W. G. Sebald and Anglo-Saxons). *Frankfurter Allgemeine Zeitung*. 2 March 2000: 49. This newspaper article explores the phenomenon of Sebald's success in the English-speaking world, and contrasts the hyperbolic praise of Susan Sontag, et al., with Sebald's merely peripheral respectability in Germany.

Weber, Markus R. "Phantomschmerz Heimweh: Denkfiguren der Erinnerung im literarischen Werk W. G. Sebalds" (The phantom pain homesickness: mental figures of memory in the work of W. G. Sebald). In *Neue Generation—Neues Erzählen: Deutsche Prosa-Literatur der achtziger Jahre* (New generation—new narrative techniques: German prose fiction of the 1980s), edited by Walter Delabar, Werner Jung, and Ingrid Pergand, 57–67. Opladen: Westdeutscher Verlag, 1993.

Williams, Arthur. "The Elusive First Person Plural: Real Absences in Reiner Kunze, Bernd-Dieter Hüge, and W. G. Sebald." In *Whose Story? Continuities in Contemporary German-Language Literature*, edited by Arthur Williams, Stuart Parkes and Julian Preece, 85–113. Bern: Peter Lang, 1998. A stylistic comparison of three variously "relocated" German writers with special attention to *The Emigrants* as Sebald's major achievement.

Williams, Arthur. "W. G. Sebald: A Holistic Approach to Borders, Texts and Perspectives." In *German-Language Literature Today: International and Popular?* edited by Arthur Williams, Stuart Parkes, and Julian Preece, 99–118. Bern: Peter Lang, 2000. A demonstration of how Sebald's transgresses boundaries, merges perspectives, and quotes from varied sources while maintaining a unified vision of art, life, and history.

Books

Loquai, Franz, ed. *W. G. Sebald*. Eggingen: Isele, 1997. This edition of the Isele *Porträt* Series contains, next to reviews from *Die Zeit* and other important newspapers, a selection of critical articles in German called "Mitteilungen über Max" (Communications about Max) on pp. 151–44.

Reviews of Sebald's Books, Interviews, Obituaries

Selected Reviews: Non-Fiction

Butler, Michael. "The Human Cost of Exile: *Logis in einem Landhaus* by W. G. Sebald." *Times Literary Supplement*, 2 Oct. 1998: 10. Butler praises Sebald's illuminating discussions of Swiss and Alemmanic writers and identifies the unspoken connection of these literary essays with the final one on a contemporary painter called Jan Peter Tripp.

Daviau, Donald G. "Winfried Georg Sebald, *Carl Sternheim: Kritiker und Opfer der Wilhelminischen Ära*." *Germanic Review* 47 (1972): 234–36. Daviau is hostile to what he sees as Sebald's overly sociological—and negative—attitude towards his subject, and to his vitriolic contempt for literary criticism and literary critics in general. To find "all the elements of Nazi literature" in Sternheim's works, as he says Sebald does, is a distortion and patently unfair.

Reiter, Andrea, "*Unheimliche Heimat: Essays zur österreichischen Literatur*. By W. G. Sebald." *Bristol Austrian Studies*. Edited by Brian Keith-Smith. *Modern Language Review* 88 (1993): 803–4. Reiter praises Sebald's attempt to find a sociological common denominator among the many writers with whom he engages, especially in his treatment of "exiles within Austria" such as Peter Handke and Gerhard Roth.

Rundell, Richard J. "*A Radical Stage: Theater in Germany in the 1970s and 1980s*. Edited by W. G. Sebald." *Theatre Journal* 43 (1991): 263–64. Rundell notes that Sebald's book, with its "lucid preface," is prompted by the recognition that the years between 1968 and 1980 were some of the most interesting for German drama in the twentieth century. Heiner Müller emerges in the volume as the rightful successor to Bertolt Brecht.

Selected Reviews: Fiction

The Emigrants

Aciman, André. "In the Crevasse." *Commentary* 103, no. 6 (1997): 61–64. Aciman recounts how he was won over by Sebald's "elusive blend of eloquence and silence, riddle and revelation." The review is itself an eloquent statement of Sebald's achievement, the empathetic return to the past through the medium of "a consummate act of artistic fatedness."

Annan, Gabriele. "Ghosts." *New York Review of Books*, 25 Sept. 1997: 29–30. Annan knows Sebald's German fiction and refers to it in discussing the nature and history of his "hybrid format." His style is "limpid, calm, and modest," and his subjects are the people that haunt him. The major influences Annan finds in Sebald's work are Nabokov and the Biedermeier novelist Adalbert Stifter.

Anonymous. "Ein Häufchen Knochen" (A pile of bones). *Der Spiegel*, 4 Jan. 1993: 129–31. This review emphasizes the figure of Nabokov as the embodiment of

Sebald's three main themes: emigration, memory, and the act of writing. Sebald's ability to create a "peculiar, shimmering mood" and a complex, multilayered structure of associations makes him much more than a mere recorder of episodic narratives.

Baron, Ulrich. "Dem Mäusevolk gilt heute meine Hoffnung" (Today my hopes lie with the mice). *Rheinischer Merkur*, 15 Jan. 1993: 20. This early German review of *Die Ausgewanderten* (*The Emigrants*) hailed Sebald's stories as some of contemporary German literature's best and most moving works. Sebald shows that modern literature does not have to be rigorously realistic to be serious, or repugnantly naturalistic, to be pertinent to modern life.

Brady, Philip. "Ghosts of the Present." *Times Literary Supplement*. 12 July 1996: 22. Brady is familiar with Sebald's German work and is able to draw comparisons between *The Emigrant* and *Die Ringe des Saturn*, with its "more linear structure," and "the elusively centred" *Schwindel. Gefühle*. He praises Sebald's eloquence and "multitude of moods and voices."

Cohen, Lisa. "Prose: *The Emigrants* by W. G. Sebald." *Boston Review* 22 (February 1997): 44–45. Cohen emphasizes Sebald's contention that his "medium is prose, not the novel." She interprets the butterfly collector Nabokov as a double for the narrator himself, who tells the story of his characters in an attempt "to pin the elusive sorrow of [their] lives to the page." Sebald is "a witness after the fact" who as a writer never loses sight of "either the power of metaphor or the viciousness of history." History itself cannot be treated as a sequence of events, but must be explored with a referential and personalized approach like Sebald's.

Steinberg, Sybil S. "*The Emigrants* by W. G. Sebald." *Publishers Weekly*. 19 Aug. 1996: 51. This is one of the earliest reviews in English and is quite brief. Steinberg mistakenly characterizes Ambros Adelwarth and Dr. Henry Selwyn as victims of the Holocaust. The cumulative effect of Sebald's photographs and seemingly authentic circumstantial detail is that of "an eerie memento."

Wolff, Larry. "When Memory Speaks." *New York Times Book Review*. 30 March 1997: 19. This admiring review locates the power of Sebald's writing in its "poetic obsessions with the past." Wolff notes similarities to the memoirs of Gregor von Rezzori.

The Rings of Saturn

Aciman, André. "Out of Novemberland." *New York Review of Books*. 3 Dec. 1998: 44–47. Sebald's tone is described in this review as "somber, cadenced, liturgical." Aciman devotes a good deal of space to discussing the first story in *The Emigrants* in order to demonstrate that Sebald's use of "languor and resignation" as the most plausible substitute for a dogmatic explanation of history and the suffering it demands. But Sebald continually circles the ineffable—a literary tactic not uncommon among contemporary European novelists—and the evasion of outright expression renders *The Rings of Saturn* ultimately sterile and forced. Everything seems to come together successfully only for a brief moment in the book, when Sebald takes on Michael Hamburger's persona as he recalls his return to Berlin in 1947. Otherwise, Aciman considers *The Emigrants* the superior book.

Frank, Edwin. "Prose: *The Rings of Saturn* by W. G. Sebald." *Boston Review* 23 (December 1998): 60–61. Frank contrasts *The Rings of Saturn* with *The Emigrants*, noting that the artful conception of the first book is replaced in *Rings* by apparent "happenstance" in the second. In the final analysis, *Rings* has "the relentless unity of obsession." Frank is wrong about the subject of *The Emigrants* being "the stories of four people whose lives have been caught in the Nazi mangel" (two of the four are not Holocaust victims in any immediate sense), but he is absolutely right about Sebald's use of photographs in both books—they suggest "experience's elusiveness as much as its indelibility."

Howell-Jones, Gareth. "A Doubting Pilgrim's Happy Progress." *The Spectator*. 30 May 1998: 34–35. With all its emphasis on calamities and the passing of time, this review emphasizes the consoling power of the novel. It is a book which does not pretend or hope to explain the strange predicament of mortal life, but to reflect life's "consonant order" in elaborate narrative patterns and connections.

Jefferson, Margo. "Writing in the Shadows." *New York Times Book Review*. 18 March 2001: 27. Though initially suspicious of the "canonization" of Sebald's works by novelists and critics, the reviewer finds *The Rings of Saturn* and *The Emigrants* hard to resist. She admires the fixed and stately rhythm of Sebald's "nocturnal prose." She notes that many of Sebald's concerns were addressed in his first novel, *Vertigo*, and she believes his once novel approach has become repetitive.

Mason, Wyatt. "Mapping a Life: A Review of W. G. Sebald." *American Book Review*. May/June 1999: 19–20. Though it is a "hero's quest without destination," the book is considered highly compelling for its "archeology of consciousness." The reviewer praises Michael Hulse's translations. Montaigne is held up by this reviewer as a kindred spirit.

McCrum, Robert. "W. G. Sebald: *The Rings of Saturn*." *Observer*. Review Section. 7 June 1998: 15. McCrum recalls the success of the strangely original book *The Emigrants* and identifies the new "clues" provided by *Rings* in comprehending the aesthetics behind Sebald's creations. The most compelling insight of the review is McCrum's comparison of Sebald's style to a kaleidoscope in which brightly colored subjects "exhilaratingly . . . hypnotically . . . blur and merge and reform, blend and reshape and re-emerge."

Stow, Randolph. "The Plangency of Ruins." *Times Literary Supplement*. 31 July 1998: 11. Stow identifies Sebald's theme as ruin and decline. The associative narrative style is nonetheless reassuring in its decorous, anachronistic tone. Sebald creates an atmosphere of melancholy plangency.

Wood, James. "The Right Thread." *New Republic*. 6 July 1998: 38–42. Sebald's appeal as a writer stems from "the delicacy of his patterning" as well as his "unscrupulous uncertainty." Sebald's postmodernist innovation is to bind facts so tightly into his narrative that they become fictive, as they had never "belonged to the actual world." In this he works in the opposite direction from writers such as Umberto Eco and Julian Barnes, who destabilize facts within their fictions. Sebald's world, though not without its humor, is tragic, and his spirit melancholy. Eco's semiotic playfulness, on the other hand, gives his work a "'factional' breeziness." Sebald's pessimism is not metaphysical or theological, but aesthetic—a tendency or mood rather than a system. Wood correctly identifies a major influence on Sebald's style: the nineteenth-century Austrian novelist Adalbert Stifter. A slightly revised version of this article appeared under the title "Sebald's Uncertainty" in Wood's book *The* √*Broken Estate: Essays on Literature and Belief.* New York: Random House, 1999. 232–41.

Vertigo

Di Piero, W. S. "Another Country." *New York Times Book Review.* 11 June 2000: 20. The poet W. S. Piero calls Sebald a "a thrilling, original writer." When he first began reading *Vertigo* he knew he had entered "The Sebald Zone," where "events and encounters align themselves into an ominously smooth tissue of coincidence." Vertigo is the sensation of one who strives to be fully aware of oneself in time—Sebald's narrative totters between recollection and present-day search, offering itself as a "model of consciousness" as well as a tale of pilgrimage.

Dirda, Michael. *"Vertigo* by W. G. Sebald." *Washington Post Book World.* 25 June–1 July 2000: 2. Dirda holds the premise that literature can be divided into two categories; "novels that readers love, and . . . texts, fictions, experiments that critics rave about." Sebald belongs to the latter. He is eminently European in his recursiveness; his wistful, hallucinatory, essayistic, and sometimes lyrical prose reminds Dirda of the mood in Rilke's *Notebook of Malte Laurids Brigge.* But being a notebook-memoir of sorts, the book will confound some readers—they will simply not know what to make of the questions Sebald raises but does not answer in his "third masterpiece."

Fian, Antonio. "Ein paar Vorurteile angewandt auf W. G. Sebalds *Schwindel. Gefühle"* (A few prejudices aimed at W. G. Sebald's *Vertigo*). *Wespennest* 83 (1991): 76–78. This scathing review reduces Sebald to an elitist hack whose appeal can be attributed to the pretensions of an audience that believes itself capable of solving arcane riddles drawn from literary history. His prose is exceedingly calculated, but at the same time its structure is marred by the most "threadbare" transitional techniques. Sebald's use of the word *zusammengefangen* ("rounded up")—clearly a repetition of a wartime euphemism—is enough to close the coffin on *Vertigo*, a dead book that never should have seen the light of day in the first place.

Hackett, Joyce. *"Vertigo* by W. G. Sebald." *Boston Review* 25 (summer 2000): 34–35. This review is one of the most insightful studies of Sebald's style, which Hackett sees as designed "to keep the reader off balance." She emphasizes Sebald's use of silence to create juxtapositions that point to meanings "in negative space." She finds *Vertigo* more abstruse and "less tight" than *The Emigrants*, but each book is a fascinating creation, and each is bent on demonstrating the yawning gap "between image and fact, between visceral truth and historical packaging, between our dreams of forgetting and the way our legacies hunt us down." Hackett is a novelist in her own right.

Iyer, Pico. "The Strange, Haunted World of W. G. Sebald." *Harper's Magazine*. October 2000: 86–90. The cultural critic Pico Iyer discusses all of Sebald's books in this excellent stylistic analysis. He emphasizes the strange appeal of "unease" in the author's work, identifying the abiding theme as the literary effect of "restlessness, of panic, of being pursued through an echoing dream." That effect is largely a Kafkaesque one, and Iyer puts considerable emphasis on Kafka's story of Gracchus the Huntsman to which Sebald refers. Sebald has an "almost posthumous calm . . . all life is a memento mori."

Lane, Anthony. "Higher Ground: Adventures in Fact and Fiction from W. G. Sebald." *New Yorker*. 29 May 2000: 128–36. Lane, like Iyer, engages in some satirizing of Sebaldian style, but his too is the flattery of imitation. For Lane, Sebald is a writer with few rivals among English-speaking novelists for "the reach and play" of his work. This review highlights the parallel world of the past embedded in Sebald's universe. His prevailing mood of unease is indebted to Kafka, but Lane also notes, appropriately, the influence of the German film director Werner Herzog, whose *Enigma of Kaspar Hauser* is mentioned explicitly in *The Emigrants*. To call *Vertigo* "the most marine of works" is also fitting, for the novel, like *The Rings of Saturn*, thrives on aquatic and maritime similes. In Sebaldry—Lane's coinage, by the way— there is always a calm that belies the "worryingly turbid [waters] below."

Sontag, Susan. "A Mind in Mourning." *Times Literary Supplement*. 25 Feb. 2000: 3–4. This review is much quoted in blurbs and advertisements for its glowing praise of Sebald as a rare contemporary example of literary greatness. Sebald succeeds, according to Sontag, in establishing the "effect of the real," and carrying it "to a plangent extreme."

Austerlitz

Annan, Gabriele. "Ghost Story." *New York Review of Books*. 1 Nov. 2001: 26–27. Sebald is described as "one of the most gripping writers imaginable." Annan rejects the charge that Sebald's license in mixing fact and fiction is mere self indulgence.

Banville, John. "The Rubble Artist." *New Republic*, 26 Nov. 2001: 35–38. The accomplished Irish novelist John Banville retraces Sebald's career in this highly complimentary review. He regards Sebald's work as "the triumphant culmination" of a process of change and experimentation in fiction that saw the rise of Milan Kundera, Claudio Magris, and Roberto Calasso. Like many other reviewers before him, Banville regards Sebald as the creator of a new and unique category of writing.

Dirda, Michael. "*Austerlitz* by W. G. Sebald." *Washington Post*. 14 Oct. 2001: BW 15. This review summarizes the story of Austerlitz and describes the novel as yet another "original and exhilarating" product of Sebald's pen.

Freund, Wieland. "Belgische Begegnungen" (Belgian encounters). *Rheinischer Merkur*. 23 March 2001: 14. Wieland sees in the protagonist Jacques Austerlitz a more distinctly fictional character than those found in any of Sebald's other books. Sebald is presented in this complimentary review as the legitimate inheritor of Thomas Bernhard's mantle of literary greatness, though without the vitriolic tirades.

Kakutani, Michiko. "Life in a No Man's Land of Memories and Loss." *New York Times*. 26 Oct. 2001: E 40. This review finds shades of Kafka, Proust, and even Ingmar Bergman's film *Wild Strawberries* in Sebald's "vaguely sinister" twilight world. With *Austerlitz*, Sebald revives the "harrowing emotional power" of *The Emigrants*.

Lubow, Arthur. "Preoccupied with Death, but Still Funny." *New York Times*. 11 Dec. 2001: E 1–2. Published three days before Sebald's death, this interview-article makes much of the author's conviction that the border between the respective realms of the living and dead is porous, i.e., that there is a "gray zone." Lubow analyses the function of photographs in shaping as well as documenting Sebald's stories. His fascination with death began at the age of five, when he saw a picture of his father's friend, who had been killed in an automobile accident. Sebald's work in progress was to relate some of Sebald's family history.

Markovitz, Benjamin. "What Was it That So Darkened Our World?" *London Review of Books*. 18 Oct. 2001: 23–24. Markovitz argues that this story of recovering the past is more conventional that previous plot lines, and that Sebald's style is not well suited for it. The book succeeds, but its cumulative effect is in no way satisfying, because the title character does not develop, but only "fills a gap."

Mendelsohn, Daniel. "Foreign Correspondents." Review of *Austerlitz* by W. G. Sebald and *Flights of Love* by Bernhard Schlink. *New York*, 8 Oct. 2001: 70–73. Mendelsohn notes the necessarily "hollow core" of the book in the tragic loss of a child's identity, but also praises the novel's "denseness" and universality.

Radisch, Iris. "Der Waschbär der falschen Welt: W. G. Sebald sammelt Andenken und rettet die Vergangenheit vorm Vergehen" (Raccoon of the false world: W. G. Sebald collects mementos and saves the past from passing). *Die Zeit*. 5 April 2001: 55–56. Radish emphasizes Sebald's antiquarian method and suggests this fourth "non-novel-non-memoir" is a potboiler offering nothing but the same shopworn techniques and the same ultimately tasteless pretensions to historical and literary profundity. Radish questions Sebald's positioning of the Holocaust alongside varied and random curiosities, as just another item in his literary "museum of lost things."

Tindall, Gillian. "The Fortress of the Heart." *Times Literary Supplement*. 19 Oct. 2001: 21. This review emphasizes the role of theme in Sebald's prose, at the same time noting that *Austerlitz* makes more use of narrative structure than any of his previous books. The English novelist Tindall calls *Austerlitz* a "spellbinding, accomplished . . . wonderful book."

Interviews

Anonymous. "Ich fürchte das Melodramatische" (I fear the melodramatic) *Der Spiegel*. 12 March 2001: 228–34. Sebald discusses the genesis and evolution of the novel *Austerlitz*.

Atlas, James. "W. G. Sebald: A Profile." *Paris Review* 41 (1999): 278–95. This is the record of an extended visit with Sebald and is perhaps the most in-depth description of the writer available.

Baker, Kenneth. "W. G. Sebald: Up against Historical Amnesia." *San Francisco Chronicle*. 7 Oct. 2001: R 2. Sebald comments on stylistics, including the character of the narrative voice in his works.

McCrum, Robert. "'Characters, Plot, Dialogue? That's Not Really My Style . . .' W. G. Sebald: The Books Interview." *Observer*. Review Section. 7 June 1998: 17. Asked about his late start in writing fiction, Sebald replies that the German novelist Theodore Fontane started writing fiction at 76 and wrote 10 books before his death at the age of 84. Sebald reveals in this interview that the "most dramatic events" in a book like *The Emigrants* are in the main factual or "documentary," while the details and "the margins" have been changed and manipulated.

Wood, James. "An Interview with W. G. Sebald." *Brick* 59 (spring 1998): 23–29. Sebald discusses the relationship between documentation and illustration, fact and fiction, emphasizing the importance of uncertainty in fiction.

Obituaries

Anonymous. "W. G. Sebald." *The Times*. 17 Dec. 2001: L 17. A lengthy profile of "one of the most remarkable talents to have emerged in recent times." This obituary emphasizes Sebald's scholarship as well as his literary originality. *Austerlitz* "consolidated a reputation already secure, and promised a great deal more." That the *Irish Times* called *The Rings of Saturn* the best book of the decade of the 1990s is all the more reason to regret the end of Sebald's life and career.

Gussow, Mel. "W. G. Sebald, Elegiac German Novelist, Is Dead at 57." *New York Times*. 15. Dec. 2001: C 16. This tribute is essentially a digest of critical comment on Sebald's work. Gussow misrepresents one of Sebald's books, the volume of essays titled *Luftkrieg und Literatur*, describing it as a novel about the bombing of Dresden.

Homberger, Eric. "W. G. Sebald." *Guardian*. 17 Dec. 2001: 20. Sebald is praised for his oblique approach to tragedy, which eschews both sentimentality and numbed acceptance. This obituary is in large part a biographical essay, tracing Sebald's intellectual and artistic development, with an emphasis on his preoccupation with the Germans' "willful forgetting" of what they perpetrated during the Third Reich, not to mention the massive destruction visited upon their cities in response.

Reynolds, Susan Salter. "The Literary Journey of a Wandering Soul." *Los Angeles Times*. 18 Dec. 2002. E 1, 4. Includes comments from Susan Sontag, who admired Sebald more than any other writer while he was alive. Reynolds calls Sebald's experiments with the form of the novel "revolutionary" in a way comparable to what Joyce achieved with *Finnegan's Wake* or Pynchon with *Gravity's Rainbow*.

Vollmann, Rolf. "Schwarzes Segel der Schwermut. Zum Tod des Schriftstellers W. G. Sebald" (The black sail of melancholy. On the death of the writer W. G. Sebald). *Die*

Zeit. 19 Dec. 2001: 36. Sebald finally succumbs to the object of his preoccupations, this reviewer observes: mortality and the passing of time. In this gentle lament of Sebald's passing, Vollmann praises Sebald's use of language, comparing his style to the placidly beautiful prose of Adelbert Stifter.

Index